"Dr. Baum's new book, *Got the Baby, Where's the Manual?!?* is a valuable resource for parents seeking information about their new roles and how they can best help their children grow and learn. Dr. Baum helps the readers identify old parental behaviors they want to leave behind and offers guidance on the wonderful, but sometimes challenging transition from couple to parents." **National Alliance of Children's Trust and Prevention Funds.**

"Joanne Baum has written a highly readable and practical book for parents of young children. This is a book that respects both children and parents. I recommend it highly for parents who want something that can truly help them become effective and reflective in caring for their children." **John Hornstein, EdD, Brazelton Touchpoints Center, Children's Hospital, Boston.**

"Dr. Baum's respectful approach to parenting is deeply humane for both children and parents. This is a much-needed book." **Michael Gurian, PhD, author of** *The Wonder of Boys, The Wonder of Girls, A Fine Young Man,* **and** *Boys and Girls Learn Differently.*

"Respectful Parenting combines the latest research on human brain development with the real experiences of today's families. The book offers both practical strategies and friendly encouragement—two things every parent can use!" **Dana Wolfe Naimark, Deputy Director, Children's Action Alliance, Phoenix, Arizona.**

"Dr. Joanne Baum empowers parents by presenting a philosophy of parenting that will enable a parent to spontaneously invent his or her own behavior in any parenting situation. This book is an excellent guide for parents who want to raise a child who has a strong sense of self." **Robert LaCrosse, PhD, co-author of** *Learning from Divorce* **and** *Working with High-Conflict Families of Divorce.*

"The book is obviously a wonderful combination of professional findings and personal discovery...laced with humor and compassion." **Foster W. Cline, MD, co-author of** *Parenting with Love and Logic,* **as well as numerous other books and co-founder of the Love and Logic Parenting Institute.**

"Dr. Baum proposes and convincingly defends an alternative child-rearing paradigm—parenting with empathy and respect for a child's needs ... adults soon discover they can pass on a healthier legacy to their children and at the same time heal their own personal histories." **Marianne Neifert, MD, author of** *Dr. Mom.*

Got the Baby, Where's the Manual!?! is a delightful, informative read for all parents-to-be and new parents. Dr. Baum presents a powerful and useable paradigm shift from shame based parenting to respectful parenting." **Jim Fay, Love and Logic Institute, author of numerous books and audios including *Parenting with Love and Logic, When Kids Leave You Speechless.***

"Your book is a delight—interesting and simply stated." **Marsh S. Hawler, Erikson Institute.**

"Dr. Joanne Baum's *Respectful Parenting: From Birth Through The Terrific Twos* is what every mother, father, and grandparent needs to read….It is written in a wonderfully understandable way, leaving the reader full of energy and excitement." **Dr. Carl Hollander, EdD, TEP, LMFT, DPA, The Hollander Institute.**

"This is the first parenting book I have seen that addresses the long-term effects of early trauma and traumatic relationships on adults as they begin to parent. The book offers realistic and useful suggestions and examples that makes the material alive and available to the reader. I appreciated the way Dr. Baum used examples throughout the book. I will be recommending it to parents." **Vivienne Roseby, PhD, co-author with Dr Janet Johnston of *In the Name of The Child* and *High Conflict Families: A Treatment Manual for School-Age Children.***

"Making babies is easy. Raising them to be just, compassionate, and free human beings is something else entirely. *Got the Baby, Where's the Manual?!?* is a wise and practical guide to shifting your parenting perspective from shaming to honoring." **Rabbi Rami Shapiro, philosopher and author of numerous books and poems including, *Wisdom of the Jewish Sages, Hebrew Prophets,* and *Hasidic Tales.***

"Respectful Parenting offers parents terrific options in raising children with healthy self-esteem and healing themselves at the same time. This book is certain to help many partners stay together in lasting relationships as parents." **Shirley Thomas, PhD, author of *Parents Are Forever.***

"Joanne Baum, PhD ably presents a loving, respectful way to parent babies to three year olds. Her insights into recognizing and satisfying the needs of children in those early years will clearly enhance their autonomy and self esteem in the years to come." **Ann Moore, creator of the Weego (the original Snugli baby carrier).**

"The strategies (in this book) are particularly helpful. I've used it professionally as well as personally." **Donna Martinez, coordinator, Su Bebe program of Denver Area Youth Services.**

"I now have a book I can give to parents to read that will help those who are perfectionist to take it easy and those who are learning a new skill to tune in to the language of the baby, infant and toddler." **Frank Leek, PhD, founder and author of Shared Parent Support Program.**

"I completed the book and found the information and format of the book immediately useful. This is an important piece of work." **Shirley Dodd, MSW.**

"At the heart of the book is Dr. Baum's belief that parenting should consist of a healthy respect for your child's total being and the development of a healthy interplay between parent and child that will promote growth on all levels of development... also addresses special issues in parenting for adults who have experienced trauma in their own childhood." **Linda Luther-Starbird, PhD.**

"I immediately realized that this was something different in a very good way... if more parents adopted this form of parenting we'd see a lot fewer problems in middle school children. Respectful Parenting will result in children having higher self-esteem, better coping skills, and more confidence. Where was this book twenty-five years ago when I was having babies?" **Nancy Visocky, MA, Middle School Guidance Counselor, Evergreen, Colorado.**

"This book provides a beautifully simple guide to parents who are interested in raising children who value respect, humor, and love. A great book for doctors to give to new parents." **Sue Peper, MS, LPC, NCC, New Dimensions.**

"Getting your child off to a good start can make a lifetime of difference. The Respectful Parenting strategies are realistic and child-focused. The stories and examples are particularly helpful for parents. Another important aspect of this book is the advice for parents whose own parents were less than perfect. I wish I had this (book) when my children were young." **M. Kay White, MA, LPC.**

"I have thoroughly enjoyed *Respectful Parenting!* Surely this will catch people up in what a creative, unfolding, collaborative enterprise raising a child is—while at the same time, being punctuated with some episodes of maddening frustration....This is a terrific book." **Jean LaCrosse, PhD.**

"I really liked it a lot. In fact we are going to start recommending it in our parenting classes and incorporating some of the ideas into our classes." **Ruth Artis, MS, Parent Education Department, Emily Griffith Opportunity School, Denver.**

"The endeavor of childrearing is as old as the second generation of humanity itself. Our Biblical heritage is filled with the trials and tribulations of parenting as endured by Abraham, Isaac, and Jacob. Respectful Parenting is a balanced, child-centered approach, which is healthy not only for the children, but for the entire family. The Respectful Parent realizes that children need boundaries and limits in order to feel safe and secure, and need to receive guidance on the choices they make as they continue to grow and develop." **Rabbi Bernard Gerson, Congregation Rodef Shalom, Denver, Colorado.**

Got the Baby, Where's the Manual?!?

Got the Baby
Where's the Manual?!?

Respectful Parenting
from Birth Through the Terrific Twos

Joanne Baum, PhD

Mountainside Press

This book is typeset in Adobe Garamond. The paper used in this book meets the minimum requirements of ANSI/NISO Z39.48-1992 (R1997).

∞

Designed and typeset by Barbara Werden Design (www.BarbaraWerdenDesign.com)
Author photo: Wendy Schott (www.WendySchottPhoto.com)
Logo development: Lori and Ted Garcia (www.tlcunlimited.com)

Dr. Baum is available for Respectful Parenting training seminars for professionals, parents, and community groups. Please contact us for details.
respectfulparenting@msn.com
www.respectfulparenting.com

Mountainside Press
mountainsidepress@msn.com
303-679-1949
800-519-6003

ISBN 10: 0-9785914-0-2
ISBN 13: 978-0-9785914-0-3
Library of Congress Control Number: 2006908404

Printed in the United States of America at McNaughton & Gunn

06 07 08 09 10 11 12 13 14 / 9 8 7 6 5 4 3 2 1

Dedicated to MJM

Contents

Contents

Introduction

ARE YOU WONDERING how to be a really good parent? Would you read a parenting book that promised to give you ideas that make a lot of sense but that you hadn't thought of before? The ideas behind Respectful Parenting, which you will read about in *Got the Baby, Where's the Manual?!?*, make sense, they work, and you can learn how to use them by reading this book. You will gain valuable parenting skills you can use for every parenting situation and challenge that comes your way. Getting your child off to a good start can make a lifetime of difference.

My goal in writing this book is to provide new moms and dads with the knowledge, understanding, and skills to parent wisely, kindly, and respectfully. Respectful Parenting is beneficial for both children and their parents. Parents will help their children establish positive self-esteem and a solid sense of confidence in themselves, while teaching skills that enhance their learning experiences in preschool and school. Parents will also be able to teach their children how to think things through, how to talk about their ideas, how to become solid decision makers, and how to respectfully negotiate appropriate limits. When you carefully choose thoughtful words to respectfully communicate with your child, and you hear your own words spoken out loud, it actually heals and strengthens you as those same words nurture your child.

Respectful Parenting teaches you how to filter out your past family history, so that you can avoid repeating what annoyed, hurt, or bothered you while you were growing up, and at the same time, you can embrace those things you fondly remember from your childhood. Respectful Parenting requires slowing down from an adult sense of time to a child's, which has a different rhythm. When you slow down and listen carefully, using all your senses, it's easier to take the time to think about what you want to do next, thereby avoiding acting on automatic pilot. You will find you have more solutions to problems when you think about how you can be respectful of your baby's needs, your toddler's needs and wants, and your two-year-old's definitively stated needs, wants, and desires.

When you slow your thinking process, it allows you to see your baby's cries as his own language rather than becoming frustrated and wishing he could tell you what he needs in a language you're familiar with. Instead of dwelling on what he can't tell you, you lovingly go through the possibilities of what he might be communicating: "Please feed me, I'm hungry;" "There's too much going on here. I need to go someplace quieter where it can all sink in before I get any more stimulation;" "Please get me someplace where I can sleep, I'm so tired;" "You haven't given me any attention in a while and I need some snuggles and hugs;" "You probably didn't notice that my diaper's dirty. I know you have a clean one in that bag. Please change me so I'm more comfortable."

When you get the right answer and take care of your baby's needs, he stops crying. Gurgles of delight replace his upset facial expressions and cries. You become awestruck by how your baby can communicate, by how you can respond, and by the positive results for both of you. You are satisfied and so is your baby.

When your two-year-old has a temper tantrum in the middle of a store you'll be able to handle her calmly and kindly rather than being embarrassed and reacting with anger. Instead of responding harshly ("Stop that nonsense right now!"), you can look at your overwrought child and your heart can go out to her. You'll understand she's telling you something really important that she probably tried to tell you in more subtle ways, but you didn't hear or you ignored her because you wanted to do one more thing before going home. You can respectfully respond to her overloaded system by reassuring her that you are going to take care of her. You'll know to bring her to a calmer environment where she can feel comfortable. Then when she's calm, you can talk and figure out what's best for her. You learn that your child can't take as many errands as you'd like to, so next time you shorten your list, and you both have a pleasant experience doing things in a way she can handle. That's what Respectful Parenting will do for you and your family.

Parents often say they want to be gentler and more understanding with their children, but many are afraid they'll "spoil" them if they're "too nice." When they take the time to examine the philosophy and strategies of Respectful Parenting, they discover that there are ways to be kind and gentle without creating a family free-for-all. Respectful Parenting definitely advocates setting and consistently using limits, consequences, and boundaries with children. By being consistent and caring as you use these limits and boundaries you create a mutually respectful relationship with your children. And by embracing this philosophy, moms and dads are often able to prevent the negative aspects of their family history from continuing into another generation, thereby avoiding chaos, pain, guilt, fear, or intimidation. The parents I've worked with have shared with me how helpful it is to stop long enough to ask themselves, "How do I want to react today, as an adult, with all I've learned in my life?" They're often pleased when they can answer that question with creative choices. The key ingredient is mutual respect rather than forced compliance through fear, guilt, or intimidation. The most important benefit might be that parents truly enjoy, not just endure, their daily lives with their children.

I developed the theories and strategies that have become Respectful Parenting as I worked with adults and families from 1981 to now. I clearly see the benefits for both children and their parents when moms and dads consciously choose to parent their children with respect and kindness. Just as I advocate *learning from* your child and *learning with* your child as you *teach* your child, I've learned so much from the parents I counseled in my private practice. This book is a result of that learning process.

Recently, brain science researchers and child development specialists have learned more about brain development. They've found that a child's social, emotional, and cognitive development are interconnected. I'm happy to report that scientific evidence now demonstrates that the kinds of parenting methods Respectful Parenting advocates will help optimize a child's overall development in all these areas.

Becoming a mom or dad is an awesome stage of life. Congratulations and best wishes as you take on one of the most exciting, satisfying, challenging, and meaningful experiences in life—becoming a parent.

Got the Baby, Where's the Manual?!?

Respectful Parenting

THE BIGGEST FRUSTRATIONS for new parents seem to come from: feelings of inadequacy because of a lack of knowledge (there's a huge learning curve); feelings of insecurity because you don't have much experience and you're not sure if you're doing the right thing; and wanting to avoid things said or done to you as a child, but finding that the thoughts, memories, words, and sometimes actions come pouring out of your mind, mouth, or hands even though you swore you would never repeat them.

The first two frustrations will decrease as you gain knowledge from being a parent and as you learn from and with your baby. This book will help you recognize and absorb those valuable lessons. The third frustration, repeating or almost repeating an action you didn't like while you were growing up, will also be dealt with, and you will learn how to deal with and avoid those old patterns. It's important to know that you are not alone in wanting to parent at least somewhat differently from how you were parented but finding it more difficult than you thought it would be. One of the main reasons for this difficulty is that we humans seem to learn best by example. Show us something or let us experience something, and we will learn much more easily than if we are only lectured about the topic. It also appears true that experiencing something day after day, year after year (such as how your parents behaved toward you when you were growing up) will leave an indelible mark on your brain. The actions or words imprinted in your mind can pop out at the most opportune and inopportune times. This "role modeling," which is essentially learning from what you see and what you experience, is a very powerful way we learn. And it makes sense that what your parents taught you through their actions about how to parent is now imprinted in your unconscious and conscious mind. Thus, things you liked or didn't like while growing up are stored in your brain, almost like automatic tapes, waiting for an opportunity to come forward.

When you were growing up, were there times when you said things like this to yourself? "When I have kids I'm going to _____ instead of what my mom just did." Or "I hate when he does that; I'll never say that to my child." Or "I can't wait to be a parent because I'll never do *that* to my child." Were there also times when you thought, "I like what my mom just said; I hope I remember to explain it the same way to my child," or "My dad was so nice about that, I want to treat my child the same way when I'm a parent."

As a new parent or even as an experienced parent, there will be times when you'll find yourself about to say something you swore you would never repeat. At those times, it's important to be gentle with yourself and understand that it's human to repeat what you experienced in your own childhood. Then take the time to offer yourself some alternatives, including taking a few minutes to calm down and come up with a new, creative option or two to try with your child. You can avoid repeating the old familiar patterns and start to replace the old tapes from your childhood. The more conscious you can be and the more time you can allow yourself to create new scenarios, the more satisfied you will be in your role as a parent. This book will present many options for creating new, positive experiences.

A Brief History of Parenting

Looking at parenting from a historical perspective can be helpful in understanding where we are today and how we got here. Up until 100 or 150 years ago, children and women were seen as the possessions of their parents (or husband), without any legal rights of their own. Women and children were allowed to be beaten by men as they saw fit, and children could be exploited in any number of ways. At the turn of the twentieth century, American culture reflected Victorian-era philosophies about child rearing, which were summed up in expressions such as, "Spare the rod, spoil the child" and "Children should be seen and not heard." The first expression not only condoned but recommended hitting children to prevent them from becoming spoiled. In a sense, the Victorian era was about breaking children's spirits so they would be seen and not heard.

Children were expected to be responsive to their parents' needs. They were expected to have a compliant demeanor that did not include boisterous behavior, participating in parental decisions, or making demands for themselves. Surviving took most of the parents' efforts and time. People's life expectancies were shorter and their work was often physically taxing. Back then, you were being a good parent if you kept a roof over your children's heads and food in their bellies. There wasn't a lot of extra time for things like recreational activities, socializing, sharing quiet cuddly moments, having long, heart-felt discussions, or "hanging out" with the family. The field of psychology was in its infancy, and no one realized how important it was to nurture a child. The idea of nurturing was just not part of the collective consciousness.

One thing that has changed over the last century is the growing view of children as people in their own right, who are deserving of their own legal rights, legal protections, and personal freedoms. They are no longer seen as merely extensions of their parents. Laws have been created, such as those preventing child abuse, child labor laws, and laws providing for the prosecution of parents for murdering or abusing their children, and even those protecting children who are successful in the entertainment business, dictating that a child's earnings be kept in trust instead of spent by the parents. As society's view of children as possessions changed, we experienced an evolution of parenting along the same lines. Now, instead of existing for their parents' needs or pleasures, children are seen as individuals with needs and rights of their own.

Those Victorian days were only four or five generations ago. For some readers that generation would have been your great-grandparents interacting with your grandparents. Your grandparents, who might have been raised with rigid disciplinary guidelines to prevent such horrors as spoiled children, raised your parents, who, in turn, raised you. Thus, the philosophies of "children should be seen and not heard," and "spare the rod, spoil the child," are not so far removed from your life. I call this type of parenting "old-style parenting."

Today, however, there is wide recognition that early messages, both positive and negative, affect people throughout their lives. The first few years of a child's life leave indelible messages in his or her mind. We also know much more about early childhood development, brain development in particular, which includes cognitive, social, and emotional development, than when you were growing up.

The first widely acclaimed child development specialist to influence people raised by Victorian-era parents and grandparents was Dr. Spock. His earliest books became popular in the 1950s. Although his ideas later changed, his early work encouraged rather rigid schedules for eating and sleeping along with watered-down versions of Victorian-era disciplinary practices. Many people raised like this went on to raise their children along the same lines, but others rebelled against the rigid routines and went in the opposite direction, giving in to all of their children's demands and whims. Some parents talked until they were blue in the face and then acquiesced, others were influenced by the hippie movement and adopted a laissez-faire parenting attitude. In more extreme cases, this attitude became benign or not-so-benign neglect, often exaggerated by parents' drug and alcohol use. These parents forgot that children need boundaries and limits.

Respectful Parenting is a balanced, child-centered approach that is healthy for children and for the entire family. When you parent your child respectfully you realize that children, like adults, have feelings and needs of their own, including the need to feel listened to and considered so that they have some sense of control over their lives. A respectful parent realizes that children need limits, boundaries, and consequences (discipline) in order to feel safe and secure. Children also need guidance for the choices they make in their lives in order to adapt successfully to the world as they grow and develop. An important part of giving your child guidance about making choices is teaching your child the basic building blocks of effective decision making. You can do this by explaining how and why you're making decisions and, as your child becomes old enough, asking your child to explain how he's coming up with his decisions, discussing his thoughts, and guiding him through a solid decision making process.

When you are respectfully parenting your child, you view your child as a young human being who deserves your appreciation, consideration, time, and love. You see your child as someone you can learn from, someone you can learn with, and someone you can teach about life. Your parenting decisions and actions are predicated on the basic belief that you and your child will give each other respect and understanding. You will set limits, but they will be reasonable, negotiated when possible, and you'll give a warning before you act on them. Respectful Parenting is time consuming and takes a lot of energy, but it's worth it because parenting in this way rewards both you and your child on many levels.

Being in awe of your child and being in awe with your child are ways you can help yourself get into the Respectful Parenting frame of mind. When you're in awe, you're in a very open minded place. You can see the world differently. You can respond to the world differently. So, when you switch out of your usual adult way of operating in the world by being in awe of what your baby is doing and discovering, you're leaving yourself open to a new perspective and new ideas. This is true from the time your baby is a few hours old and teaching you his various cries, which mean different things, to when your child is a teenager and awesomely challenging the limits you've set. The following are two examples of a parent being in awe. Starting with a mom and her eighteen month old and how the day changed when mom allowed herself to get into her child's world instead of rigidly sticking to her adult agenda. She still accomplished her agenda, but she had the gift of looking at the world differently by being in awe and following her child's lead and noticing how her child was reacting to her little world.

What Parents Say

Linda: I think my daughter was about eighteen months old when I started realizing what a cool sense of humor she had. One day we were in the vegetable garden, and bees kept coming through to the flowers beyond. She was getting scared of the bees, and I thought we might have to go inside. Instead, I took some time, gathered her in my arms, and talked to her about bees: how they weren't there to bother or hurt us, they just wanted to get to the flowers so they could make their honey. I tried to reassure her that they wouldn't hurt us if we didn't hurt them.

I could tell she felt better, and when I asked, she said yes, she did want to stay and garden some more. A little while later, another bee went flying right by her head, and she pulled back a little and said, "Excuse me, bee!" I was so amazed. Thinking about it later, her response showed such a sharp sense of humor, plus she must have really understood and been reassured by what I told her. . . . Pretty incredible!

At around the same time (eighteen months) I noticed how responsive my daughter was to other children, especially babies. Like in a mall: if we were walking along and she heard a baby crying, she'd say something like, "There's a baby crying. He needs his Mommy," or "He needs to nurse." Sometimes if we could see the baby and his or her mother was ignoring him, she'd ask, "Why isn't that Mommy holding (or nursing) the baby? He's crying." She would be so concerned. I'd try to explain that not all mothers raise their children the same way I was raising her, and then she'd be even more confused and concerned.

I had trouble explaining why, if she asked for more of an explanation, because I don't know why all Moms don't respond quickly when their babies cry. But I do know that how my husband and I parent is unfortunately in the minority. I'm reminded of that most times we're in public places and each time we go see our extended families.

Her compassion for others still impresses me. I guess it's because she's been responded to so much, her needs have always been addressed, that's all she knows . . . role modeling, huh? It seems to go a long way.

When we go see relatives who parent differently, who yell at their kids, or spank their kids, or whose kids get told they're "bad" and "in trouble," my daughter just stands back, hangs close to me, and watches. They think we're "just lucky" to have such a mellow kid. They also think some of our parenting ideas are at least a little weird. Actually, I think they think we're really out there. They don't associate how we parent, so gently and responsively to her needs and desires, as a reason why we have such an easy, mellow little girl. It's not luck at all. She's shown love freely. We talk about her in positive terms, she gets praised a lot. And she herself is loving.

* * *

Sarah: When my son was not quite three years old, I had to leave him to go to my grandmother's funeral. I explained to him that I would be leaving him with his daddy for a few days because my grandma had died. He asked me why she had died, and I told him she had been very old and frail and just didn't have the strength to live anymore. I reminded him of how small she had been when we last saw her and told him a little about how she used to be and why I had loved her so much. He knew she hadn't been able to hold him six months before when we had visited because she was so little and frail. So he had some understanding. He even assured me that he and Daddy would be okay.

About a week after I came back, he and I were in the bathtub and he said to me, "Mommy, when you're old and little, I'll hold you and take care of you." My eyes filled with tears as I gathered him in my arms and hugged him. "Really, Mommy, you hold me and take care of me when I'm small, and when you get old and small, I'll take care of you." What a sweetheart he is. I hugged him and told him that would be lovely. I was in awe of his understanding and ability to know that, someday, I, too, would be old and need help.

Old-Style Parenting versus Respectful Parenting

Here are a number of old-style parenting lines many people heard when they were growing up. Hearing these one-liners often resulted in a child feeling hurt, ashamed, fearful, or guilty and later, as an adult, having a low self-esteem. Do any of these old-style one-liners sound familiar to you?

"What were you thinking?"
"Why? Because I said so."
"Why? Because I'm your mother/father."
"If you don't stop crying, I'll give you something to cry about!"
"You should be ashamed of yourself."
"I'm going to kill you if you don't stop . . ."
"Because I said so, and if you don't do it now, you're in big trouble!"
"Why are you doing this to me?"
"How could you be so stupid?"
"What's wrong with you?"
"You're a *bad* girl!"
"You need to *obey* me."
"How come you can't be good like David down the street?"
"Do you ever think before you do anything?"
"What the hell's the matter with you?"
"Who do you think you are?"
"How dare you?"

If you heard some of these lines when you were growing up, you were raised with old-style parenting techniques. You'll find sections throughout this book entitled "Eliminating Old-Style Parenting Patterns," which will give you specific techniques to use so you can become a more conscious and respectful parent starting right now. Please keep in mind that even the most enlightened parents a few generations ago had very different expectations of children and very different ideas of parenting than we have today.

Think about times you've heard a parent angrily *demanding* that her child listen to and respect her. Just by demanding this, the parent is being disrespectful to the child. Why should the child respect a disrespectful parent? And how is the child going to learn how to respect another person if he or she is not being treated with respect? Respectful parents realize that they must *show by example* and be role models for how to treat others and how they want others, including their children, to treat them.

Here's an example: let's say a parent has said, "Justin, go wash your hands, it's dinnertime."

"I don't want to," Justin replies.

The old-style parent immediately responds in an angry tone of voice, "I told you to go wash your hands! Now listen to me!"

"But they're not dirty," the child implores.

The parent responds, with more anger, "Stop talking back to me. How dare you be so disrespectful. I told you to go wash your hands. Now go do what I said right now or you won't get any dinner."

"But why?" the child replies reasonably. "They're clean."

And the parent might very angrily reply, "Because I told you to. Now that's it! You go do what I told you to right now or absolutely no dinner!"

Where along the way was that child's reality taken into account? The parent repeatedly demanded adherence to the rules but did not stop long enough to consider the child's point of view. In these kinds of situations a child will often comply out of fear, but fear and compliance are very different from respect. In this example, the child could easily go off to the bathroom (disrespectfully) muttering under his breath . . . and why not? By being disrespectful to the child, that parent was perpetuating the negative behaviors she was trying to stop.

Instead, the following respectful conversation could have resulted in the child feeling good about why he's washing his hands.

"Justin, would you please go wash your hands? Dinner's almost ready." (A less harsh request with a gentle *please*.)

"I don't want to."

"Why not?" (Listening to child's opinion and validating it by addressing it instead of just ignoring it.)

"I'm playing."

The parent walks to where the child is playing (again, acknowledging the child's reality). "Oh, I can see that. Well, dinner is just about ready.

How about washing your hands and eating, and then you can come back to play some more after dinner?"

"But they're not dirty."

"Let's see . . . I don't see any dirt on them either. But you know what? Unless you've just washed them, it's still a good idea to wash your hands before eating, even when you can't see dirt, because sometimes tiny pieces of dirt or germs can be there even though you can't see them, and they might get inside your mouth and body when you eat. So, to stay healthy, it's a good idea to always wash your hands before you eat."

"Oh, okay," the child says somewhat reluctantly but understandingly.

"Thanks for listening," the parent might say cheerfully, reinforcing the child's cooperation. Or, if the child had recently washed up, the parent might simply say, "You're right, they do look clean. Thanks for showing me. Come on in and eat." Again, this technique will validate the child's reality and, at the same time, will teach your child why you want him to wash his hands and will show your child how to be respectful.

Respectful Parenting does not mean repeatedly discussing and negotiating the same issue each time it comes up. For instance, you don't want to have a long conversation every time you ask your child to wash his hands. If you've gone through this before, you would use a shortened version: "Remember we've talked about germs and hidden dirt and washing your hands before eating so you can stay healthy? Hopefully your child will then nod or say something about remembering, and you could add, "Well, here's your opportunity. Go ahead and then we'll eat."

Another example is when a two-year-old decides he wants to get out of the car on the opposite side of where his parent is standing and holding the door open. He normally gets out through this door, but now he's standing at the far door and clearly wants to get out on the other side.

Old-style parents might respond in this way: The parent stands at the customary door and says gruffly, "No, I'm not going to walk around the car. You come here." The parent's tone of voice sounds unnecessarily harsh, as if her two-year-old had said something inconsiderate or disrespectful. The parent's tone of voice implies that the child's behavior (wanting to exit through the other door) is somehow wrong or bad.

The Respectful Parenting model would go something like this: "Oh, okay. Do you want to see what it's like to get out on that side of the car?" Or, "Sweetie, see all my packages? It would be easier for me if you'd come out this way right now. We'll try it your way next time when my arms are free." Or even, "No thank you, I'd appreciate you coming out over here, where I'm standing."

It's true that the shortest distance would be for him to come out nearest the parent, but who says we have to be totally efficient at all times? With old-style parenting, the child was reacted to in anger and the message from the parent's gruff tone of voice was, "How dare you request such a thing!" or "What's wrong with you?" or "Who do you think you are? I'm not going to walk all the way around the car for a two-year-old." The child was not being bad with his simple request, it may have just been curiosity at work, and he didn't need or deserve a negative interpretation of his simple request.

There are a number of ways you can respond to a request like this, all respectful, from giving in to your child's curiosity and walking around the car and opening the other door to letting your child know that you understand his request but it's not going to happen at this time. When you recognize and understand your child's request the respectful parenting response allows the child to make a choice of his own and models behavior that accepts another person's wishes. If you decide to grant the request, the child will see what getting out on the other side of the car is like and, within a short period of time, he'd probably be back to getting out on the side you opened. Or you would be able to remind him of your preference while allowing for his own experience. When you treat your child this way, you're setting an example of how you want to be treated. You develop a respectful reciprocity between you and your child. Children of respectful parents sense their interest, love, caring, awe, appreciation, and respect. When they feel it from you, they'll often respond to you in a similar fashion.

Eliminating Old-Style Parenting Patterns

Respectful Parenting offers you a way to improve on how you were parented and to heal some of your old hurts along the way. With very few exceptions, how you were brought up wasn't all bad, but you can make some improvements—especially in those areas where you remember thinking, "When I'm a Mom (or a Dad) I won't . . ." Unfortunately, as many of you may have found already, being the kind of parent you want to be is not as easy as you once thought. Let's examine why. As stated earlier, what you experienced your parents doing to you (role modeling) is what you probably learned. Your parents were, throughout the years you lived with them, role models of how to *be* parents. Thus, you are living with the reality that what you saw when you were growing up has been consciously and unconsciously programmed into your brain. The things your parents said and did will come out of your mouth and hands automatically, like replaying old tapes, the good along with the not-so-good.

That's why you may find yourself saying and doing things you promised yourself you'd never do. In extreme examples, it explains why adults who were physically abused as children often grow up to abuse their own children. It's important to realize that those old, familiar tapes are in the back of your mind, waiting for an opportunity to be replayed. Any changes you want to make are going to have to be concrete and conscious choices on your part. While people from healthy, loving homes can often rely on their intuition to parent in a healthy, loving manner, all parents will sometimes need extra help. Remember, your brain has stored all of your life experiences, and it can only supply you with the options it has on hand, no matter where your heart is. If you were not parented respectfully, then your brain cannot give you that option unless you have seen it someplace else or you consciously set out to learn how to be respectful today.

Luckily, the strategies and techniques of respectful parenting can be learned. The strategies provide the framework you'll need to come up with new, kind, and creative parenting options. You'll probably have to practice them a few times before they begin to feel natural. You can learn how to stop the old tapes and replace them with healthier alternatives so you can fulfill your goal of being a kind and gentle parent who sets limits in a calm, respectful manner.

You will heal old wounds left over from your childhood when you hear and watch yourself treat your child in ways you wish you had been treated. In some ways the young person you were when the hurt first happened is still there, deep inside you, needing what it didn't get. That ever young person inside you is waiting for someone to come along who can provide what you've been waiting so long to receive: that love, respect, compassion, and understanding somehow you knew you needed. When you parent your child with respect, you're also re-parenting the child within yourself. Both children, the real one in front of you and your own inside, will appreciate and grow healthier from hearing and experiencing you respectfully parent your child. Your self-esteem will improve. You'll get respect from your child by offering your respect. You'll get lots of hugs and appreciation in return for giving lots of hugs and appreciation.

You will also rekindle positive memories that you had forgotten as you hear yourself saying or doing things that, on some primitive level, feel familiar. Sometimes old, bad memories overshadow the good ones, but the process of growing up and growing beyond your childhood will be aided by remembering the things that your parents did well. You'll feel healed when you intuitively know that the sweet thing you just did with your child was done with you.

Respectful Parenting Strategies

A philosophy can explain what's happening, but it doesn't provide you with the tools to change. The strategies suggested in this book will give you direction, guidance, and tools you can use. They will also provide the framework you'll need to come up with new, creative, and healthy parenting options. Some will seem very broad, others will seem specific, and you'll find there are plenty of different techniques you can do within each of these strategies. The following list summarizes the respectful parenting strategies and prepares you for the road ahead.

- **Begin with the understanding that you will learn from your child, you will learn with your child, and you will teach your child.** In other words, be a mutual learner rather than a know-it-all teacher. You'll avoid many of the inherent power struggles found in old-style parenting by having a more flexible, responsive style.
- **Slow down.** This cannot be stressed enough. An adult's pace is very different from an infant's, a baby's, a toddler's, or a small child's pace. You will miss too many cues from your child if you are thinking or acting (or *reacting*) too quickly. Even though you're trying to fit a lot into your day, it will actually go more smoothly and you'll accomplish more when you slow down. If you find yourself saying "what" or "hurry up" repeatedly, you're going too fast.
- **Listen carefully, using all your senses.** See, feel, and hear what your child is saying. This is important not only for your preverbal child, but for school-aged children as well. In spite of their verbal abilities, young children often have difficulty articulating their emotions be-

cause their vocabularies are limited. This is why psychologists often ask children to draw what they're feeling. Another tactic is to have your child describe her feelings by telling you what it feels like physiologically (inside her body). She might describe butterflies in her tummy or a happy glow inside, and then you can give your child a word to associate with that feeling. You'll get a more accurate and complete message when you use all your senses to listen.

- **When you listen, be open to changing your mind or compromising with your child if she suggests something sensible that you had not considered.** If your child offers a good alternative to your plan, be flexible and do it her way. You don't want to do this every time, because then your child will think she is running the show. But children like the idea that they have some control over their lives, and they will be much more cooperative if you also use their ideas. By following your child's lead instead of imposing your own agenda every time, you'll be led into the slow-moving, enchanting world that children inhabit.

- **Focus on your child.** We often interact with our children while thinking of something else. If you're preoccupied, you're more likely to misinterpret or miss signals from your child. Focusing on your child by looking at your child as you're listening and talking, will help you understand what he is feeling and make your child feel worthwhile and important.

- **Be in awe with your child.** Recapture the innocent delight in life that babies and small children naturally have at their disposal. Appreciate your child's perspective of the world.

- **Be in awe of your child.** See how terrific she is. Feel how excited she is about life. Hear how involved she is. Feel how incredible it is that your little one is learning all about the world at an incredible rate.

- **Give your child positive messages.** Rather than saying, "Don't spill your milk," say "I like how carefully you're holding your cup." Our brains often ignore negative words like "not" and end up doing the very things we want to prevent. Wording messages positively helps assure you of the responses you want.

- **Validate your child's ideas.** You can do this by listening carefully, commenting on his input, eliciting his input, and doing what he wants when you can. You can tell what a preverbal child wants by watching his facial expressions and listening to the types of sounds he's making.

- **If you don't like how you're viewing your child's behavior, refocus your view.** This means look for another, more positive angle from which to view the current situation. When your child cries in the middle of the night, feel good that she trusts you enough to cry out for what she may need rather than being angry that your sleep has been interrupted.

- **Look for the positive intent in your child's actions.** If your child pulls all of the plastic containers out of the cabinet, see it as a game he's trying to play with you rather than as extra work he's trying to create. Laugh with him and then show him how much fun it can be to get the containers back in the cabinet. See if he can hand you one and then comment on his ability to help you. Have fun with him.

- **Don't sweat the small stuff.** Think about whether an uncomfortable situation is worth pursuing. Save your creative energies for the big stuff. If your toddler won't leave the buttons on your phone alone, move the phone (you can even put the phone in a time-out until she knows it can't be touched like that) and find something she can touch. In a few months, those buttons won't be so tempting and it will no longer be an issue.

- **When in doubt, ask for help.** Sometimes we can't see the positive options ourselves, and sometimes we are just human and need a break. Hopefully you have someone to contact whom you trust. Alternately, numerous parenting websites and chat lines can help you pick up new ideas, answer questions, and get support, including www.respectfulparenting.com. If you need something immediate, you can appeal to a higher power (pray), or it can be very helpful to simply say out loud, "Help, please!"

- **If you find yourself in a power struggle with your child, back off for at least thirty seconds.** By backing off, you'll clear your mind a little and remind yourself that you're the adult. Give the situation a calm perspective rather than getting caught up in a power struggle. There's almost always a different way to handle the situation rather than head on. Backing off gives you the breathing room to figure out a more creative and peaceful solution to the dilemma at hand.

Eliminating Old-Style Parenting Patterns

If you are a parent healing from a less-than-ideal childhood, the following are additional strategies and reinforced methods you can use to parent more respectfully.

- **Give yourself messages using positive wording.** Instead of saying, "I don't want to hit my child" or "She's driving me crazy," tell yourself, "I'm going to take the time to slow down and accept the fact that my baby is having a bad day. I will tell her that I wish I knew how to help her, but until I know how, I will at least hold and comfort her."
- **When in doubt, ask for help.** This is especially important for you. When you ask for help, you are admitting you don't like what you're doing and you're leaving yourself open to new ideas. All kinds of new options may come flooding in. Parenting can be a lonely business. It always helps to have someone to share your feelings with and to hear how someone else deals with similar problems. If there's nobody around to talk with, you can always pray and turn it over to your God, the universe, or the cosmos. When you offer up your questions, and you're willing to hear new ways of doing things, answers often gently present themselves to you.
- **Take note when you do things well.** Keep a journal to provide yourself with ongoing feedback about your parenting. It can remind you of techniques that work with your child, and it can reinforce your positive efforts. If you don't like writing, at least take the time to give yourself positive verbal feedback rather than taking your efforts for granted. When you handle a potentially difficult situation well, you may want to recall what life was like for you as a child in a similar situation, and congratulate yourself for handling it better.
- **Forgive yourself when you slip.** When you forgive yourself for not being the perfect parent, you will free up a great deal of energy that can be used to be a much better parent the next time you find yourself feeling challenged.
- **Use Time-Outs with a mirror.** If you go into a room where you can see yourself in a mirror, it's easier to focus on who you are today and how you want to respond. You can see yourself as the adult you are rather than the child you were. You can even say, "Okay,

here I am [___name___]. It's [___date, including year___]. I'm
_____ years old. How do I want to handle this situation today?" Somehow, seeing your own face helps to consciously clue you
in to the adult resources you have rather than falling back on the
automatic responses that were unconsciously programmed in your
childhood.

- **Enjoy the process.** Many positive changes are going on in your life:
  changing your behavior as a parent, watching your child's reaction,
  feeling better about yourself, and healing your old hurts by hearing
  yourself being kind and respectful to your child. Savor these moments.

- **Recognize that parenting is a process:** You're going to have your
  good days, your great days, your not such good days, and your days
  you really wish you could just re-do as a parent. The days you want
  to re-do are often days marked with more anger than you want to
  be feeling.

- **The Shield of Anger:** If you begin to look at anger differently, as an
  emotional charge that surges through your body periodically, you
  can begin to develop a different kind of relationship with your
  anger. Right now you probably feel like it has control over you. But
  if you reframe your anger and see it as a defensive shield, like warriors used in the old days of fighting with bows and arrows, protecting you from your more vulnerable underlying feelings, you'll be
  able to defuse the anger by recognizing it as a defense and not your
  true feelings. The next step is to look "beneath" the shield at your
  underlying truer feelings of fear, hurt, sadness or frustration. When
  you figure out which feelings are the real ones, you can begin to
  talk to yourself before your anger reaches that boiling point. In order to do that you need to have "smart feet." Smart feet will take
  you out of the room (where your anger is charging through your
  body and about to come out of your mouth or hands) to a place
  where you can ask yourself the following questions: a) If I wasn't
  thinking I was angry right now, what am I really afraid of? b) If I
  wasn't thinking I was angry right now, what am I really hurt about?
  c) If I wasn't thinking I was angry right now, what am I really sad
  about? d) If I wasn't thinking I was angry right now, what am I really frustrated about? When you can get in touch with the truer

feelings underneath the defensive anger shield you can decide if what you're really afraid of, hurting about, sad about, or frustrated with is something real or if it's an irrational reaction that's fueling your anger. If it truly is one of those underlying, more vulnerable feelings, that's a lot easier to express and channel in productive ways than anger. You'll find yourself immediately becoming gentler in your approach with your child as you deal with your true feelings rather than getting out the cover-up shield of anger.

- **Map of Anger:** Sometimes dealing with the shield of anger isn't as easy as you want it to be. Sometimes you can't find your smart feet and can't get yourself out of the room so you can calm down enough to ask yourself those key questions. If you'll look carefully at your anger and draw a map of your anger within your body, you'll begin to learn where and how the emotional charge feels as it moves through your body (physiologically) and when you can have smart feet and leave. If you follow the idea that anger is a strong charge surging through your body and out of your mouth (or hands) you can trace a path from where it starts out as a bother, an irksome issue, or a frustration to where it travels in your body as it builds into a rage. You could draw the sequence in boxes as though you were drawing a series of pictures in a comic strip. Each frame is another area where your emotional charge is building and traveling before it comes out of your mouth. You don't have to be an artist to do this. Stick figures will do; just make sure you draw your emotional charge in a way that you can become acquainted with your own map of anger. Each time you get angry try to find where it was before it came out your mouth, and before that, and before that. Drawing out the anger-building process will help you learn to find the physiological responses in your body that indicate a problem before it is out of control. Then you can pinpoint the time to use your smart feet and stop the process in its tracks. When you can find the emotion before it becomes a rage, you can use your smart feet to take yourself out of the room where your emotional charge is building, look in a mirror, and ask yourself the questions (in the previous section, on page 16) to get behind your shield of anger to your truer, more vulnerable feelings underneath.

Forgiveness and Understanding

Parenting the way you really want to and becoming a creative and respectful parent is challenging at times because you're bucking your own personal history, combined with your parents' personal history, combined with their parents' personal history. That's a lot of momentum. In order to understand your parents and be able to forgive them for their mistakes, it is often helpful to look at how they were parented. When it becomes clear that they did the best they could given where they came from, it's even easier to accept who they are, understand them, and possibly forgive them for what they did and how that affected you. Once you can do that, it becomes easier to forgive yourself for not being a perfect parent, thus freeing your personal energy to gather new ideas and become a respectful, creative, and kind parent.

Two

Making the Transition from Couple to Family

HE BIRTH OF A BABY launches two adults into a major transition from "couple" to "family." With love, understanding, and support, each couple welcoming a baby into its home can become a family that works for them. The amazing thing is that each new family's transition process is uniquely their own. For some it's such an easy transition that it seems like both people were born to be parents. For others it can be easy for one parent and more difficult for the other. For many it's harder than either new parent had imagined, and they're both caught off guard, left wondering what they've gotten themselves into and how they're going to deal with this new family they've created.

It doesn't matter if the child is born into a traditional marital relationship, into a committed but unmarried heterosexual relationship, into a same-sex couple, to a single mom giving birth, or a single parent adopting a baby. In all circumstances the arrival of a baby signifies the formation of a new family. This chapter will address the transition process as adults become parents. The term couple will be used, which includes traditional and non-traditional families such as blended stepfamilies, unmarried families, and same-sex couples becoming families. The use of *couple* is not meant to leave out single parent families, it's simply used to simplify the prose. Another simplification is using *marriage* where *relationship* may apply.

No matter how you enter into your new family, the learning curve for new parents and their infant is incredible. Even when they have been planning for months or years, most new parents are surprised by how different really having the baby is from what they imagined. As soon as they leave the hospital both new parents must face additional responsibilities and challenges in a sleep-deprived state. It is a time when parents learn to juggle being a mom, a wife, a husband, a dad, a friend, a worker, and a doer of household chores. Amazingly, it does happen for most people, life goes on, even if it seems daunting at first.

One woman said she was overwhelmed by the enormity of the tasks facing her. She said, "For the first few days it was just me, my husband, and the baby. I never felt so close to him, and I was absolutely in love with our baby. Then my parents came. It was so nice to share our new family with them. I'd nurse the baby, they'd burp him. I'd change the baby if they didn't do it first. And then one afternoon I realized that my parents were leaving in two days, my husband was back at work, and I was still exhausted. I sat and cried and blubbered out loud, 'But how will I nurse the baby, play with the baby, change his diapers, go to the grocery store, shower, cook, and take care of other things around the house while *he* works? You're all doing most of that now. I won't be able to do it all because I'm only one tired person, and in three months I have to go back to work myself. Then what?'"

She said her mother assured her that although it seemed like too much when they were there to help, once they left she'd figure it out. And she did. She said she learned very quickly to sleep when the baby slept and let her house be messier than usual. She made simple nutritious meals, and she loved taking care of her baby. Her husband would come home anxious to be with the baby, and she could do something else such as rest or enjoy seeing her husband and baby together. She said it was all very sweet but still tiring. It was her new family and she loved it, tired and all.

Avoiding a Bumpy Transition

If you and your partner were playmates before becoming parents, sometimes one or both of you will have trouble buckling down and facing the responsibilities this *parenting thing* involves. Situations where one parent gives all to the baby and the other parent carries on with life as before will not work in the long run. Tensions can easily build around who's doing what and who isn't. Tempers flare. Blame is placed and denied. A tremendous amount of resentment can build up within the parent taking primary responsibility. It's impossible to predict how you and your partner will relate to all the changes that happen as you become parents and a family. These necessary changes affect the couple's relationship tremendously, and they can be dealt with effectively. However, if they're not managed with care, the transition to family can be stunted or unsuccessful.

Unfortunately, a growing number of people with young children have trouble transitioning into a family. In fact they often have so much trouble, and consider their efforts so unsuccessful, that combined with other reasons, they decide to divorce. As a result, more than half the current divorce cases in U.S. courts involve at least one child who is five or younger. This is indeed a scary notion, especially when compared with how hopefully two adults conceive a child, bring it into the world, and look forward to becoming a family.

Perhaps the big question is how to avoid such a bumpy transition that it ends in the nightmare of divorce, and instead find another route that leads to a happy, intact family life. Planning, communicating, respecting each other, maintaining a sense of humor, being flexible, partnering, which demands a true give and take with responsibilities so that it feels like you're sharing the responsibilities rather than fighting each other about who is doing more, being in awe of your baby and your partner, celebrating small miracles such as your baby turning over for the first time, all of these things contribute to your new family life. They are moments you can keep as mental snapshots. You can bring them out and talk about them with your partner. "Remember when . . ." is a fun and warm family game. You begin to create your own family history. Creating and savoring these memories directly eases the transition because you're focusing on the positive aspects of your new family life rather than feeling burdened. It takes a lot of thoughtful, conscious effort to juggle caring for your baby, yourself, your spouse, and your work. You can't think it will happen naturally, rather it takes real work on everyone's part to make the family and the couple come alive and stay alive as viable co-existing units.

New parents must realize how much their relationship affects their children's emotional and cognitive development. The less stress a child feels the more he can develop to his full potential in all areas, including emotional, social, physical, and cognitive development. Thus, when parents get along well and there is little stress in the environment a baby feels safe, happy, and is free to easily learn about the world around him.

Parents should make sure their intimate relationship is based on a mature closeness that can withstand attention and affection being shared with a (necessarily) demanding infant. Ideally each adult will be mature enough to truly share their partner with a baby who will always take precedent. At the same time, new couples will need to save enough energy and love for each other and not give all of that good stuff to the new baby. As you nurture your child and each other, pay attention to and learn from your partner's interactions with your child, and watch your child's awesome reactions as she begins to recognize both of you as *her* parents.

Communication is the first step in the transition process. It will be very helpful to talk about what you remember about your childhood, including how you were parented and how that felt to you. You'll both want to share your ideas on parenting and explore what you want to repeat from your parents and what you want to do differently. You'll begin to see where your parenting ideas are compatible and what areas need to be worked on. To avoid no-win power struggles over how to raise your child, neither one of you should be convinced that *"my way is the only right way to do it."* That kind of parenting power struggle leaves new parents feeling angry, distant, and unappreciated by their partner. Those kinds of feelings create fertile ground for resentment and distance to develop. By discussing how to handle the baby from the very beginning, parenting ideas that need to be adjusted can be managed through a respectful dialogue. If they come up again later, you'll know how to communicate (after you've both had some rest) and you can move forward in a positive direction. Just as you'll be learning from and with your baby, allow yourself to learn from and with your partner.

It's difficult to predict how you or your partner will behave once your baby comes on the scene. The more you can talk with your partner as you're making this transition, the better off you, your partner, and your baby will be. As you discuss your similarities and differences, remember it's normal to *not* be parenting clones. You both come from different family backgrounds. You both have conscious and unconscious memories of your early family life and how you were parented. Those imbedded memories are going to affect how you parent today. You both have ideas, some strong, some not so well defined. But the more you can make conscious choices together about how you want your new family system to work, the more prepared you'll be, and the smoother your transition will be. Knowing that at times you'll disagree, you should even discuss how you want to deal with the inevitable parenting conflicts before they arise and decide how you want to handle parental disagreements.

Hopefully, after sharing your hopes, dreams, and fears about parenting, you'll find yourself respecting and understanding your partner's differences. Effective strategies for fostering your communication and relationship include: respecting each other's differences, remembering that you love this person, accepting that your partner may have a good idea even when it's different from yours, and that it's not about being right or wrong. Another effective approach is to try out different parenting ideas and see how your baby reacts to them. Let your baby's moods and behaviors guide you as to which parenting techniques work best. On some days your baby may react to your ideas better than your spouse's, and on other days your spouse's ideas may be more effective.

Agreeing to follow the child development ideas and parenting philosophies that make sense to both of you will help you bridge the differences between your family backgrounds. The more you both can become conscious of how you were treated and what you want to do differently, the more you can support each other in making conscious parenting decisions every day. When you work together you can come up with creative new approaches that work for you as a new family. The goals are to have lots of parenting options at your disposal, to ask your partner for help when you're stuck, and to accept the help offered even when it's something you hadn't thought of trying.

While you are making this crucial transition from couple to family it's important to know that the couple doesn't die the day the family is born, just as the individuals you were didn't disappear when you two became a couple. The couple and the individual adults are still very much alive, but these identities move backstage for a while as the baby takes center stage. He needs much more attention than the couple or the adults. Of course the couple still needs attention and nurturing, even though the world provides you with only twenty-four hours in a day. Because all your responsibilities just expanded and because you were not handed more hours to accomplish everything as you left the hospital with your baby in your arms, you might become overwhelmed very quickly.

Don't worry! It's possible to practice Respectful Parenting and raise a healthy baby with good self-esteem by re-prioritizing things, shuffling responsibilities, becoming more flexible, respecting your partner's input, and not being a "know it all new parent" with your partner. Keeping the couple alive will mean making some adjustments. You may not be able to have weekends away in romantic places for a while. You may not even be able to go out for dinner and a movie for a while. But you *can* have a candle-lit dinner at home and watch a video as you nurse your baby and cuddle with your partner on the couch. You can have intimate discussions where you talk about life as it is evolving. Is your relationship different than it used to be? Absolutely! But different doesn't mean "less than." Your scale for viewing your life and what's ideal for you as a couple will change. Use the same types of conscious discussions you're having about how to parent to also talk about how to maintain closeness and intimacy in your life as a couple. You can each talk about how you'd like your new life as a couple to look, feel, sound, and work now that you're parents and not solely lovers.

You should talk about your *needs* and *wants.* Try to build in ways you can each get those needs met. Understand that wants will probably have to be shuffled so you each get some of them met. Hopefully each of you has learned to distinguish between your own needs and wants. And hopefully you have the *waiting* part down, and you can tolerate not having all your wants addressed in a timely manner. It's good practice now, as you'll have to teach your baby the differences between needs and wants and the art of waiting as he approaches the terrific twos.

Another important aspect of this transition is to remember that it *is* a transition. It may take some time, and it probably won't always be smooth sailing. The first time you disagree on how to diaper the child is *not* time to panic, tell yourself "this won't work out," and start retreating and planning how you can raise your child alone. Both parents need to realize that different techniques for diapering don't have to be bad or inadequate. Flexibility and acceptance of each parent's methods within the context of the agreed-upon parenting philosophy are the keys to avoiding panicky feelings. When you work together one parent never feels the other is always telling him or her how to do it *right.*

Another way to avoid the panic is to remember that the first few months are a sleep-deprived reality that is not the most emotionally balanced time in your life. Important decisions like whether to stay together or not will be influenced by this. Once your baby starts sleeping through the night, your perspective will be different. Remembering that everyone's plate is more than full and that everyone is new at this thing called parenting will allow for more patience and understanding between you and your spouse. Remembering to respect each other's differences also helps.

Understanding how your spouse's early family dynamics contributed to who he or she has become and accepting your spouse's foibles helps you to be more kind, compassionate, and respectful of your partner's shortcomings. All of these things will help you keep your perspective and help avoid an insurmountable confrontation.

The other end of this continuum is to embrace your new experiences together. Give your partner compliments and praise when you see her having effective parenting interactions with your baby. A sense of humor is important in this process: laugh over mishaps instead of blaming each other. Enjoy each other's stories about what happened while you were away. Slow down and watch your baby together. Try to see your baby's mind working, taking in his environment. Be in awe together.

Although regular communication is the best way to navigate the transitional period, other tools can also be used. Parenting classes or sharing parenting books that make sense to you can put you both on the same page. Sometimes one parent is a reader while the other is not. If you as the reader highlight key paragraphs in a book and your partner is willing to read or listen to them, then you can form a unique "we" way of learning and parenting as a team. Identifying problems and resolving them as they come up, rather than ignoring them, is an effective way of keeping them from accumulating and becoming overwhelming. Family counseling can also help alleviate stress and resolve problems. Try to remember that this parenting thing is new, being a family is new, even partnering with a young child is new. You're not going to be good at all of it right away. Even if you're an overachiever, there will be a steep learning curve and a few backslides. You loved each other enough to make a family, it's worth whatever energy to takes to make your new family work well.

Common Pitfalls and How To Avoid Them

■ *Trouble working through disagreements.* If you come from a family where your parents were not able to successfully work through disagreements and stressful times, you may not have the communication skills to work things through to a useful solution with an intimate partner. Somehow issues with your spouse become much more emotionally charged, more quickly than with coworkers, acquaintances, and friends. There is an art form to communication and how to deal with emotional issues without getting all charged up about it. If you can begin by acknowledging to each other, out loud, that this is a rocky area, but you want to communicate as kindly and gently as possible, taking breaks whenever either of you needs to, you will set a cooperative tone from the beginning.

■ *Short-hand speak and how to communicate more effectively.* Couples often get stuck in what I call "short-hand speak." The pattern goes like this: your partner says something. He has the best of intentions but somehow the message he thought he sent was not clear. Perhaps he didn't give the reasoning behind what he said, or perhaps it was a very short, incomplete message, leaving plenty of room for interpretation. You make an assumption about what's just been said (usually the assumption implies something negative about the speaker or assumes the speaker has just put-down or misunderstood you, the listener.) Based on that incorrect assumption, you put a negative twist on the statement your partner made. You get upset because of what you assume he meant. Instead of stopping the conversation for a moment and asking him to clarify what he said or meant, you (who heard and misinterpreted the first message) send a new, somewhat caustic message back to him. Note that you have just reacted defensively (or aggressively) from an upset place due to your misinterpretation of his message rather than the message itself. This is where things begin to escalate. He hears disgust or anger in your voice and he's momentarily confused. He knows he didn't say or mean anything negative in his original message that should have set you off. He's disturbed by your caustic response to his innocent remark. He responds defensively, in anger, because he perceives he's just been attacked for no good reason. A second unnecessary escalation of negative emotions has just occurred. Your partner could have avoided escalating the situation by asking why you are upset, but he doesn't make that kind of "process" inquiry. He simply assumes he's been attacked (for no good reason) and attacks back.

From there the problem continues to escalate because you thought he was mean-spirited in the first place (when he began the conversation), and his second statement is equally if not more aggressive or negative than the first. You are not aware that your own misinterpretation and negative response triggered the second negative response. You still feel your response was justified based on your misinterpretation, but you don't know it was a misinterpretation from the beginning. All you can think of is his second, nasty reply. You are sure that your original (mis)interpretation was accurate and your righteous and angry response was entirely appropriate. Therefore, you respond a second time, increasing the level of emotion in the conversation. The conversation has quickly become an upsetting experience for both of you.

The problem continues to escalate from there with both people feeling attacked, counterattacked, misunderstood, and righteous in their responses. The end result is a good, old-fashioned stalemate (at best) or a huge fight with one of you stomping off (at worst). The saddest part is that both of you started this conversation with the best of intentions, but it quickly disintegrated as each side made (inaccurate) assumptions and interpretations. And you didn't check those assumptions out because of an underlying assumption of the worst, instead of the best, about your spouse.

If you stop long enough when interacting with your spouse to really look at him and remember, 'I love this person, I didn't marry a malicious individual.' Then if you *ask* that person what he meant by his last remark in a kind voice instead of assuming the worst, you'd get along better, you'd be communicating more effectively, and you'd avoid many unnecessary, hurtful fights.

Ask before you assume the worst or before you put a negative spin on someone else's message to you, "Did you mean _____?" The next thing you have to do is *believe* him when he tells you what he really meant to say, which you didn't hear. Surprisingly, people often cling to their own versions instead of believing their partner's original intent. Even when they stop and ask themselves, "Does this person normally lie to me?" and the response is, "No, of course not," they still tend to maintain their negative spin. I think it comes from a need to protect themselves from more hurt. To get unstuck from that defensive mode, ask yourself, "Why would I want to believe that my spouse is lying to me or purposely being mean to me instead of believing he meant what he's telling me he meant?"

If you ask your spouse and yourself those kinds of questions as you begin to feel a conversation going down a negative road, you may stop and think something like, "Oh, I don't have to feel attacked right now and escalate this conversation into an argument. There's really nothing to argue about. We're both talking respectfully, I'm simply not hearing him clearly."

If you don't believe your spouse's explanation, repeat what you heard, explain why you perceived it the way you did, and ask him if that's what he meant. The final step is for you to listen to him openly and believe his explanation.

When you send messages, make sure you use complete sentences and share your underlying thought process with your partner. It's easier for him to get a complete message and understand where you're coming from when you give more information than a phrase or two. If you can master these skills, you will find that you and your partner are able to communicate in a kinder, more effective manner.

■ *The 50-50 myth.* Most people have the 50-50 myth in their head and compare their marital relationship to the myth. The myth says, "I do half the work and my spouse does half the work." Rarely is this the case. You may do 70 percent in some areas and 30 percent in other areas. And your partner may have different strengths and do the majority of work that relies on those strengths. Avoid keeping a carefully calculated list in your head or if you find yourself in the "taken advantage of" category talk to your spouse and ask her what she's doing that you are not noticing. See if you need to re-evaluate what each of you needs to do in order to have a well-balanced home where you feel it's a partnership rather than an "all me" situation.

■ *The blame game.* Another myth is, "I'm a good team player at work, why is this so hard? It's my spouse who can't do it. I talk to people at work and we resolve issues. It's got to be her who's the problem. I think I'll talk to an attorney since I'm clearly the one with the skills." That's what I call the blame-game myth, which is blaming your spouse for all the problems in a marriage. It really does take two. I know it's easier to see your spouse's problems, but if you can identify and work on your part, amazing things sometimes happen. Remember the expression, "Every time you point your finger at someone else, there are at least three pointing back at you." See if you can do something differently. The first thing you might try is to voice your concern in a non-threatening way, such as, "I'm not feeling very good about _____. Can we put our heads together and figure out a different way of handling this so we both feel comfortable?" By stating your concern that way, you become a team with a common goal rather than a blaming adversary. It's important to remember that negotiating at work and negotiating at home involve two different skill sets and two different emotional levels; you probably need to be gentler and kinder at home.

■ *Intimacy complicates things.* Intimacy entails its own set of emotional entanglements and complications. Sometimes you need a therapist to help you sort out what's yours and what's your spouse's; other times you can do it on your own. Recognizing the complexities of life and accepting them rather than thinking, "This should be easy," helps. Intimacy takes time and work, resources that are particularly scarce as you become a new family.

There's an expression I read that applies here, "We won't always see eye to eye, but we can see heart to heart." Respecting each other's differences instead of putting a negative spin on your differences can go a long way toward creating a happy, comfortable home life.

■ *If I ignore it, it will get better.* One of the problems for people transitioning from couple to family seems to be that one spouse, often the wife, will talk about what's bothering her and what she wants to work on changing. While she identifies problems, her husband often minimizes her complaints and doesn't work on changing or accommodating her wishes. The woman feels invalidated and may get tired of waiting for a more effective response from her husband. By the time the husband accepts that his wife's been making some valid points, she's thinking about or initiating a divorce. It may be too late for that couple.

If your spouse complains and says he or she really wants to figure out how to do this family thing differently, try respecting his or her feelings. See what each of you can do differently to help the family function so everyone is satisfied. If you deny or minimize the problems your spouse is identifying, you may find yourself living alone. Individual counseling and marital therapy can be very effective. Even if you've never contemplated it before, if your marriage is rocky, before it's *too late,* try seeking help from a professional therapist. Going for therapy or counseling is certainly a lot less expensive, emotionally and financially, than going through a divorce. If you think of going to therapy as a way of adding more skills so you can help create a growing, intimate partnership rather than looking at what's "wrong" with you or your partner it may be easier to engage in therapy. You'll feel better and your partnership will be stronger for having weathered a storm and learned how to avoid the next one.

I would highly recommend that if you're having trouble in your marriage, please seek help from a marital or family therapist. Don't wait until there's so much water under the bridge that divorce seems to be the easiest answer. Remember that you may successfully divorce your partner, but you'll have to see and interact with your partner for the rest of your child's life. If divorce seems to be looming on the horizon read Chapter 15 carefully. It has additional tips for how to avoid a divorce if possible, and if you can't avoid it, the chapter presents ideas on how to handle divorce so as to minimize its negative effects on all of you.

Summary

The keys to successfully making the transition from couple to family seem to be respecting each others' strengths and struggles, nurturing each other through the process, and accepting that even though this may not be an easy transition, it can be a respectful, thoughtful, conscious, mindful, and loving transition.

There is a myth that because forming a family is a natural process, it should be easy and smooth. So, if you're struggling or feeling like you're alone, everyone else can do this but you, this is terrible and can't be fixed, you're not alone. All young families hit rough spots. If you're kind, gentle, and respectful to yourself, your partner, and your baby, and know you're all learning together it will make things easier. If you also remember that you want to learn together and get better at parenting and being a family, you can have the patience to ride through a transition that can take a few years before you get your roles down smoothly. Even then, smooth means some rocks and boulders will get in the way. That's life. If the boulders become too big and you recognize that you need to learn some new communication skills or additional coping skills go to a good therapist, counselor, or coach. You can go alone or with your partner. Recognizing you or you two need some new skills takes courage, but getting the skills is a relief, and you can move into the next stage knowing help is out there when you need it.

Successful family life can be seen as staying together and working out how to get over the rocks and around the boulders that life dishes out. It's not about smooth sailing and having no rocks or boulders to deal with. If one is realistic about family life and knows it takes conscious effort, commitment, respect, and emotional involvement with your child, yourself, and your partner to do well, then you can make it. If you expect a continual scene of running through a meadow of wildflowers in slow motion with a romantic pinkish haze filter to smooth the rough edges, you'll opt out, but you'll be missing a glorious bumpy ride called *family*.

Three
Nursing

ORE WOMEN ARE NURSING their babies today than they have in at least 65 years. Nursing is enjoying a resurgence as the medical, physical, and emotional benefits of breastfeeding are recognized within the medical community and the community at large. Prior to the twentieth century women either breastfed their babies or they hired a wet nurse for their babies. Having a wet nurse became so popular for women who could afford it that by the mid-eighteenth century in Europe there were government run bureaus that registered wet nurses. The idea to feed human babies animal milk began to grow in popularity in the nineteenth century. It took a while for people to realize that the raw cow's milk they were spoon feeding human infants was often making them sick.

The first baby formula was developed in 1860 by Henry Nestlé in Switzerland. He was trying to figure out a way to decrease health problems in babies and lower the infant mortality rates in foundling homes. Nestlé's formula was made with malt, cow's milk, sugar, wheat flour, and was mixed with water rather than heated cow's milk. Nestlé began selling his formula in the United States in 1870. At about the same time, Justin von Leibig, a chemist in Germany, developed the first commercial baby food. His formula was a powder made from wheat flour, cow's milk, malt flour, and potassium bicarbonate added to heated cow's milk. Leibig's formula was sold in groceries in the United States starting in 1869. By 1897 the Sears catalogue was selling eight brands of commercial infant foods.

At the time, formulas were too expensive for most families and many mothers continued to nurse.

At the turn of the last century, as the industrial revolution developed and more emphasis was placed on the importance of scientific inquiry and modern advancements, physicians and nutritionists began to monitor babies' growth patterns more carefully. They looked for ways to increase a baby's weight and lower health risks. Their work led to a more scientific approach to early infant feeding and new formulas were developed. By 1915 the trend was to try to create an infant formula that closely resembled human milk. Scientists, physicians, and advertisers were so successful in their campaign to have babies fed in a more scientific, modern manner (rather than a mother's breast milk) that between the 1940s and 1960s most infants were formula fed rather than nursed. During this period, formulas were often made or mixed with evaporated milk and babies were given vitamins and supplements. It is estimated that by 1960, 80 percent of bottle-fed babies were using a formula with evaporated milk. By the mid 1970s the number of women who breastfed their babies reached an all time low of 25 percent.[1] Scientists, physicians, and parents had come to believe it was easier and better to feed a baby a bottle and the cost had come down so it was "affordable." Pediatricians were not encouraging women to breastfeed as they thought the scientifically formulated products were more beneficial for the baby.

As more studies were done on nursing babies versus formula fed babies, scientists and physicians realized that breast milk is the most nutritious way to feed your infant and that there's nothing more beneficial to a baby than a mother's milk. The women's movement and La Leche League helped spread the word. With the growing "back to nature" and "health oriented" attitudes prevailing from the late 1960s through today, there has been a large, willing audience who responded well to the new information about breastfeeding. What could be easier than nursing? What could be less expensive than breast milk? Some of the old myths perpetrated by the formula manufacturers began to fall on deaf ears. Women rediscovered the pleasures of nursing and realized how nutritionally sound and how nurturing breastfeeding is for their babies. As dads became more active in the parenting process they supported their wives breastfeeding and saw how quickly a crying infant could be comforted. The benefits of breastfeeding began to be discussed in the news media; parents started paying attention.

In 1991, 50 percent of women leaving the hospital were breastfeeding their babies, and by 2001 that number had increased to 69.5 percent of newborns were breastfed at birth.

To Nurse or Not to Nurse?

How do you make the decision to nurse or not? How do you decide how long to nurse your child? How do you handle the reality of nursing and working? How do you handle family and friends' reactions if you choose to nurse past infancy, or six months, or even nurse your toddler, new walker, or two year old? For many couples it's a joint decision, for others, one parent or the other feels particularly strongly and convinces the other. The decisions are unique for each family, but the answers to these questions should be explored from the start. This chapter and the stories within will provide a foundation for that exploration.

One of the biggest considerations of whether or not to breastfeed revolves around the mother's schedule. A working mom faces particular challenges, but they can certainly be managed with accurate information and the right tools. Because regular nursing or pumping is important to keep your breast milk supply flowing adequately, you need to make arrangements if you work full-time or even part-time to make sure you drink plenty of water and you take time out of your work day to pump milk so you can keep your supply up. That way, on weekends and on your days off when you can nurse throughout the day, you have enough milk for your baby. A working mom can buy a small breast pump that can be taken to work so she can pump milk during the day in order to keep her milk supply up throughout the day and be available when she gets home and her baby is hungry. Parents can also rent (or purchase) a larger, more efficient breast pumping machine to pump extra milk at home or at the office so the baby can always have his mother's breast milk, even when she's unavailable. Moms can also hand pump milk without the aid of a breast pump at work or when they're away from their baby for a few hours. Pumped breast milk can be frozen and later thawed and heated up when the baby needs it if mom isn't available.

Many other nursing aids make breastfeeding easy and comfortable. The Boppy company in Golden, Colorado (www.Boppy.com) produces an award-winning nursing pillow that fits around a woman's abdomen so the baby can be cradled at just the right angle while nursing. A regular pillow can also be used to make the baby more comfortable and to help the nursing mother be more comfortable and not strain her back by holding the baby up and sitting during the hours she nurses. Soft baby carriers, such as Weegos (www.weego.com), are also a wonderfully nurturing way of holding or carrying your baby when you breast feed in public places so you have privacy. The Weego is an updated version of the original soft baby carrier, which has safely and lovingly held babies close to their parent's heart since the mid-seventies. You can adjust the baby carrier to easily hold your baby in a comfortable, private environment where you and your baby can relax and nurse. Alternately, a light baby blanket draped over your shoulder and chest can also provide you and your baby with some privacy.

The Benefits of Breastfeeding

There are many physical and emotional benefits associated with breastfeeding for you and your baby to share. Many women approach breastfeeding with enthusiasm, but if they encounter problems during those first few days, they may give up too soon. It can be disappointing and intimidating when a new mom encounters difficulties nursing her baby. She can judge herself harshly thinking, "This is such a 'natural' process, why can't I just do it? What's wrong with me?" When a new mom feels insecure it may seem easier to her to stop trying and mix up some formula. If you experience these kinds of concerns or insecurities, before you give up look on the Internet or in your local phone book for some help—websites, lactation consultants in your area, or La Leche League will provide free or paid services.

There are lots of ways someone more knowledgeable about nursing can help you smooth the transition and teach you helpful tips. The following are a few tips you may not have known about.

Tips for Easier Nursing

- It's easier to nurse when you hold your baby up from your lap and at an angle.
- Your nipple should be as far back in your baby's mouth as possible to minimize nipple soreness.

- Using a pillow or two across your lap helps—your baby will be in the correct position and you won't have to support your baby's weight with your back.
- You need to drink plenty of water and liquids to keep your milk supply up (at least six to eight glasses per day).
- Nurse on demand to stimulate your breasts to produce plenty of milk.
- Let your nipples air dry at first until they toughen up to prevent cracking or infection. If your nipples do crack, you can try putting some breast milk or other natural moisturizers on them. Vitamin E oil or lanolin are often used, but be careful if you use Vitamin E or lanolin because some babies are allergic to them.
- Eat well so that you will have proper nutrients and energy to pass on to your baby when you nurse. You'll need at least 500 extra calories a day to nourish you and your baby.
- Get as much rest as possible, which often means sleeping when your baby sleeps, even if it's only for an hour or two at a time.
- Avoid introducing an artificial nipple, such as a pacifier, for a week or two, because sucking on a pacifier or a bottle nipple requires a different sucking action than real ones. Your baby is learning how to nurse and you don't want to confuse her.
- Your milk will flow more easily if you're relaxed, so if you're feeling anxious about the nursing process, try relaxing music, meditating before you start nursing, or creating a calm nursing environment in your home where you and your baby can go.

Recent studies suggest that nursing your child is the most nutritionally sound way of feeding your baby, and the most nurturing foundation you can provide. Breast milk has just the right amount of lactose, water, fatty acids, and amino acids necessary for human digestion, brain development, and growth. Breastfed children seem to have higher IQs than formula fed babies. Breastfeeding protects your baby in countless ways because breast milk is a complex, natural formula that strengthens your baby's immune system. When you nurse your baby you transfer your own antibodies for diseases to your baby, helping to prevent diarrhea, rashes, allergies, asthma, ear infections, respiratory infections, pneumonia, botulism, bronchitis, staphylococcal infections, influenza, and German measles. Nursing babies are also at lower risk for developing tonsillitis, obesity, sclerosis, inguinal hernia, undescended testicle, reflux or gastroesophagel reflux disease, diabetes, Crohn's disease, Hodgkins disease, urinary tract infections, and juvenile rheumatoid arthritis. A mother's breast milk changes as her baby grows to continually supply the most balanced source of nutrition your baby needs. You can continue to breastfeed after you introduce solid foods to your baby thus continuing to protect your child with your antibodies and have a ready way to nurture and comfort your growing young child.[2] In addition, nursing promotes good jaw development in your baby. Nursing takes more effort from the baby as he/she sucks than using a bottle, and that effort strengthens your baby's jaw and encourages teeth to develop in a straight, healthy way.

Babies can only focus about 12 to 15 inches from their eyes, so when you're nursing your baby is able to focus on your face and you're able to focus on your baby. This eye to eye contact helps you and your baby connect and form attachment bonds, which are vital to your baby's emotional, social, and cognitive development. The tactile sensations of cuddling skin to skin with you are also emotionally nurturing to your baby. You and your baby experience a sense of warmth and security from being that close to each other. It's healthy for you and your baby to feel relaxed and focused on each other. This kind of emotional closeness is very beneficial to your baby's optimal development.

Mothers benefit directly from nursing too. It's easier to nurse than to worry about bottles to wash, formula to prepare, and nipples to sterilize. Lactation helps the mother's uterus contract back to its original size. Nursing helps a mother lose the weight she gained in pregnancy. Nursing releases the hormone prolactin, a naturally relaxing hormone. Many moms talk about how good they feel while they're nursing. Part of that good feeling is likely the prolactin which helps them relax with their baby. Women frequently say nursing helps them maintain a sense of balance in their life. Nursing mothers are able to quickly make the switch from working woman to Mom by sitting down, rocking, and nursing their child soon after they come home in the evening.

The only disadvantage to continuing to breastfeed until your child is ready to stop is the comments you may get from relatives, friends and associates. As long as you believe in the benefits of nursing and are feeling good about your nursing relationship with your child, all those comments can be dealt with. Other people's concerns do not have to become your own. You can educate people who aren't as familiar with the benefits of nursing or you can simply say something like, "I understand you think that way, but I see it differently. Thank you for your concern, but I'm really very comfortable with what we're doing."

Breastfeeding can be painful at times, especially in the first few weeks. Women can experience sore and cracked nipples, clogged milk ducts, breast infections, and engorged breasts (breasts can become overly full of milk and hard and painful). All of these issues are temporary and can be dealt with by using home remedies, homeopathic remedies, or antibiotics if necessary. These issues should not lead you to stop nursing if you want to continue. Do get help and don't ignore these problems as they're likely to get worse if they're not treated. They can easily be remedied if you stay tuned to your body and recognize and treat the problem when it develops.

What Parents Say

Sarah: For some reason, all during my pregnancy I knew, in a completely nonwavering way, that: a) I was going to nurse my baby; and b) there would be no problems doing so. I had heard stories of women who had "too much milk," "not enough milk," babies that weren't interested, or who had only nursed for a few weeks. But I wasn't going to be one of those. I was fervently committed to six months of nursing because I had bad allergies and I didn't want to pass them along. I had inklings that there might be more nurturing reasons to nurse my baby, but basically, I justified it to the doubters in my life by citing my bad allergies and the idea that I could make sure my baby didn't develop them. I had seen friends nurse babies and it always looked so natural; except for one friend who had nursed her toddler; now that I found a little absurd. I remember conversations with my husband where we both expressed our disapproval and knew we'd never do that; six months was fine but once a child was walking, give me a break. . . . I really don't know why I was so confident about my nursing abilities, because I wasn't as confident about anything else having to do with this upcoming motherhood thing.

I'm not sure who was more surprised, my husband or me when I was still nursing past six months, into toddling, walking, and running. I just became more flexible about it the more I read about child-led weaning and the more I experienced the benefits of easily comforting my child when he cried. I felt so close to my baby, and neither one of us wanted to stop. Luckily, my husband supported my decision to continue to nurse as long as our son wanted to and as long as my milk held out.

* * *

Judy: Within seconds of his birth, my baby latched right on as if he had been doing it for years, I felt absolutely incredible being involved in such a miraculous occurrence. Having this newborn in my arms, feeling his little life beginning, and feeling my love well up in waves from my body, enveloping his. . . . I instantaneously knew there was more to this nursing thing than I had imagined. My whole life changed in that millisecond, never to return from where it had come. There truly was a colossal shift in my being, my reality. As my child was born, so was my parenting.

Strategies for Successful Nursing

The following strategies for successful nursing go hand-in-hand with the strategies for Respectful Parenting.

- **Slow down.** Again, slowing down cannot be stressed enough. When you slow down, you're calmer and your milk will flow more easily.
- **Drink lots of water, eat really well, and take vitamins.** Nursing and producing nutritious milk are very demanding on your body, so you should take good care of yourself, both for you and your baby.
- **Follow your child's lead whenever possible,** rather than imposing your own agenda. If you nurse when your baby wants to rather than imposing your own schedule, life will be smoother for you and your baby.
- **If your baby has a nursing strike** and refuses for a couple of nursings or a couple of days, pump through, offer to nurse but don't push the idea, and then start up again when he's ready.
- **When in doubt, ask for help.** Hopefully someone whom you trust will be available either in person or by telephone. You can also call trained lactation consultants listed in the phone book, through the La Leche League, or on the Internet.

Following Your Baby's Nursing Lead

An added benefit of nursing is that it actually does make your life easier in some ways. If you're worried about when to nurse, how often, or how long to nurse, the best rule of thumb is to follow your baby's lead. Your baby feels hungry when his little tummy is empty, and he will stop nursing when his tummy is full. Sometimes your baby will want to nurse for comfort, and what a wonderful way to comfort and nurture your child. Your baby will end up being calmer, happier, and less fussy if you follow his needs for nursing. When you're going out for a few hours, you don't have to worry about taking bottles and formula—you have your milk in place. Likewise, if you find yourself and your baby stuck somewhere unexpectedly, feeding your baby is not a problem. When your baby voices her "I'm hungry" cry, you just find a place to sit and quietly provide what she needs.

For example, when my infant was four weeks old, I joined a group for mothers and their infants offered by the local adult education center. After the second meeting I suggested to a few mothers that we go out to lunch at a restaurant across the street. They thought it was a novel idea and with some trepidation we set out the following week. There were six of us with six infants, the oldest only eight weeks. All was fine until one of the babies started crying. The mother looked upset and asked, "What should I do?" "Nurse her," I said. "Here?" she asked, blanching as she looked around. The restaurant was packed with the lunchtime crowd, and aside from our table, not a single customer was under sixty-five. The restaurant was in a small shopping center at the entrance to a large retirement community.

I said, "What choice do you have? Otherwise, you'll have to leave and you just ordered." It made sense to me. She said, not too enthusiastically, "I guess I could try. . . ." and she lifted her blouse as discreetly as possible. Her baby latched on happily, and quieted down immediately. Within fifteen minutes, and from then on, at least four of us were nursing at any given time. Far from disapproving, I don't think any of the older folks left without stopping by our table to comment on how wonderful or delightful it was to see young people in the restaurant and to see young mothers nursing again. They all hoped we would be back. It was such a pleasant surprise. I know it helped me to "launch" my public nursing in such an accepting and approving atmosphere.

When you breastfeed your baby you establish an important "nursing relationship" with your baby. Your family becomes a "nursing family." You develop such close emotional bonds with your baby as you're able to quickly respond to your baby's hunger and emotional needs wherever you are. It's important to feel comfortable when you're nursing so your milk flows easily for your baby. When you're in public you can use a light baby blanket over your shoulder to provide a private and personal space for you and your baby, you can sit a distance from people if you feel like you or they would be more comfortable, or you can use a baby carrier to assure you're not "exposing" yourself in public. Hopefully, a nursing mother can feel confident that she's providing her baby with the best beginning possible by nursing and be able to know if someone is judgmental that's their problem. You can accommodate to a degree, but it shouldn't stop you from providing your baby with the benefits of breastfeeding. Here are some women's stories about their nursing relationships with their babies.

What Parents Say

Judy: One day, when my mother was visiting and sitting with us as my child nursed in my arms, she said, "What a wonderfully safe place for him to begin his life; hanging out in your arms for the first few months . . . that child can't help but feel good about himself when he grows up, after such a long beginning of almost constant hugs and cuddles." Now that's the kind of love and support nursing mothers need.

* * *

Sarah: When I had to go back to work part-time I was very sad and knew I'd miss spending all day with my baby, but the financial reality was such that we had no choice. Once I started back I realized how incredibly blessed I was to have a flexible schedule, and handy childcare arrangements. I'd wake up at 5:30 and have a half hour or so to: pump milk for my baby, think, meditate, and just be all by myself. Then around 6:00 or 6:30 my baby would wake up. We'd nurse and have our cuddly playtime in bed.

As he got older our routine solidified to a degree. We'd take a bath and nurse in the tub, which must have felt as safe, warm, and cozy as anything; I imagined it felt rather familiar and womb-like. A little later we'd nurse into a nap together, nap, wake up, nurse again, and then, once he was on solids, we'd have lunch and go off to child care. I was able to, an hour-and-a-half to two hours later, drive the one mile to the child care center, nurse him and visit with him there, then go back to work for another two or three hours and then pick him up for the evening. Sometimes, they'd give him a bottle of pumped milk in the late afternoon. Later, we always had one nice long nursing to sleep. There isn't anything much better than helping your child drift off into a deep peaceful sleep, or being able to hold and nurse them when they're upset about something, or if they've gotten an owie, or are simply ready for those warm cuddly nursings just because.

* * *

Judy: I think it was around three months, maybe earlier when I wondered why I had had a self-imposed six-month rule to stop nursing our child. I think it was from back in the days where I saw nursing as a more clinical approach to preventing allergies. But fairly early on I could see that barrier melting as I think I replaced it with nine months, and kept the idea of even extending to one year on the back burner. I still saw nursing a walking child as unnecessary, and stretching this wonderful nursing thing a little too far. So I thought I'd wean him around the time he began to toddle.

You know how time has a way of moving very quickly? All of a sudden he was crawling and shortly thereafter toddling. By then I had loved our nursing relationship so much, I knew he did also, and everything I had read said it was perfectly healthy to take the child's lead in weaning rather than impose a parental ending point. So I began to slowly introduce that idea to my not so willing husband.

I guess it took hold, because at some family gathering, where people were giving me a hard time, asking whether I planned on nursing him through college, I heard my husband say, gently but with conviction in his voice, "We never thought she'd nurse him for so long, but they both like it so much and it's clearly so good for him that we're just going to see where this goes." I felt truly supported and loved by him at that moment, amid a rather large number of raised eyebrows.

* * *

Sarah: When our child was almost two-and-a-half, I was delighted to meet another woman who was nursing her almost three-year-old. It was the first time I was beginning to feel a little antsy about nursing and actually on some days could foresee an end in sight that would be okay with me. I don't know why I was feeling like that, but I was . . . I remember her saying that she had heard, children often make the break around three, and she was waiting . . . a little hopefully, feeling like maybe it was almost time. When we met again a few months later we commented on how supportive our first meeting had been. Both our children were still nursing, and we had each re-relaxed into it for the duration.

Fathers and Breastfeeding

It's important to talk honestly, openly, and calmly with your spouse and make sure you're both onboard with nursing your new baby. Hopefully, you and your partner already share common beliefs about nursing and how to make it work together. If not, respecting each other's feelings and working through any problems rather than becoming upset with each other's stubborn stances will help you resolve them peacefully. Respecting potential differences and acknowledging the challenges often brings couples closer. In his book, *Becoming a Father*, William Sears writes, "Breastfeeding is a lifestyle, not just a method of feeding. Providing understanding and support for the breastfeeding pair is one of the most valuable investments you can make in the future health and well-being of your family."

Fathers sometimes do feel left out when a mother nurses her baby, especially if the nursing relationship extends beyond infancy or the first six months, which wards off later allergies and strengthens the baby's immune system. But if you can view your little group as a nursing family rather than as a nursing mother and child, the father doesn't have to feel left out. A good way to start is for the father to understand all the physiological and emotional benefits of nursing and to see how healthy his baby is. It's also helpful if the mother can pump extra milk so the father can feed his baby and feel that special closeness that comes from feeding. It's a good idea to wait until your baby is six to eight weeks old before you begin bottle feeding your pumped breast milk to your baby. By then you and your baby will have a strong nursing relationship and you'll avoid confusion which sometimes results because there can be a faster flow of milk from a bottle than a breast. Sometimes, if you introduce a bottle too soon, the baby prefers the bottle and that can interfere with your nursing relationship. In the meantime, a father can bond and feel close to his baby when he's not involved in the feeding process by interacting with, playing with, and carrying his baby.

What Parents Say

Cindy: People don't talk about it often, but breastfeeding can cause tension in a marriage. I know it has in mine. My husband and I are both committed to it, and we know in our heads and hearts this is the right thing to do. But periodically my husband says things like, "I know it's great what you're doing with our baby, and how much time you're willing to let her nurse. But I miss you! You're in there with her, sweetly nursing her to sleep every night for forty-five minutes, while I'm out here twiddling my thumbs and waiting. Sometimes you fall asleep, too, and you don't come out here to the living room to join me at all.

We used to have our evenings together and now we get so little time, just the two of us. And no, I don't want to lie beside you two and watch her drift off to sleep. That's okay now and again, but not every night. Sometimes I'm jealous and I don't like that you're so dedicated and I'm supposed to be so dedicated, too. And sometimes I feel left out. And those times I wish you'd stop nursing already."

I can see his point. I really can. Sometimes I'm sympathetic to him and try to accommodate him, but other times, I react angrily because I'm scared he's going to start really pressuring me to stop. I want to nurse till she wants to stop, not till my husband wants me to stop. I love nursing her and I know he needs me, too. But he's an adult, he should be able to wait. And so sometimes, it's difficult.

The Logistics of Nursing

Unfortunately, women often feel pressured by well-meaning friends and relatives, particularly those who were parenting in the days when doctors unanimously recommended formula feeding or only nursing for six months, to stop nursing at some set date. These friends and relatives are operating from a false belief that there is a "right" amount of time to nurse your baby and a "wrong" amount of time to nurse your baby. If you have confidence in your knowledge of the benefits of nursing (as long as it is working for your child, you, and your partner) you can hear what they say and make your own knowledgeable decision remembering that all the scientific evidence backs up your efforts.

If you're wondering how do you know when your baby is hungry, when you should nurse your baby, and how long you should nurse your baby each time, watch and listen to your baby carefully. Children have a way of telling you when they're hungry or when they need to nurse for comfort. Infants have an "I'm hungry" cry. When they're verbal, they'll ask or tell you when they're ready. If you're concerned about how other people will react if you're nursing a young verbal child, and your child asks to nurse in public, you and your baby can come up with a special word or expression for nursing so you know what your child wants but others won't necessarily know. My child came up with the expression "nigh, nigh" so when we were in public and he asked for nigh nigh, people thought he was so sweet to know he was tired and needed to go to sleep. I'd take him to a private, quiet place to nurse him. He usually did fall asleep, and people did not have to know that I had nursed him to sleep.

Children who are being nursed longer than six months will often have a couple of nursing strikes where they seem uninterested in nursing. They can last a couple of nursings, a day, or a few days. If you drink lots of water and pump through the time to keep your milk supply up, and offer to nurse but don't force it on your child, your child will let you know when and if she's ready to nurse again. In the meantime, offer your baby your bottled breast milk so you know your baby is continuing to get the nutrition she needs. On the other hand, a nursing strike may be the beginnings of child-led weaning, and your child may be telling you she's had enough. You may not know for a few days, so be patient. Whichever it is, a nursing strike or the end of your nursing relationship, it helps your child if you're calmly following her lead.

Let your child know whatever decision feels right to your child will be fine with you, so there is no pressure one way or the other. If she's less than six months old, you may want to continue to pump and feed her breast milk to help boost her immune system. If she's over six months you can know your nursing relationship with your baby ended peacefully and at a pace she initiated. When you follow your child's lead, you're telling her on an unconscious level that she has good ideas. You're helping to shape her positive self-esteem by letting her know she's worthwhile. You can contact other breastfeeding mothers, nursing websites, or organizations like La Leche League if you start having doubts about when stopping is right for you. The following are some parents' stories that may relate to your concerns and your joys about nursing.

What Parents Say

Sarah: Our baby was three weeks old, when my mother-in-law visited for the first time. Within hours of my mother-in-law's arrival, she had decided that I must not have enough milk (because our baby cried after he nursed.) She told me that she had tried to nurse her oldest child, but hadn't had enough milk. She thought that was my problem. I listened and tried to reassure her that the doctor had said our baby had underdeveloped intestines and the best thing I could do was to continue to nurse him. She continued to think I should stop nursing. Finally, after hearing this numerous times, I pointedly said, "Look, he's gaining weight beautifully. I'm not worried about having too little milk for him." I think I put her off a little, and that was all we said on the subject that day.

The next morning, when our baby started crying again shortly after he had nursed, she said, "You're probably right. It's probably not that you don't have enough milk, you probably have too much milk. You should supplement your feedings with formula; then you wouldn't produce as much, and he'd be okay." I just stared at her thinking, 'I thought you were coming to help. I don't need this.' The third time she brought her new theory up, I said, "I don't think I have too much milk. I don't think there is such a thing as too much or too little milk. I've seen a lactation consultant and I've talked to the La Leche League and to the pediatrician. They've said this is one of those many normal things that sometimes happens and to keep nursing because I'm doing the best thing for my baby." She responded strongly saying, "The La Leche League! Don't they advocate nursing? What do you expect they'd tell you?" I just had to let it be, as I didn't think she was open to new information so it wouldn't even be worth the effort. Sometimes you need to accept people where they are and know you have your own good reasons whether they agree or not. By three months, all our baby's gas was gone, his intestines were fully developed, and we were still happily nursing away with my milk being his only nutritional intake.

When You Have Trouble Nursing or Decide Not to Nurse

Some mothers find that they're unable to nurse or don't want to nurse even when they understand that nursing is definitely the best thing they can do for their babies from a nutritional and nurturing standpoint. It's important to acknowledge that for various reasons, not everyone can nurse their newborn babies, and not everyone wants to nurse their babies. If you want to nurse, and you're having trouble, before you give up, seek some help. Lactation consultants are listed in the phone book. You can find a local chapter of La Leche League (in the phone book or on the Internet), and their leaders are very willing to help. Or look online for nursing websites that have valuable information and tips.

Today's working women sometimes find it difficult to breastfeed as long as they would like. They don't have private places where they can relax and pump milk during the workday to maintain their milk supply. Some moms can't take the time to pump at work. Some women find it difficult (or impossible) to relax enough within a thirty-minute or even a one-hour lunch break, to eat and pump. Many are forced to cut back on their nursing and only nurse in the morning and night. Others say the stress of trying to juggle all of life's demands cuts down their milk, they become frustrated, and so do their babies.

In these circumstances, women often feel guilty about not being able to live out their breastfeeding dreams. They really don't need that guilt when they're doing the best they can to juggle work, home life, and a personal life. So, if your breastfeeding career is not exactly what you had hoped for, accept the fact that you're doing the best you can given life's reality, and let go of the guilt.

The nurturing involved with nursing can be replaced when you and your husband give your baby lots of cuddles and loving. You can nurture your baby by holding her, rocking her, walking with her, and carrying your baby close to your heart by using a soft baby carrier, such as a Weego. The more you can provide your infant and small child with lots of hugs, understanding, and respect, the more your child will have a wonderful, healthy beginning even without breastfeeding.

If you are looking at adopting a baby and think you can't breastfeed, please check with La Leche League in your area. They may be able to help. Here is one mother's story who ended her nursing relationship earlier than she had expected, how she struggled and came to peace with the reality of her situation with her daughter.

What Parents Say

Jeanne: I tried to breastfeed for two weeks, on and off, but it was clear she preferred the bottle. I had to admit she had made her choice, and I had to stop trying to convince her that my preconceived notion was the way to go. I realized I had my agenda, she had hers, and she was perfectly happy without breastfeeding. I was causing her frustration by trying to get her to like something she had no interest in.

When I finally made the decision to stop trying to nurse, I could feel a big difference in myself. I relaxed more, accepted her decision, and now, six months later, I feel terrific. I don't think it did anything to our bonding. If anything, because I respected her choice, maybe I was telling her something. She's a cuddly baby, so she certainly gets her share of hugs, holding, cuddling, and touching in all those important ways.

Summary

From the 1940s through the late 1960s, the possibility of beginning your life with a close, warm physical relationship with your mother, as she quietly breastfed you, was just not considered an option for many people. The scientific and medical community largely advocated the scientifically developed formulas thinking they were more beneficial to babies. It has only been through newer research coupled with the rise of the women's movement, the environmental/ecology movement, breastfeeding support groups, and women and men who began thinking for themselves and reading some of the newer materials comparing breastfeeding and formula fed babies, that nursing has enjoyed a much needed resurgence.

How much more nurturing can you be than to hold your crying infant in your arms, bring him or her close to your warm body, and provide the kind of comfort that only closeness and intimacy can bring? At the same time, you provide the incredible benefit of perfect nutrition. Some people will question why you're nursing and not using bottles. Others will question why you're "still" nursing. Others may even be embarrassed. But if you, your baby, and your partner are in agreement and sharing the benefits of being a nursing family, you'll come up with some creative responses when the situation arises. Remember to look to your baby for cues. When you see your baby resting peacefully in your arms, nursing into a blissful sleep, with a perfectly calm face, free from anxiety, you'll know there's no need to stop.

Notes

1. Contemporary Pediatrics.com/contpeds/article/article Detail, "A Concise History of Infant Formula (twists and turns included)" February 2003.

2. See www.fda.gov/fdac/features/895_brstfeed.html, www.AskDrSears.com, or www.lalecheleague.org/NB/NBJulAug01p124.html.

Four

To Spoil or Not to Spoil

ALL PARENTS SHOULD BREATHE a sigh of relief as they read the next nine words: There is no such thing as "spoiling" an infant. The old-style parenting fear that a child could be ruined at an early age if parents responded too often when their infant cried is groundless and false. Children may be spoiled when they are given everything they want, but an infant does not have any *wants,* only *needs.* An infant's needs include: nourishment for an empty tummy, being held, being nurtured, some quiet time when she's overstimulated, interactive playtime when she's awake, a soothing environment to fall asleep, and a clean diaper. Infants are not spoiled when their needs are taken care of. In fact, they feel good, they begin to trust the world around them, they establish strong bonds, and they begin to feel good about themselves when their needs are addressed. An infant communicates his or her needs by crying, and parents can be assured that they're taking care of all their baby's needs when they respond to his or her cries promptly and caringly.

Today, child development specialists advocate that parents need to stay tuned-in to their children's needs and provide infants with appropriate nurturing geared toward the specific developmental stage of their baby's life. I will go into these stages in greater detail in the next chapter. But for now, remember that it's important for you to respond caringly when your infant or baby cries and tries to tell you something, because you're helping your baby develop a healthy self-esteem.

You're not just caring for the physical needs of your baby when you respond to her cries; you're taking care of her emotional needs as well.

When you convey a deep, strong, continual love to your child she will feel good about herself and will be more likely to behave in a positive and compassionate way. Compare an infant's needs with an adult's needs for intimacy, for comfort, for closeness, for human contact. Most adults, when they marry (if not before), sleep together. Why? Because they don't have enough beds to sleep apart? No. Because they like the comfort, the softness, the intimacy of cuddling or being close to another human being whom they care about. Did they develop that need at the altar or when hormones raced in adolescence? No. Most human beings are born with needs for attachment and closeness.

One woman who came to me for therapy had become a mother in the early 1970s. She experienced a great deal of family pressure to maintain rigid feeding schedules and give fairly limited comfort to her crying baby. She was repeatedly told, "just let him cry it out." But she felt something was wrong. Intuitively, she wanted to respond to her son's cries more lovingly. Sadly, because of her own personal background of physical and verbal abuse, she didn't have the confidence to follow her instincts in the face of her husband's threats, her in-laws' advice, and her parents' disapproval. She was ridiculed for being a baby herself and not realizing that this infant had to learn to wait until his next mealtime or to comfort himself. She reported the following: "I could hear my son crying and wanted to go to him. He was so small, so defenseless. Yet, when I'd start, my husband would berate me for spoiling him. I often got as far as his closed door, where I would sit on the floor and cry quietly, wanting to have the courage to go in, but afraid of defying my husband, my in-laws, and my parents, who demanded that I teach our son that he was the child and we were the parents, and we would say when it was time to eat and when it was time to play. I hated it, but I did it.

Now I know I taught him not to listen to his own instincts and that he wasn't important. By the time our son was seventeen, our whole family was in therapy so we could unlearn those early oppressive messages. I was relieved that finally someone was telling me that my more loving instincts had been right. Maybe we'll have a chance of becoming a healthy family. I just hope it's not too late for our kids. I don't want them to repeat what my husband and I passed down to them from our parents."

Dr. Marianne Neifert, in her book, *Dr. Mom*, warned people not to make the mistake of thinking that a good baby is undemanding or that a demanding baby is bad. She offers the perspective that a demanding baby is a healthy baby and that the demands present opportunities to teach your baby that he's loved and can count on you. If this information had been available when my client was a young mother, she might not have had to suppress her loving instincts and adopt her family's more stern approach. The rigid parenting techniques and ensuing emotional pain that reigned in her family for the next seventeen years could have been avoided.

In close, respectful parenting relationships, babies seem to *take* a lot. Outsiders who don't understand what's going on wonder about parents who seem to give *so much*. By giving lovingly, the respectful parent is establishing healthy building blocks for the baby's self-esteem. Parents who are parenting in this newer way feel so rewarded by their child's appreciative responses that it's easy for them to keep giving. The simplest guideline I can offer parents is: respond lovingly to your infant and young child's needs when he or she expresses them.

Some of today's parents are still afraid of spoiling their children, therefore, they believe responding to all their young child's needs is an unnecessary and ridiculous way of parenting. Often well-meaning parents and in-laws try to influence or pressure you with their perspectives. It's difficult to buck those pressures, but if you and your partner are in agreement, you can. Others may say things like, "You have to impose a feeding schedule on an infant as soon as possible." Newer parents need to remember that it used to be the goal to have a child fit into your world and to meet your needs, the needs of an adult. But that isn't the goal anymore, because we know that the best way you can help your infant attain high self-esteem and establish self-confidence is to take care of your infant's needs first. Here is one mother's story.

> **Linda:** Never before in my life did so many people have so many things to tell me about how to run my life. It mostly had to do with my baby. I shouldn't hold him as much. I shouldn't nurse him as often. I shouldn't coddle him. I'll spoil him. If it hadn't been for nightly teary-eyed discussions with my husband, who felt the same way I did, I don't think I could have gotten through those first few weeks of well-meaning friends and relatives. The ones who agreed with me were reassuring, but the others really tested my confidence as a new mother. I had my instincts, which said to hold my baby as much as I

wanted and to respond to him immediately, but I also knew my background hadn't been so good, and I didn't want to go overboard in the opposite direction. It really helped a lot that my husband knew about this stuff from his work and continually reassured me that I was doing a great job. I don't know where I'd have been without his support. Now that my baby is ten months old, everyone says I have such a happy baby—even some of the same people who tried to get me not to hold him just a few months ago. It's funny, but now I just tell myself, "They mean well," and I do what I believe is right.

In *Dr. Mom,* Dr. Marianne Neifert suggests what a healthy parent should do in order to prevent intimacy problems in adulthood. "When [an infant] has a need and it is satisfied, he learns that the world is a safe place and he is loved. By trusting, he begins to learn to communicate. . . . Follow your instincts and hold, hug, talk, and attend to your baby without limits. You *can't* overdo it. If you are excessively affectionate, you'll end up with a responsive, secure, happy baby who knows he is loved and will love in return.

Crying or Communicating?

When an infant cries, he's telling you something. A child doesn't cry without a reason. Crying can be an intelligent form of communication. As stated before, we recognize today that infants have no wants, only needs. These needs are felt and expressed in an urgent fashion. More importantly, a baby's needs should be taken care of in a timely and loving manner. Needs only go away when they have been taken care of—they cannot be ignored away.

It's important to learn what your baby's cries are saying. If you're not sure, pick him up so you can figure out what he's trying to tell you. If he stops crying when you pick him up, there's your answer; he wanted to be held. If not, then go through the basics to find out if he's telling you: he's hungry, he needs to be changed, he's tired, he needs less stimulation, or he simply needs some closeness and comfort. If your baby is still fussy, simply talk to him calmly about what is surrounding him in the world. Hold him gently as you talk to him unless holding him increases his fussiness. If his fussiness increases try taking him to a quieter, less stimulating environment, where he can focus on your soothing words and gentle presence more easily.

Eliminating Old-Style Parenting Patterns

I have worked with people whose need for closeness has been suppressed by childhood trauma. Their only defense was to erect rigid, impenetrable boundaries around themselves. There are others who were neglected or left alone so much as infants and small children that they suppressed their needs for closeness to cope with the pain of early rejection and abandonment. These circumstances notwithstanding, most adults do need, desire, and enjoy some degree of closeness with other adults even though they have knowledge, experience, and tools to cope with life's stresses. Why wouldn't a newborn infant, a baby, a toddler, or even a small child who doesn't have these resources to comfort himself be entitled to comfort from you?

Yet it can be very difficult for people who were raised the old-fashioned way, left to cry it out or responded to with anger or frustration, to come to understand that babies' cries are an expression of need rather than an unreasonable demand for attention. How can an adult relate to this? Have you ever really needed to go to the bathroom? It is a physiological need. It can't be put off for long. It must be responded to quickly. That's what an infant has—immediate needs that must be responded to quickly. And when a parent respects those needs by responding lovingly and understandingly, the infant begins to learn two vital things: her needs can be met and she is capable of getting her needs met. You may be doing all the work for a while, but the infant learns she has the personal ability to get her needs met and she begins to trust the world around her.

Many adults never developed those two basic beliefs in themselves. These adults usually share some of the following beliefs: they don't believe they can get their needs met, they don't think their needs are legitimate, they think they're not capable of getting their needs met, or, worse still, they don't believe they deserve to get their needs met. Life often has supplied these people with family members, friends, lovers, partners, or spouses who have told them their needs are not important, that they're being demanding or ridiculous. Is it a coincidence that oftentimes these people find similarly unresponsive mates? I don't think so.

When parents ignored their child's cries as an infant and small child, when they made that child wait until it was convenient for the parent to take care of him, that child also (unconsciously) learned he was not worthwhile or important. If you add the gruff parental one-liners from Chapter 1 to those kinds of nonverbal messages, the end result is a wounded adult who does not see himself as worthy or worthwhile. These kinds of early old-style parenting messages set a person up to find people in their adult life who will repeat the invalidating messages he is used to. When he continues to hear those kinds of negative messages, life feels normal and familiar on an unconscious level, even though consciously he may feel hurt, alone, and inadequate.

Learning to respectfully parent will produce three positive results in your baby. First, the more secure he feels, the calmer, less fussy and demanding your baby will be, and he will eventually be an "easy" toddler. Second, as you nourish a rich love that grows out of emotional give-and-take, you will enjoy a greater closeness with your child than you shared with your parents. Third, you will begin to feel better about yourself as you see yourself parenting kindly and hear your loving words. You'll know that just as your baby deserves love for being who he is, you too deserve love for being a caring human being.

When You Take Care of Your Baby's Needs

When you take care of your baby's needs, your young child may seem overly dependent in her early development. She will probably stay close to you because she feels loved, she knows she's safe with you, and she knows that you will meet her needs. As these children grow, and their small world continues to feel safe and loving, they have confidence in themselves, and they will eventually be more comfortable about venturing away from you and into the world around them. Over time, as your child grows older, you'll help your child learn about the difference between needs and wants. She'll be able to satisfy her needs and understand that her wants sometimes go unanswered because you'll have taught her about the difference as she develops wants that feel as intense as the needs used to feel. When you respectfully parent as your children grow they seem to have more patience, perhaps because they have a deep-rooted trust in others, and can wait for things to happen without going into a panic-like reaction that nobody will be there for them. They have a level of self-assurance, what we call high self-esteem, which allows them to venture off and feel good about themselves.

All this because they were nursed or fed on demand? All because they were held when they needed to be? These may not be the only reasons, but what a wonderful foundation! What a terrific way to begin to learn so many things: I am loved, I am terrific, people respond to me, I am appreciated, they think I'm important, they can do for me, I can do for myself, I can do for others, and my world is a safe place.

While you were growing up, a child who thought or said those things might have been accused of being egotistical or having a swelled head. How absurd that a child who legitimately thinks he is unique and special would be criticized. What's wrong with appreciating yourself and feeling good about yourself? It's not the people who feel good about themselves that do all the boasting as teens and adults. People who truly feel good about themselves often tend to be more humble about it. They know who they are and are often generous with others. It's often people who feel poorly about themselves who try to cover up that reality by boastful talk and actions. The boasters are not people who have an underlying healthy self-esteem, nor have they been loved, held, coddled, appreciated, or respected as infants, babies, toddlers, and young children.

A child who is respected and loved, who is responded to on demand for the first year or more, will be a calmer, happier toddler and grow up to be more self-assured than a child who is forced into your schedule and whose needs obviously take the back seat to yours, the parents. There is plenty of time later on, after establishing this healthy internal base, for the child to learn the differences between needs and wants, and to learn about waiting. Children will learn these lessons. They'll also realize that other people in this world deserve compassion, understanding, and respect. They'll know how to do that from what Mommy and Daddy taught them through their actions, which is what we call role modeling. And they'll probably take the time and effort to find friends who will treat them well, because they know they deserve to be treated that way. It will feel normal on a conscious and unconscious level to be treated well, and they won't tolerate or accept the kinds of disrespectful (mean) behavior that a child who isn't treated with respect thinks is normal.

$\mathcal{F}ive$

Brain Science Research, Respectful Parenting, You, and Your Baby

OR YEARS PEOPLE have wondered if babies were born with set moods, emotions, and intelligence (cognitive ability), or if most learning took place after birth. Thanks to recent brain science research and child development studies we know that a baby's brain is not fully developed at birth. A complex interaction of genetic input and life experiences determines how each person's brain grows and develops. Early life experiences are particularly influential to the developing brain in all areas: cognitive (intellectual and academic), social, emotional, and physical abilities.

Helping Your Child Reach Full Potential

The most intense brain development occurs during the first three to five years of life, when about 80 percent of *how* a child will learn is set. During this relatively short time period the brain seems to have the most flexibility, experiences more growth, and makes more vital connections than during any other period in life. These ideas may change as researchers learn more, but the first few years are expected to remain a critical period in a human being's life. It takes about fifteen to twenty years for the brain to fully develop. As people grow and continue to learn they seem to rely on early connections to process later information.

The brain is often associated with thinking-type activities (cognition and intelligence), but the brain is more complex than just acting as the center where thoughts are generated, it's also the origination point for emotions, social behaviors, and physical behaviors. Thus the intellectual brain, the social brain, and the emotional brain should be studied independently and as an interdependent group. For instance, research has shown that if a baby doesn't get enough nurturing (holding, soothing, loving attention, understanding interactions) she is likely to have problems with human interactions and learning throughout her life span. If a child doesn't get enough nurturing, and she is also exposed to prolonged stress (parents fighting, economic problems, violence in the home, fear in the home) her brain can be permanently re-set from how she was born to having difficulties in cognitive, social, or emotional areas she would not have had without the neglect and stress she experienced.

The opposite is also true. When a baby gets lots of nurturing and love, that baby will form early and important personal attachments and be able to blossom to her full potential. The power of human interactions with infants, babies, toddlers, and young children should not be underestimated. A baby's personality, moods, thinking patterns, learning abilities, emotions, communication skills, coping skills, and physical coordination are influenced by the type of care that baby receives. Respectful Parenting encourages beneficial parenting practices you can use with your child from the day your baby is born. When a child has been

- nurtured,
- loved,
- held,
- talked to in full sentences and paragraphs,
- given complete explanations,
- encouraged from an early age to participate in creative play,
- encouraged to think for himself,
- taught decision making strategies,
- appreciated for her uniqueness, and
- knows you love, adore, and respect her,

that child does much better in school and in later life.

As a parent, you can be your child's most significant teacher. The quality of the relationship you establish with your child will serve as the foundation for her social, emotional, cognitive, language, and motor skills development. By practicing Respectful Parenting techniques, you will help her grow into her full potential. However, if you respond in harsh, inappropriate ways, you'll actually diminish her potential.

Touchpoints

Dr. T. Berry Brazelton has developed ideas about child development patterns. Development used to be thought of as linear, meaning each step building on the step before and proceeding in a positive, linear fashion. Dr. Brazelton, instead, recognizes time periods in the first few years of life when a child may regress and have a few difficult hours or days preceding each developmental milestone. During these times it appears as though the baby or child is taking a step backward or slowing progress. Dr. Brazelton describes these time periods as "predictable bursts of regression" called "touchpoints."[1]

Touchpoints seem to happen at three weeks, six to eight weeks, and then at four, seven, nine, twelve, fifteen, and eighteen months. They then begin to spread out, occurring a few times a year, between the ages of two and six. A child experiences a fairly predictable disorganization at each of these points as he prepares for the next stage of development.

Touchpoints are often a challenging time for the entire family. The adults in a baby's life may get anxious when they see a baby who has been developing in a somewhat linear pattern regress. They may wonder, "What's the matter? Why is this happening?" Parents and childcare providers can be less anxious when they understand a child will often experience unusual behaviors as he takes a regressive, disorganizing step just before he moves forward to the next developmental accomplishment. The touchpoint occurs before a child learns something new such as rolling over, sitting up, pulling himself up, taking his first step, or announcing a real word. It's helpful to talk with your child's caregivers during these difficult touchpoints. Ask what they're seeing and how they're handling any changes your baby may be experiencing. When you support each other's efforts, the time periods pass more easily, minimizing stress for your baby, you, and your baby's caregivers.

The First Thirty-Six Months in Detail

This section outlines an infant's, baby's, toddler's, and two-year-old's healthy development and demonstrates how Respectful Parenting can help your child's cognitive, social, emotional, language, and motor skills blossom. Keep in mind that every child develops at his or her own rate. Your child's development may naturally vary from the progression described below. The guidelines in this section are a distillation of information contained in a set of hand-outs developed by Zero To Three and the American Academy of Pediatrics called "Nurturing Children's Development from 0 to 36 Months: Healthy Minds, 2003," along with Respectful Parenting ideas and techniques based on my experience in private practice. If after reading this section you're concerned about a set of behaviors you see in your child, read Chapter 13 for more direction.

Birth to Two Months Old

Brain science researchers, child development specialists, and early childhood educators indicate that from birth to two months infants are learning how to feel comfortable in the world. They're learning about eating, sleeping, and emotions and communicating through gestures, sounds, and facial expressions. Your baby will invite socializing by watching your face and exchanging looks with you. She will ask for a break from interacting by looking away, arching her back, frowning, or voicing a particular "I've had enough" cry.

Your young infant has lots of ways to play. She can connect with sounds and loves being talked to or sung to. She enjoys seeing objects and can begin to track them with her eyes and later with her head. It's easiest for her to focus when the objects are held about eight inches to a foot away. She likes being able to grip an object and hold on. Infants use play to engage and interact with you, forming the foundation for a strong attachment bond with you. Play is not about winning, losing, or competing at this age, it's about connecting with you and feeling safe and cared for.

When your infant interacts with you by watching your eye movements or gestures, she's actually developing social and emotional skills. Her efforts to engage you by looking and making sounds to get your attention are part of her developing cognitive, social, and communication skills. The actions are also early lessons in cause and effect; the baby learns that if I look and make a sound, Dad notices me, looks back, and smiles. That feels good. When you play peek-a-boo your infant is learning that things go away and they come back. They begin to anticipate what comes next. It's important for an infant to begin to learn that she can control and affect aspects of her world. That knowledge builds trust and confidence.

When you follow your infant's needs and desires to play you're enabling her healthy development. However, it's important to listen and watch for her limits and not encourage stimulation overload. When she's had enough and needs to rest she'll let you know. If you don't respectfully respond to those limits, your infant will feel as though you're bombarding her senses. You may end up feeling unsafe to her. If you consistently disregard her limits, the whole world ends up feeling unsafe. That feeling can hamper healthy development.

Two Months to Six Months

Babies this age love making sounds, cooing, and babbling. They often start with vowels, then they try out the *P*s, *M*s, *B*s, and *D*s. You and your baby can have conversations back and forth by listening to your baby's sounds and then responding with a mixture of his sounds and real words. Babies also love to imitate. If you stick out your tongue, your baby will probably do the same back, and then when you do it again, watch as your baby giggles with delight. He is probably beginning to explore more, especially by checking out how objects feel and taste in his mouth. As a result, you need to make sure the toys he plays with can't fit entirely into his mouth.

At around four to six months old your baby may begin to roll back and forth, and he will be delighted with his accomplishment. That delight comes from his desire to see new angles and different scenes. You can also put your baby in a safe place or hold your baby in a variety of positions that will allow him to see as much as possible.

It's important to child proof your house so your baby can move and explore things freely, being safe as he rolls about. If you can encourage your baby to enjoy his movements in a safe place, you'll help him learn to trust the world, feel safe, and feel confident in his progressing abilities. If you admonish him or tell him he shouldn't move so much or he could fall, you'll discourage his explorations and the world will begin to feel unsafe.

Talking with your baby and reading to your baby encourages language, social, and cognitive development. Talking about feelings and putting labels on your child's emotional reactions encourages emotional intelligence. Sometimes it feels like you can see inside his brain as he wrestles with a problem. A look of delight comes over his face and body as he realizes he's figured it out on his own. If he has enough words he'll delightedly share his discovery with you. If his language skills get in his way he may get frustrated. You can help him find words and let him know you can tell he's excited. Encourage him to try to use a combination of words and actions to share what he's discovered. Reading and talking with your baby about the pictures in the book also encourages creativity, which in turn fuels a young child's emotional, cognitive, and social development.

Six to Nine Months

Your baby can begin to copy you pushing buttons and learn more about cause and effect at this age. She will also make lots more sounds and maybe even begin to put vowel sounds together with consonant sounds as in *dada* or *mama*. Responding to your baby's attempts to talk in your baby's own type of language encourages her to talk more and feel confident in her language development and her ability to interact and socialize.

You can also introduce more objects, such as playing with plastic containers in the bathtub. You can pour water out and encourage your baby to mimic you. Talking about what you're doing, why you're doing it, and what your baby is doing and accomplishing helps her understand and learn more about the world. As your baby listens and interacts with you, social, cognitive, and language connections are being made in her brain.

When your baby feels safe as a result of your consistent, kind, and gentle attention she responds by clinging to you. You'll know she trusts you. That trust is further evidence that her social and emotional development is progressing. When a stranger is nearby your baby may cling to you until you've assured her the stranger is safe or until your baby has convinced herself the stranger is safe. If you push your child too fast to someone new because you want your friend or relative to see how friendly she is, you're not respecting your child's limits or her need to figure things out. You'll also discourage her abilities to discern for herself safe people and objects from unsafe ones. That response is old-style parenting; with Respectful Parenting you'll help your child develop her own way of assessing people and situations. You can encourage and reassure your baby without forcing her to respond within your time frame.

At this age your baby may begin to grab food from your hands while you're trying to feed her. She's learning about cause and effect, trying to learn independence by wanting to feed herself, and developing her fine motor skills. Allowing her the freedom to feed herself makes eating a messier and longer process, but when you can do it in a positive, encouraging manner, you'll help your daughter build self-esteem, confidence, language, and motor skills. Cries and gurgles are early language development, and your baby's sounds, gestures, and facial expressions are all becoming more complex, indicating more sophisticated language skills.

Nine Months to Twelve Months

Babies at this age are able to express their feelings through gestures, sounds, facial expressions, and physical movements such as crawling or even walking to or away from things and people. They're more certain about cause and effect: "If I smile Mommy usually smiles back" or "If I cry, someone comes to see what I want." A nine- to twelve-month-old's memory has formed enough to know, from living in a relatively trustworthy world, that if you leave (you being a parent or caregiver), you will come back. It may not be right away, but you'll be back. You've taught your baby this lesson through your behavior. If the world has not been relatively stable and trustworthy, then a baby at this age will not have learned this lesson and will experience much more stress. His development will probably begin to suffer, if it hasn't already.

Repetition helps babies build their memory and self-confidence. Parents sometimes get bored with repetitive play, but it's great for a baby's development. If you get bored, you'll want to shift your focus from the activity itself to your awe at your baby's interest. Then continue the interaction by following his excited lead and allowing yourself to bask in awe with your baby's persistence, ability to focus, and long attention span. In order to encourage the natural progression of learning that helps your baby use his brain, his emotions, his developing self-esteem, and his ability to discover different cause and effect relationships, your baby needs your active, engaged, and respectful involvement.

When you comfort your baby when he cries you're acknowledging his uncomfortable feelings. Your baby feels validated and learns that he has a sense of control over himself and his environment. He was able to use social cues to grab your attention and he used his communication skills (crying) to get you to respond. When you respond your baby's emotions shift from uncomfortable to comfortable and positive feelings increase.

At this age you can encourage your baby to communicate more by interacting with him in thoughtful ways. If he reaches for a toy, ask him if he wants the toy rather than simply handing it to him. By asking questions you are inviting your baby to practice his communication and social skills. You're also engaging his brain with a decision: do I want it or not? When he decides and tells you, he's practiced decision making, communication, and social skills. When you give him the toy, thank him for letting you know what he wanted. He'll be pleased that you understood him and that he was able to get what he wanted. At the same time, you'll teach him subtle social skills.

When you play with your child at this age you can do more than repeat movements (although he still likes that a lot). You can encourage your child's participation by doing something like building a tower as a joint venture. Tell your child, "You can do this now. I'll show you how, and you do it." And then exclaim how well he did on his first try. If he needs more help, do it again, positively and patiently. This kind of play is another time when you need to slow down and follow your child's lead.

While you're doing these simple, pleasurable activities, your baby's brain is making rapid connections, developing an ability to think things through, remember things, figure things out, and learn more about the world. It truly is amazing what's going on in your child's brain. As you're looking at this small, sweet face in front of you, the synapses in your child's brain are firing off about 3000 connections a second. The more you interact in a gentle, kind, affirming way (the basis of Respectful Parenting) the more connections and understandings your child will establish.

From Twelve to Eighteen Months

Toddlers learn new words every day, and they really like using them. As you continue to watch your child's actions, such as where they point, and listen to their words or attempts at words, you're encouraging your child's full development. Another way a toddler communicates and expands her creativity is through creative play. A child may take a common object such as a toothbrush and turn it into an airplane. Rather than saying, "That's not an airplane. It's a toothbrush. I'll make you a paper airplane." Ask your child what the toothbrush is. If she says "airplane" or makes flying noises, comment on her creativity. Let her fly the toothbrush around for a while and then lead her to the bathroom where she can land the toothbrush-airplane in the right place, the sink counter, also known as the runway for the airport.

As your toddler takes on the skill of running and is excited about exploring new areas, you'll probably be tempted to yell warnings as she runs around. If you're scared or anxious when you call out your warnings, your child will pick up on your anxiety. When you're trying to keep your toddler safe, use positive words rather than frightened, tense, negative warnings. For instance, saying "walk slowly" rather than yelling "STOP!" encourages a child to explore safely. Or you can offer an explanation: "When you get to the ramp, wait for me, and we can run down it together," instead of yelling anxiously, "Don't go down that ramp!" You want to teach your child slowly over time to begin to think things through for herself and not always depend on others to keep her safe. Yelling, "no" or "stop" may keep her safe at the moment (and there will be times when that's appropriate) but it teaches nothing except to listen to grownups.

To avoid power struggles over objects she's not supposed to play with, such as your cell phone, give your daughter a toy cell phone of her own. Encouraging her to use her imagination with acceptable objects will help you avoid saying "no" all day. Divert your child's energy after validating her by saying something like, "I see that bowl is intriguing you. Let's look at it together. See all the colors in it? Here's blue and red and orange. Let's put the bowl where it belongs and look around the house and see what we can find that has the same colors as in the bowl." Or you can tell your toddler, "There's a pretty new plate on the shelf by the fireplace. Let's go over and look at it together. It's heavy and it can break, but we can look at it safely together." Explanations like that will need to be given a few times, but patience, persistence, and repetition will teach your child how to handle breakable objects.

You may associate learning with a classroom, but as a parent, you're consciously and unconsciously teaching your child all the time. The more you interact in a gentle, respectful, caring way, the more your child will learn.

From Eighteen to Twenty-four Months

At this age your toddler will become steadier on his feet. He can string words together, or maybe connect two or more to form a simple sentence. Young children get pretty excited about being independent. They want to be in control, to have a sense of mastery over their world. It's important to encourage their sense of competence, which builds self-esteem, while also setting caring, appropriate limits. For instance, you can feed a sense of mastery and control by having your child help you set the table. Have him place safe utensils such as spoons, a sippy cup, plastic plates, and napkins on the table while you follow with the forks, knives, breakable plates, and glasses.

Two-year-olds think just about everything is "Mine!" Some things do belong to them, so you can tell them, "Yes, that's your ball, and while your friend Diana is here to play we're going to *share* the ball with her (meaning you and your friend can both play with the ball together or separately). Then, when we go to Diana's house, we'll have fun playing with her toys. Your toys stay here when Diana goes home. But while she's here, we share." When your child is learning how to share, it can help to talk to him before a friend comes over. Remind him that you're all going to share things with the visitors. Before a playmate comes over, you can ask your child if there's anything he wants to put away so his friend doesn't play with it. Remind him that whatever is left both he and his friend can play with. If you need to remind your child about sharing again once his playmate arrives, try to do this calmly, in a private place.

Children instinctively love to move. Running, walking, jumping, crawling, and climbing actually strengthens brain connections that help with their coordination and their ability to focus. Perhaps the most difficult part of parenting toddlers is respecting and encouraging their love of learning and exploring, being independent, and doing it their way, while keeping them safe at the same time. In the face of their curious explorations, how many times do you have to remind them what's safe and what's not? You might lose your patience if you think, "He's bright and a couple of reminders *should* be enough." An important reality check for you is to understand that a couple of reminders are almost never enough for an excited, curious, headstrong toddler. He's not maliciously testing your limits, and he's not out to "get your goat," as an old-style parent might think. He's just into the moment. Toddlers aren't able to thoughtfully consider the consequences of their actions. They're spontaneous. They're excited about the world. They're young explorers with lots of territory to cover in a day.

You have to slowly, repetitively teach them the art of waiting and the art of thinking through whatever it is they might be doing. These sophisticated concepts often take years to learn. You and your child will need a lot of practice, patience, love, respect, and understanding while you instill a love for learning and exploring in your young child.

When you're a respectful, warm, caring parent, your children will turn to you when they're unsure, frightened, or wondering about life. You want to be that safe person. Sometimes your child will turn to you when you least expect it. For instance, let's say you've brought your toddler to a puppet show. It's a "children's puppet theater" but instead of being enthralled with the show your child is in your lap, hiding his face. This is not the time to tell him that he should be having fun, or he shouldn't be scared, or there's nothing to be scared of. Instead, begin by validating your child's fear: "This is something new for you. I didn't think it would be scary, but I can see it is. I'm sorry you're feeling scared. I'm here. This is a safe place, but if it doesn't feel safe to you we can go outside for a while." You may need to leave and forgo the puppet theater for a few months. Being a flexible parent is important at times like these. You don't want to force your child to stay because you thought it would be fun.

It may help if you get to a new place or new event early. Then you can slowly introduce your child to the new stimuli. If a slow introduction doesn't work, and your child is still upset, you can gently reassure him that you can leave and try it later when he's bigger. Using the puppet example, you might try simple finger puppets at home. This is a way to deal with a specific fear in a safe place. You will teach your child that sometimes things start off being scary, but once you learn more about them, they're not scary at all.

Sometimes children get so locked into their own explanation of what they think is happening that they get very upset and fearful. When a child is very upset, he can't "hear" or concentrate on your explanation. It's as though fear has paralyzed his brain. You'll need to soothe and calm him until his brain can take in new information and hear what you tell him. For instance, with the puppet show example, if the child thought the wicked witch puppet was going to come get him (in the audience) and hurt him, he could easily get caught up in the fear/fantasy. He wouldn't be able to hear or believe the explanation that he didn't have to worry, because his fear had become his reality. When you take your child outside, where the wicked witch can't get to him, and you are calm and understand that he's frightened of something, ask him to tell you what it is. Then you can calmly address his specific fear in a safe place. He can hear your reasoning. Young children are concrete thinkers—the puppet witch is as real to him as you are. They are also black and white thinkers, without complex or analytical thinking abilities. Your child can follow your reasoning, but only when it feels safe to him, so that he can give up the fear/fantasy that has become his reality.

Twenty-four Months to Thirty-six Months

By this age your child has become proficient at all the skills you've helped her develop. She will talk more and put longer sentences together as she approaches the three-year-old marker. She will enjoy talking with you. If you're a responsive listener your child will like answering your questions. Having simple conversations helps two-year-olds feel competent and increases their social and language skills. Even though their skills are growing, it's important to remember that two-year-olds understand a lot more than they can verbalize. Although they may be talking more, they're still unable to communicate as well as they'd like to, and that can lead to overflowing feelings and frustrations at times.

When you're talking with or playing with your two-year-old and her mood begins to change, try to find out what may have triggered the difference by asking gentle questions. If you were playing with a toy that required fine motor skills, did that become frustrating for your child? Did she knock over what she wanted to build up? Did she get distracted by something else? Did she attempt to redirect your play or add onto it but you wanted to do it your way? Perhaps you forgot to ask what she was doing so you could understand the shift instead of assuming she was distracted and didn't want to play anymore.

A good example of this misunderstanding would be something like the following. You're playing dress up and you're both wearing necklaces and carrying handbags. All of a sudden your two-year-old goes running out of the room. Instead of thinking, "She's not cooperating," and reacting to that false assumption, ask her what she's doing in a curious way. You may get a surprising response that indicates she's still involved but has added another dimension. Your two-year-old may say, "Forgot baby. Need baby," as she comes back holding her favorite doll. She's ready to keep going. You can thank her for remembering baby. Your child will appreciate your feedback and you can happily resume playing.

An old-style parent might gruffly say, "We were playing. What's the matter with you? Why'd you run away? You have to stick with something you start." Assumptions were made and acted on without consulting the child. And what underlying messages would that stern response send? The child was wrong (bad) to leave; you were directing the play and she wasn't supposed to add to it (the parent's way is the *right* way); there's something wrong with using her creativity; and there's something wrong with using her own head. Those messages are not good for a child's self esteem or cognitive development.

If What You See at Home Doesn't Match What You've Read Here

If, after reading this chapter, you're particularly worried as you compare your child's development with the guidelines offered on these pages and you're wondering what may be wrong, you have two options: wait and see if your child is in an unusual phase that will pass or seek a professional opinion from a pediatrician or a child development specialist. The wait-and-see attitude sometimes pays off: "it" passes, and you realize your child was simply going through a difficult phase. If your concerns mount, and you begin to make adjustments in how you live in order to accommodate your child's increasingly concerning behavior or moods, then it's probably time to consult a professional. If you wait too long and your child needs extra help, it's more likely to affect his self-esteem and confidence, which can then interfere with his ability to take in new information and process it effectively. Self-esteem doesn't have to be negatively affected if a child receives the help he needs at an early age. A young child's brain is developing at such a rapid rate during the first few years of life that often, if it needs to, it can incorporate new information to overcome difficulties more easily with early intervention than later in life. I will explain this process in detail in Chapter 13.

Simplifying the Brain

Now that you've seen how parents can affect their children's development, let's look at the brain itself to understand how it works. The brain has four main parts: brain stem, cerebellum, limbic region, and cerebrum. The brain stem is at the base of the brain. It's the first part of the brain to become active, and it controls automatic body functions such as heartbeat and breathing. It also houses the emotional fight or flight response. Because of the action of the brain stem your lungs move in and out so you can breathe, your heart beats and pumps blood without any thought or action on your part, and you can fight or flee from a threatening experience without much forethought. We need the brain stem to function, but we also need other areas of the brain to function properly so that the automatic "leave here immediately," or "fight to the death" responses are not triggered at inappropriate times.

The cerebellum is the area above the brain stem. The cerebellum is where movements originate. The parts of the brain related to mental focus and abstract thinking are also closely connected to the dense cerebellum. Children who don't exercise or move on a regular basis don't have as sharp thinking abilities as children who are physically active. It's important for your toddler to explore the world, to climb, jump, run, swing and move around so that the cerebellum is stimulated, thus increasing a child's ability to focus and learn about the world.

The emotional center of the brain is the limbic area. This part of the brain works differently from other areas because it contains structures that secrete chemicals into the circulatory system. These substances affect how we feel and act. One of the substances released by the limbic area is adrenaline. Another substance is cortisol, which can negatively impact a child's ability to learn in a surprising way: when babies feel stressed, fearful, or insecure, the limbic region can actually stop learning from taking place by circulating cortisol over the neural cortex (which we'll explore shortly). When it covers the neural cortex, cortisol prevents neural connections from being formed and strengthened. When stressed children are presented with learning opportunities or the appropriate stimulation in their environment, they can't take advantage of them because the cortisol has shut down the thinking part of their brain.

Because babies and young children are entirely dependent on others for their survival, their panicky or fearful reactions are triggered faster than adults. It may take less to stress a baby than to stress an adult. These stressors can be found almost anywhere. If a child's home environment is very stressful, but the child is in a great child care center, he won't be able to learn as well as he would if the home and the child care were both warm, secure environments. The reverse is also true. If home is stable, warm, and nurturing, but the child spends eight to ten hours in a stressful child care situation, the internal, physiological stress reactions will be triggered. Cortisol will begin circulating, effectively numbing the baby's ability to take advantage of the nurturing at home. Because many parents will be working and placing their babies with a caregiver or in a child care center it's important to find a safe, caring, relatively stress free, engaging, and stimulating environment (see Chapter 6). What would make a child care center stressful? Too much stimulation, the wrong kind of stimulation, not enough stimulation, neglect, or abuse. If you see changes in how your child reacts to playtime, to you, or to the things she would usually find stimulating and engaging, make a few unexpected visits to the child care provider to verify that your child isn't in a stressful environment.

If the period of stress is limited to a brief time period and then things go back to being calm, stable and healthy, a child can learn to the best of her ability. But if the stressful period is prolonged or repeated the results can be very serious and far reaching. During the first three years, as neurons are building in the cortex, the emotional (limbic) center of the brain is also growing, forming, and developing. If a young, growing child is in repeated or prolonged stress, the brain gets used to having cortisol around, and the child can actually seek out experiences that will release cortisol, because it feels "normal" to her. Children who live with stress and have cortisol released frequently will, in essence, begin to rely on the emotional (limbic) area of their brain for coping rather than the front, thinking part of their brain, because it (the limbic area) works more easily and the thinking part has been cut off from functioning well by the extra cortisol. The limbic area will become overdeveloped and the cerebrum and frontal cortex can be underdeveloped.

What kinds of far reaching effects can that uneven development have? As the baby grows up, she will misinterpret many situations as fight or flight problems rather than thinking about the situation, looking at all of the perspectives, and coming to a peaceful or thoughtful response. These children often have problems with authority figures. They can't see alternative solutions and tend to act impulsively. Additional negative effects can come from prolonged exposure to stress combined with not receiving enough love: babies can become depressed, experience a loss of impulse control, and display aggression as they get older. All these behaviors make it difficult for them to do well in school. They carry these problems into adulthood and are often addicted to "high drama," are drawn to stressful situations, or react as though they're being attacked when they're not.

The flip, or positive side of this coin is also clear. Providing young children with positive and engaging relationships with their parents and caregivers seems to be the key to a child's intellectual and emotional health throughout life. The Respectful Parenting techniques and philosophies discussed throughout this book provide you with the tools to optimize your child's development.

The part of the brain farthest away from the brain stem is the cerebrum. This part of the brain deals with thought processes. The frontal cortex, at the top and front of the cerebrum, is not fully formed until a child is about eight years old, which is why young children tend to be concrete, simple, black-and-white thinkers. More sophisticated thinking takes longer to develop. You can help your baby's frontal cortex develop by giving full explanations and asking questions that trigger connections in the frontal cortex. By doing this, you help your child learn how to think abstractly, how to begin making solid decisions, and how one thought or feeling leads to another.

The outside covering of the cerebrum is called the cortex. Neurologists once believed the cortex was fairly uniform in thickness in most people, but new research has revealed that the thickness of the cortex varies. Further research seems to indicate the thickness of the cortex is related to how quickly and thoroughly people can solve problems and learn new tasks. Here's where you come in as a parent: a child's early life experiences seem to determine the thickness of her cortex. Providing a nurturing environment and interacting with your baby using stimulating, safe objects and lots of explanations of what you're doing and why, along with positive comments about what your baby is doing seems to help her cortex thicken, which enables her to learn and cope well throughout life. Research demonstrates that stressed and neglected children's brains do not have the kind of thickened cortex that children who have lived a less stressful life possess.

The cortex is made up of cells called neurons. An infant is born with about one hundred billion neurons. At first, a neuron looks like a spindly young tree without any leaves. Each one is on its own, isolated from all the others. The neurons will then either grow branches and form connections with other neurons, or the neurons will wither away without connecting to other neurons. What determines the neurons' paths? As infants are exposed to stimuli that engage their senses of sight, touch, taste, sound, smell, their neurons begin to grow and branch out. The branching and connections are what enable a baby to learn and function.

The more you communicate with your infant and the more she begins to realize words and events are connected or can be used for many purposes, the more the neurons branch out. A couple of examples of your infant's early thinking could be: 'I can grab the rattle mommy is holding out to me' or 'If I cry daddy comes and holds me. I like when he holds me.'

From a field of spindly, isolated "trees" a full, dense forest of neurons communicating and connecting with each other grows in the baby's brain, thus stimulating even more growth and learning. The cortex becomes thicker as the network of branches continues to grow and connect with each other.

It's during the amazing time between birth and three years old that researchers think this type of brain activity is more vigorous than any other time in life. PET scans comparing the brains of healthy children who are developing well with children who have been neglected reveal that the brain growth described above is much more dependent on the environment than on heredity. Therefore, caregivers can help babies the most during this vital time by providing them with nurturing, caring, interactive, and engaging play and communication. They can, essentially, help set the stage for a child's lifelong learning and coping abilities to flourish.

Summary

A baby's brain is not fully developed at birth, and it seems that babies are born with a range of abilities and capacities for coping and learning. Their early life experiences influence how much of that range they'll develop. The more positive, nurturing, respectful, understanding, interactive, supportive, and engaging you are with your baby, the calmer and less stressed your baby will be, which in turn allows his brain to develop to its fullest capacity. Stressful and scary early life experiences, especially in the first three years, can negatively impact your baby's emotional, social, and cognitive abilities.

Everything Respectful Parenting advocates helps ensure this healthy development. The emphasis on respectful interactions from day one makes sense and is reinforced by research into the physical development of a young child's brain. Your roles as supporter, encourager, narrator, interacting partner, caring observer, and respectful parent are critical to your child's development.

Note

1. National Association for the Education of Young Children, Annual Conference, November 2003, Chicago, Illinois.)

Six
Looking for Child Care

PERHAPS ONE OF THE MOST important decisions you will have to face is who will take care of your baby when you aren't able to provide full-time child care yourself. This chapter will provide you with guidelines for questions to ask, standards that should be in place, credentials the staff should have, and assessing the environment at a child care center. When you've gathered all that information, visited various child care centers, and spoken with a variety of child care providers you'll be able to weigh the advantages and disadvantages of each option available in your community and make an informed decision.

Local parent resource networks and other parents' experiences can be a big help in your search for the best child care providers in your area. You'll find websites for national organizations and parent resource centers as well as local sources on the Internet. You may want to begin with:

www.naeyc.org
www.zerotothree.org
www.ChildcareExchange.com
www.cwla.org
www.childcareaware.org, and
www.nrc.uchsc.edu

Almost every state has a statewide parent resource center that lists licensed and accredited child care providers. To be state licensed a center or home-based child care provider must meet particular standards of care. In order to be accredited by a national organization such as the National Association for the Education of Young Children (NAEYC) the center or home-based program must surpass the level of care and standards that the state requires. If you're choosing between a program that's licensed and one that's licensed *and* accredited, the latter probably meets a higher standard of care, which means it will most likely be an enriching environment for your baby.

Your baby needs a combination of nurturing and exposure to early learning opportunities to enhance his or her cognitive, emotional, and social development. You'll want to find a child care center or caregiver that is attentive to your baby, his emotional and cognitive development, you, your family, and how you, your baby, and your family fit into the larger community. Your child care provider ought to be educated about the latest information on child development, including emotional and cognitive development.

Don't settle for an arrangement that's convenient; find a person or a center that's terrific. You and your baby deserve that. Keep in mind that terrific doesn't have to cost an arm and a leg. It isn't how many new toys a center has that should impress you; it's what the staff and babies do with the toys that's important. Are the toys engaging, interactive, used for self-exploration, used by the caregivers as educators, rotated, and cleaned often? If you take some extra time while you're pregnant and after your baby is born talking to staff, visiting child care centers, and seeing how you and your baby feel in them, you'll make a well-informed decision.

After your child begins child care, you'll want to make unannounced visits once in a while to make sure everything is going well. Even if you leave him with a relative or nanny, make a few unexpected visits to make sure you see what's happening while your baby is preverbal. You don't want to find the caregiver watching soap operas or leaving the child in front of Sesame Street-type programs all day. You don't want to keep a caregiver who's impatient or rough when your baby is having a difficult day.

Because so much is now known about infant and brain development (see Chapter 5), you should have high expectations of caregivers who work with infants, babies, and toddlers. You want to look for child care providers who understand the interplay between all areas of a child's early development and learning, including cognitive, emotional, social, language, and physical needs. The NAEYC offers specific standards on their website (www.naeyc.org), and the following tips are a good place to start.

A child care center should not just be a place where you drop off your child in the morning and pick him up in the evening, kind of like a glorified babysitting service. Instead, look for a program where caregivers check in with parents at the beginning and end of each day. The staff should be available to talk about problems you may be having at home with your child and offer parenting tips, parenting classes, books, tapes, and other resources to help you. If you have family problems that require outside resources such as food stamps, subsidized housing, marital counseling, or developmental testing for your child, the staff should be familiar with local offices and organizations that would offer assistance. They should be interested in your role as mom or dad in your child's life and encourage involvement from both parents. Social activities should be hosted by the center so that you have a chance to get to know other families. If you are concerned about something your child is doing the center may be dealing with similar behaviors, and they may have found an effective solution they can share with you. You should be able to observe what they're doing and learn from the staff. You want a staff that can sense changes in children, and you want them to be willing to respectfully question you or offer on-the-spot information. An early child care center's goal should be to facilitate children's cognitive, social, and emotional development.

Checklists for Evaluating a Child Care Center

STAFF

❑ Do the caregivers/teachers seem to really like children?
❑ Do the caregivers/teachers get down on each child's level to speak to the child?
❑ Do the caregivers hold babies often?
❑ Do the caregivers talk to and engage the babies when they're awake?
❑ Is someone supervising the sleeping babies and toddlers?

- ❑ Do the caregivers hold babies when they're crying?
- ❑ Do the caregivers meet children's needs quickly even when they are busy?
- ❑ Are the caregivers/teachers trained in CPR, first aid, and early childhood development and education?
- ❑ Are the caregivers involved in continuing education programs?
- ❑ Are caregivers/teachers trained and experienced in child care?
- ❑ How long have caregivers/teachers been working for the center?
- ❑ Is the director and assistant director trained and experienced in early childhood development and education with at least a bachelor's degree and two years of experience in child care settings?
- ❑ Does the lead teacher have a bachelor's degree in a child-related field?
- ❑ Has the lead teacher worked in child care for at least one year?

PROGRAMS

- ❑ Does the program follow children's changing and developing interests?
- ❑ Do the caregivers/teachers and children enjoy being together?
- ❑ Is there enough staff to serve the children? (Ask local experts about the best staff to child ratios for different age groups.)
- ❑ Is the atmosphere bright and pleasant?
- ❑ Is the program accredited and/or licensed and/or regulated?
- ❑ Are there different areas for resting, quiet play, creative play, and active play?
- ❑ Is there enough space for the children in each of these areas?
- ❑ Is there a daily balance of story time, activity time, and creative playtime?
- ❑ Are specific activities geared for each age group?
- ❑ Are there enough toys and learning materials for the number of children?
- ❑ Do the older children look stimulated and engaged?
- ❑ Do you agree with the way the center sets limits and consequences for the children?
- ❑ Do you hear the sounds of happy, engaged children?
- ❑ Are surprise visits by parents encouraged?
- ❑ Do you sense that your child will be happy there?
- ❑ From observing the older children, do you anticipate that the program will be appropriate for your child as he grows and enters the preschool years?

RELATIONSHIP WITH THE FAMILY

- ❏ Are children and parents greeted when they arrive?
- ❏ Will the caregivers/teachers tell you what your child is doing every day?
- ❏ Will the caregivers/teachers speak to you about problems your child is having and ask if you are seeing those behaviors at home and, if so, ask what you're doing about them?
- ❏ Will the caregivers/teachers share their solutions to problems your child is having with you?
- ❏ Will the caregivers/teachers share your baby's progress and accomplishments with you each day?
- ❏ Are parents' ideas welcomed? Are there ways for you to be involved with the center?
- ❏ Does the center offer parenting education?
- ❏ Does the center offer social opportunities for the families?
- ❏ Is the staff familiar with local resources families may need and can they make referrals in a timely manner?

HEALTH AND SAFETY

- ❏ Are toxic substances such as cleaning supplies and pest killers kept away from children?
- ❏ Has the building been checked for dangerous substances such as radon, lead, and asbestos?
- ❏ Is poison control information posted?
- ❏ Does the center have an emergency plan if a child gets injured, sick, or lost?
- ❏ Does the center have first aid kits?
- ❏ Does the center have information about who to contact in an emergency?
- ❏ Does the center have a plan in case of fire, tornado, flood, blizzard, earthquake, or terrorist attack in the area?
- ❏ Does the center have practice drills once every month?
- ❏ Can the staff see each other at all times, so a child is never alone with one caregiver?
- ❏ Have all caregivers gone through a background check?
- ❏ Have the caregivers been trained on how to prevent child abuse, how to recognize signs of child abuse, and how to report suspected child abuse?

- ❏ Does the center keep medication out of reach of children?
- ❏ Are caregivers trained to understand medication labels so that the right child gets the right amount of the right medication at the right time?
- ❏ Have caregivers been trained on how to keep children healthy and safe from injury and illness?
- ❏ Do caregivers know how to give first aid and CPR to young children and babies?
- ❏ Are all child care staff, volunteers, and substitutes informed of and implementing safe sleep policies (infants should sleep on their backs) to reduce the risk of Sudden Infant Death Syndrome (SIDS)?
- ❏ Is there an outdoor play area? Is it fenced and secure? Does it have a variety of safe play equipment?
- ❏ Can the caregivers/teachers see the entire playground at all times?
- ❏ Are toys clean, safe, and within reach of the children and crawling babies?
- ❏ Is the eating area clean?
- ❏ Is there a sanitized, safe area for diaper changes?
- ❏ Do all caregivers and children wash their hands often, especially after eating, using the bathroom, or changing diapers?
- ❏ Do caregivers keep one hand on the child while diapering?
- ❏ Do caregivers dispose of the diaper without dirtying any other surface, and do they clean and sanitize the surface after the changing process?
- ❏ Is the diaper changing area large enough to accommodate all of the babies in the center?
- ❏ Is there adequate supervision for other babies and toddlers when a staff member is changing a child's diaper?
- ❏ Are appropriate snacks given during the day?

Since this is a long list of questions, you'll want to make an appointment to be sure a staff member, the home child care provider, or a nanny has enough time to answer all of your questions. If it's a particularly busy day, you may need to come back a second time to finish your interview, but it's worth it to have all of the questions answered. As you interview staff at a potential center, or the person running the home-based child care, or a potential nanny remember you have the right to ask these questions. You should be encouraged to quietly observe as long as you don't disrupt their program, for as long as you want to. When you come to observe with your baby, you may want to stay for twenty minutes to a half hour the first time, and build up to an hour or two to see how your baby feels in the environment. During your visits, be sure to check out the room(s) where your child will graduate to if you stay with this center as your child grows. As you observe, get a sense of how the various staff members interact with each other and with the children. Do they seem to be enjoying their job? Is there collegiality among the staff? If you're observing one person, make sure the caregiver is relating to the children in most of the ways suggested on your checklist.

If anyone is insulted or upset by your questions and observations, you should probably leave right away. Any quality child care program or provider will greet your questions openly and honestly. The questions are intended to verify standards of care and are based on the criteria for licensure or accreditation—the staff should be prepared to demonstrate they meet the standards you desire. Your infant's physical and mental health as well as their cognitive and emotional development may depend on the answers. Keep in mind that your baby is depending on you to find him a safe, nurturing place.

Types of Child Care

There are four different types of child care arrangements: relatives, a nanny, in-home small child care programs, and large child care centers. Most formal child care settings—whether in a caregiver's home or in a child care center—offer the advantage of a state's licensing process: the provider is accountable to, and has a track record with, an official state agency or accreditation program managed by an independent organization such as NAEYC or the Child Welfare League of America (CWLA).

Using a Relative

The most informal type of child care is using a relative. Relying on a relative is ideal in some ways because you know you can trust your family. Parents often assume a relative will provide warmer, more loving care for their child, and a bond between the baby and the caregiver may already be established. That relationship can be very reassuring for a parent. The flip side of having a relative care for your child is whether the relative will practice old-style parenting or Respectful Parenting with your baby and how effectively you can deal with potential conflicts with your relative.

The obvious advantage of using a relative for child care is that the person is a known entity. Your child may also be the only child at your relative's home and thus may get one-on-one attention. Or if your child has an older sibling already being cared for, it's still all in the family. One might assume that, at least at the beginning, a relative will have an easier time bonding with your baby. (Of course you may be surprised how many child care workers have big hearts and can establish a close relationship with you, your baby, and your spouse.) A relative can also be more cost-effective and flexible than an independent caregiver or child care center. You'll need to weigh the financial cost, however, against the emotional cost of how potential conflict will be handled and how it will affect the whole family. Family dynamics will clearly be different from independent, objective personal interactions. But, when you have a relative you adore, who you know is loving, respectful, and whose influence you want your child to experience, then what better option can you give your child? A relative can truly love your child and give him more individual attention than he will receive in a group setting. A relative is family—an intimate part of your life and your child's life. It's a wonderful option when it works well, but it can tear a family apart if it doesn't.

If you're concerned about parenting or care giving styles matching between your home and your relative's home, it's helpful to talk about what he or she will be doing, how it will be done, and what parenting ideas he or she practices. This may prove to be a ticklish discussion, however. Relatives who have raised their own children sometimes don't like being questioned. Because they're experienced and believe they know how to do it, some relatives may even be *offended* by a new, inexperienced parent questioning their abilities. It may be very difficult to give a relative constructive criticism or suggestions. It's usually easier if the potential caregiver is approached by his or her direct kin rather than by the in-law. If you're feeling unsure about your relative, or any child care provider following your lead in terms of how you want your child cared for, you may want to give the caregiver a copy of this book so they can read it and have it on hand to refer to at different times. Let him or her know you'd like to talk about the techniques so you can make sure that you're all on the same page with regard to your baby's care. This step should be taken well before you're ready to drop the baby off for the first time because if they think these ideas are "too wild," you can look for another child care option. Leave yourself plenty of time to respectfully decline their offer of help if you need to make that tough call.

In-Home Caregivers

Another alternative for a one-on-one experience is with a person who comes to your home or lives with you. Most people refer to that person as a nanny. A nanny is usually paid by the hour unless he or she lives with you. Live-in nannies typically receive a monthly salary plus room and board. Their responsibilities are usually confined to the parents' working hours. If evening or weekend help is needed, you should expect to pay the nanny an extra, agreed-upon hourly rate. Of course any extra hours should be pre-arranged as the person cannot be expected to be on-call twenty-four hours a day, seven days a week.

The biggest advantage of using a nanny is that your child (or children) is usually the nanny's only responsibility, but parents choose in-home care for a variety of other reasons. They believe the baby will be safer and more secure in their own home. Sometimes there's more flexibility—it's certainly easier for a parent to simply get ready for work and leave after the nanny arrives. A nanny eliminates the pressure to get ready, get the baby ready, drive to a child care center, check in with staff, say goodbye to the baby, and get to work on time. If you have several children or share a nanny with a another family the price of in-home child care may not be much more than a child care center, and the children will get more attention than at a center where there may be four babies for every caregiver.

When you interview a potential nanny you will want to find out about the person's background, why she's doing this type of work, what her "parenting philosophy" is, and what child development courses she's taken. Most states don't regulate in-home caregivers, although some do regulate nanny-placement agencies. You should check an agency's credentials, screening process, and track record before hiring someone they recommend. Don't be surprised if the agency has recruited women from overseas; if the agency is regulated and recommended, you can be sure they have screened and interviewed the recruits before they arrive. Even though a nanny is not an official child care center staffer, you can use the checklists provided in this chapter to ask questions that apply to the caregiver, the program he or she would set up in your home, and safety issues. Additionally, you may want to ask about how they were parented, since some of those old parenting behaviors are likely to come out during challenging and stressful times, and there won't be anyone else in your home supervising the nanny.

You may balk at the idea of asking a stranger about her parenting philosophy because you want to be the parent. Or you may be unsure of where you will stand in your baby's eyes if you invite a nanny into your home. Those are valid concerns, but the closest thing to caregiving you can ask about is parenting. You will want to know how that person will react when your baby is having a few difficult days, when he is fussy, when he wants lots of attention, or when he is having a good day. And don't worry, even when babies feel close to caregivers, when active, involved, loving moms and dads come home the baby easily makes the transition and responds to the parent. A baby who's loved and attended to has plenty of love to return to everyone in his life.

The downside to this type of caregiver is often that the person is not necessarily trained in early childhood development. He or she is less likely to understand the importance of early emotional and cognitive stimulation for babies. The nanny may mean well but might not be as informed about opportunities to help your child develop as someone with child development and child care training will be. Nannies can end up being glorified babysitters. A thorough interview will help you avoid this problem and will help you be comfortable with your choice. If you're thinking of employing someone in your home, have that person come and visit a few times at different times of the day before you decide she or he is the one. Let them take over care for your baby while they're visiting so you can see how the caregiver and your baby get along. After your baby and possible caregiver get to know each other, and you feel like you can trust this person, you may want to leave for a few hours and see how your baby does when you return. Even after you decide, it's important to make periodic surprise visits at different times of the day. You want to verify the caregiver is being kind, involved, and interactive when your child is awake, and that she's not sitting in front of the television or on the phone with friends all day.

When I was pregnant I really wanted to have someone come to our home so my baby could have one-on-one attention while I worked, but I didn't need full-time care. When I began investigating the possibilities, I quickly found out that I couldn't afford to hire someone who spoke fluent English. I then began to interview people who did not speak English fluently and met some very warm, nice women. But I was concerned because I couldn't ask them enough about their background, their parenting philosophy, or how they were parented. The depth of our conversations was limited as a result of the language barrier. Many of them were recommended by the parent resource center in Berkeley, but I wasn't satisfied with our ability to communicate, and it was still more money than I wanted to budget for child care.

It was difficult for me to give up the dream of my baby being with one loving caregiver at home and admit that I needed to consider a child care center. I was afraid my baby would not get the attention and nurturing he needed and deserved. On the other hand, I had to be practical; it was what we could afford. So I swallowed my disappointment, hoped I was wrong about the not-enough-nurturing fear, and began to investigate local child care centers.

I found one in our neighborhood that seemed really good. I knew other people who had used the center. I liked the director and assistant director. I liked what they had to say about their programs and their child care philosophy. I liked that they were fine with me stopping in any time to check them out. When I visited the infant and toddler center, the atmosphere was so loving that I wanted to stay all day. I ended up being very wrong about my assumption that one-on-one was the best and only way to go. My child received plenty of love, attention, encouragement, engaging creative play, and nurturing at his center. He also received plenty of socializing at a young age.

It's interesting how things sometimes turn out the way they're supposed to despite your own preconceived notions. My child ended up being an only child. I think his early part-time child care center experience helped him become a caring, compassionate human being. He was one of a group and learned to share, to care about his peers, and to play with other children. He learned that the world does not always revolve around him.

He loved the child care center from the first time we visited when he was about three and a half months old. Dropping him off that first day a few weeks later was much more difficult for me than for him. He was enthralled with the other babies in the infant center. I dropped him off (which meant putting him into the arms of a loving caregiver) went into the hall where he couldn't see me, and shed a few tears. By the end of the first week he remained comfortable, and I had become more comfortable. There were no more aching-throat drop-offs for mom after the first two weeks or so.

My office was only a mile from the child care center, so I was able to go back and nurse him halfway through my afternoon. It was so much fun watching the other babies and the staff as we nursed. I share this story so you don't have to feel like you're shortchanging your child by using a child care center. There are many great child care centers that have lots of activities for your children and for families. Some centers offer parenting classes, a lending library, family nights, and other opportunities for parents to get together and become a community or extended family system.

Home-Based Child Care Setting

A home- or family-based child care setting provides your child with more socializing opportunities than having a nanny in your home, is usually less expensive because the provider is looking after a number of children at once, and offers your baby a homey environment. Most home-based, small centers will have four to six children with one provider. Some family child care providers have a few babies and small children during the day and care for older children before and after school.

Every state sets minimum health, safety, and nutrition standards for this type of provider, but not all states require home-based providers to be licensed or formally regulated. State rules are usually more lenient when there are fewer than five children. Many states use a voluntary regulation process for these very small home-care settings. You should check with your state to see what standards of care they require and how often they may visit a family-based child care center.

If you find an experienced, knowledgeable, and loving family-based child care provider your child will get everything he or she needs. He will be nurtured in a safe, home-based environment, and he will be part of a small group, which is good for socializing. Because there are fewer children than in a larger child care center, there won't be as much exposure to colds, flu, or viruses. A family-based child care provider would be a good match for a child who feels more secure in a small group.

As with any child care environment, you will want to make unannounced visits to be sure the provider is interacting with the children in a caring, engaging, age-appropriate, educational way. You'll also want to make sure the provider keeps up with recent information on child development and early childhood education by going to continuing education seminars and conferences or reading journals.

Child Care Centers

Child care centers divide the children into age groups—infants, toddlers, older toddlers, twos and threes, and so forth—and place them in different spaces. One of the advantages of a child care center is you know that if your child is healthy and you have to be somewhere, someone will always be at the center to care for your child. You won't get a call in the morning from a nanny who's sick or a family-based provider who has canceled child care for the day because her own child is sick. Some centers even have separate rooms for babies who aren't feeling well, while others may have extended hours, which means almost unlimited access for night-shift workers and parents' outings. A child care center can provide some stability for your child as she graduates from room to room and can offer continuity of care in terms of a center-wide philosophy about children's emotional and cognitive development.

Every state requires child care centers be licensed, but the requirements for obtaining a license vary by state. Unfortunately, licensing may not actually regulate the quality of care, rather it may only require meeting minimum health, safety, and caregiver standards. Inspections are made at least once a year at every state-licensed center. The standards of care reflected in the checklist in this chapter are not required by most states. Many of the items on the checklist are above and beyond what a state requires and are more likely to be met if the center is also accredited.

Becoming accredited is a voluntary effort on the part of the center. You probably want to choose a center that is licensed by your state and accredited by a nationally recognized organization (such as NAEYC). When a center is conscientious enough to seek voluntary accreditation, it clearly cares about maintaining more than minimal standards. The center will likely hire a higher caliber staff with more child development training. They probably support their staff with continuing education opportunities. As a result, the staff is more likely to plan age-appropriate activities that will enrich your child's development. These conscientious child care centers are also more likely to provide social or educational activities for the families, so you will get a built-in community along with good care for your child.

You would probably choose a child care center over the other options if you want your child to be in a larger group with multiple caregivers, where you know the staff is supervised, trained, and where you have some safeguards through state licensure and voluntary accreditation.

Summary

You'll probably want to begin looking at child care options while you're still pregnant, but leave the final decision until after you've become acquainted with how your infant does in different settings. If you have time before your baby is born, you can do preliminary interviews using the checklist included in this chapter and observing a number of alternatives. If you're beginning your quest for child care after your baby is born, you may want to do some initial screening by telephone. Once child care options have passed your initial screening, then visit the centers that seem most likely to meet your requirements and check them out as they compare to the checklists in this chapter.

Once your baby is born you want to take the information you already gathered and try to figure out which child care alternative is right for you and your baby. First look at your child's needs—does your baby do better in a smaller, more intimate setting? If so, can your baby's need for a smaller setting be met by the separate spaces within a larger child care center? Do you need to look for a qualified in-home provider or a nanny? After you've made that decision, take your baby to the places you liked best, meet with the staff or the individual child care provider, observe them with your baby, and see how your baby responds. When you're observing by yourself or with your baby, look, listen, consider, and allow your head and heart to sort out what you see, hear, and feel in each place you visit.

Seven

You and Your Infant

*T*HIS CHAPTER COVERS the earliest time period in your child's life, from birth to the first developmental milestone, when your infant becomes a baby. The word *new* is the key to this chapter. Your infant is new to this world and you are a new parent to this baby. Even if this is your third or fourth child, you don't know this unique infant, and you need to take the time to get to know each other. Introductions were made in the hospital, now comes the getting-to-know-you phase.

The same basic principles for Respectful Parenting apply even at this very young age.

- **Slow down.** Listen carefully, using all of your senses. **See, feel, and hear what your child is telling you with different cries and looks.**
- **Be in awe of them and in awe with them.** Recapture the innocent delight that infants naturally have at their disposal. Appreciate their perspective of the world. See how terrific they are. Feel how incredible it is that your little infant is learning her way around the world. Be in awe that your infant knows to seek out new information and to naturally go for what's safe (you). When your infant feels your awe, she feels pretty important, wonderful, and appreciated—and her self-esteem blossoms.
- **Follow your child's lead.** Be flexible when you can. Follow your infant's lead instead of imposing your own.
- **Address your infant's needs quickly and lovingly.**

- **Be patient** with your infant, yourself, your spouse, and your other children (if you have any)—remember you're all a little overtired and overwhelmed by the "newness" of this new life.
- **Be physically close with your infant.** This closeness will facilitate healthy bonding. Focus on your child. **Have lots of one-on-one, eye-to-eye contact when your infant is awake. Your interactions will enhance your parent-child attachment bonds, which are vital to your infant's development.**

A Whole New World

The first couple of months with your infant are characterized by intense learning on everyone's part. Usually your learning takes place through bleary, sleep-deprived eyes as your infant's personality begins to emerge. You're learning how your infant communicates his needs so you can physically and emotionally take care of him. Plus, you're trying to take care of yourself and keep up with your family's needs. An exciting juggling game is going on as you maneuver your way through what may be the biggest transition of your life. While you're going through this learning process, your infant is contending with his own changes. After nine months of slow, steady growth in a warm, darkened place, where nutrition was available automatically at all times and sounds were muffled and muted, your infant has been thrust into an entirely alien territory.

It's pretty amazing when you consider an infant's ability to learn and adapt to survive. From the moment your infant is born and the umbilical cord is cut, everything is new, not a single thing resembles his earlier existence. So, if you're feeling like everything is new and a bit overwhelming, imagine your infant's feelings and remember: he doesn't have the tools, resources, or world experience you have. From this perspective, it's certainly understandable why an infant would cry to be held. That feeling of connection he gets when he's held is vital to his sense of security. Infants need that closeness because it approximates what they felt inside when they were sheltered in mother's womb before being born and being thrust into this big world we know so well.

A baby needs to grow close to at least one human being, a parent or caregiver, during his first year of life in order to establish the essential bonds that form the basis of his sense of security. Sitting and holding your infant in your arms is a wonderful experience for him, especially when you slow down, hold him calmly and caringly, and have lots of close eye contact. You can hold your baby in your arms, you can nurse him, or you can move around with him safely cradled close to you. All these methods help your infant feel safe and nurtured. The most important gift you can give your infant at this age is to help him feel bonded with loving people.

A parent can unknowingly create a negative cycle, however. Here's an example: your infant cries and you pick him up to comfort him, but your arms are rigid because you're not sure why your infant is crying, and you don't know whether you'll be able to comfort him or not. Your son feels the tension in your body as he's being held. When your baby feels your tension, you no longer feel soft and safe to him. He's likely to react by crying more. Hearing him cry while you're trying to help can make you feel more insecure and inadequate. You may become more anxious and worry about what's happening and why you can't calm him down. Your son feels your increased tension and intuitively feels that something is wrong and cries even more. The sad part is both of you are trying to communicate with the other, but it's just not working. You need to do something different. Instead of perpetuating this anxious cycle, as your infant cries, see if you can pick him up confidently so you can give him a congruent message such as, "I'm here for you," or "You're safe now, I'm here," rather than anxiously wondering if you can help. Assume you can help and relax as you acknowledge that you'll be able to figure out what he needs.

What Parents Say

Bonnie: I was so tired one night, I didn't think I could go on, yet there she was crying again. I nursed her, but she still cried. I rocked her and she still cried. At that point I felt myself tensing up. I had an urge to shake her. Wow, I thought, that's how child abuse must start. I could see how it was possible at that moment. I was so frustrated and tired and clearly at the end of my rope . . . but I didn't shake the baby. Instead I called out to my husband.

I needed help. I was too tired to calm down or be the kind of parent I wanted to be. By the time he came in, both the baby and I were crying. I told him I needed a break and asked him to please take over. He tried to calm me down, but the baby was wailing. I told him he didn't need to worry about me, I just needed some sleep, and he needed to calm the baby. He looked a little anxious, but I was able to say, "You can do it. I know you can. I need to sleep."

It was the first time my physical limits affected the way I wanted to parent. I knew it wouldn't be my last. I was glad I had learned quickly to ask for help instead of trying to force myself beyond where I could lovingly go. And I'm grateful I was able to get that help.

Later, when I woke up, I felt refreshed. My husband and baby were playing together. I was able to gather my happy infant in my arms, give her a few kisses, and apologize for being so tired and probably seeming cranky to her earlier. Her eyes just sparkled away in response. My parents never said they were sorry or acknowledged the effects their behavior may have had on us kids. I want to do that with my child.

Communicating with Your Infant

As a new parent you should try to relax and convert any anxious energy into a loving, concentrated effort to look at and listen to your infant. Don't dwell on fear and insecurity, which will block your attempts to figure things out; instead, listen to your intuition. You have studied your infant like no one else has so you can follow her cues. If that's not working, my other suggestion is to try to slowly talk through your feelings with your infant. Avoid short statements such as, "I'm frustrated," instead really explain your thoughts and the feelings that are flowing from your thoughts. Your thought process is one you want to share with your child. If you slow down, and acknowledge what is happening out loud, your tone of voice will become calmer instead of more anxious. For example, "I love it when I can hold you and you stop crying, but here we are—I'm holding you, and you're still crying. It's not your diaper; I've checked that. I just tried to nurse you, and you don't seem to be hungry because you turned your head away. I wonder what it could be? I wish I knew. Imagine when you can talk, and you'll be able to tell me. Here you are, so little, trying to let me know something. This can be so frustrating. I do want to help. I just don't know how. Hey, your cries are getting lower. Are you feeling better? Did you just need some extra time and talking? Maybe you just wanted some contact. Oh, look at that big yawn. That's so sweet. Big stretch. That was it. You woke up and couldn't quite fall back to sleep. Thanks for letting me know. I'm glad I've been able to help you. Now, you're peaceful again."

This kind of talking is soothing for you and your infant. It allows you to connect with your infant's pace and communicate your concerns. As you talk, she can be soothed by your caring tone of voice and stop crying. You can be reassured by calmly going through what you're trying and the effects of your efforts. New options often flood in when you slow down and process your emotions. Your arms should relax as the negative, tense cycle reverses itself. Infants don't understand words, but they do respond to tone of voice and physical feelings, like a gentle person lovingly holding and talking to them.

In addition, by sharing your thought process with your infant, your words and actions are congruent, which is important to your infant's developing sense of trust. An infant is incredibly sensitive to the subtleties in nonverbal and verbal communication. For instance, if you say, "There, there, everything is fine," but your arms are tense, your infant will know on an intuitive level that something is wrong, and she won't be able to relax. A psychology professor once said, "There are no rules about communication except you can never not communicate." Assuming that's true, you may as well communicate positive, loving, appreciative messages from the start. For instance, you can thank your infant for all she's bringing into your life. By the time your baby understands words, she will "get" that: a) she is adequate and worthwhile; b) she brings joy to other people; c) she does things other people appreciate; and d) she has a positive influence on the world around her. She'll learn those lessons from what you've communicated with your words and body language. Talking out your feelings will also introduce her to manners such as when to say "Thank you" or "I'm sorry." You'll be informally teaching manners by doing them with your infant.

Some of you may be thinking, "These ideas seem okay, but not for an infant. I'll wait until my child is old enough to understand, say about four or five, then I'll talk like that." If you wait that long, you'll probably never start because other parenting patterns will already be in place. You'll have practiced avoidance or what I call, "short-hand speak" for so long it will be difficult to switch. Short-hand speak is a method of communicating where the essentials are spoken, but in such abbreviated form that the listener (your child) can easily misinterpret your message. Instead, I recommend communicating your thoughts and the processes behind your thoughts in full sentences, so that your intentions will be clear to your listener. No one will be able to put their own spin on things or be forced to figure out what you mean or why you're saying what you're saying. When you engage in shorthand speak, you'll inadvertently send mixed messages that can confuse your infant, baby, toddler, or small child. In trying to make sense from her confusion, she may learn that grown-ups don't mean what they say. Your child may have trouble developing a solid sense of trust and security.

Slow Down and Take Cues

Raising an infant involves surrendering many adult ways of looking at life. The more childlike and spontaneous you become, the more you'll enjoy your infant. Likewise, the more you slow down, the more you'll notice and appreciate your infant's perspective. If you don't focus on the minor actions and changes your infant is making on an almost daily basis, you'll miss a lot of growth, excitement, and transitions. These small but momentous happenings make all the diaper changes and late-night feedings worthwhile.

You may be so bleary-eyed from lack of sleep that focusing can be difficult. Try paying attention to little things such as smiles, coos, hand movements, eyes following objects, and hands reaching for objects. Your enthusiastic responses to your infant's movements will give him valuable feedback and tell him he's worth paying attention to. You'll also be telling him that he's a good learner, he's impacting his environment, and he's fun to be around. These early lessons contribute to your infant's self-esteem, and it's never too early for that kind of feedback.

What Parents Say

Sarah: I'm still in awe of all I learned and continue to learn by watching and being responsive to my son. It's been his lead; he's taught me. I remember saying to my husband, "How can this twenty-four-hour-old infant teach me so much? I read the books and he just is." So far it's been the nicest, most loving education I've ever received. I just never knew I'd learn so much from him so quickly.

I can remember the simple joy and loving exhilaration of playing with my child when he was two months old. I remember fun times; sitting with my back against the bed frame or couch arm, and my knees up supporting his back as he sat perched against my thighs. My arms helped balance him if he shifted his weight enough to warrant that. We talked and played for as long as three-quarters of an hour at a time. Those goos and gurgles and coos were some of the best conversations I'd ever had.

Sometimes we'd throw in tongue thrusts (sticking our tongues out at each other), arm waving, and singing, just to vary our repertoire. There I was, the "professional woman" turned into the "rhapsodically happy mom," thrilled at these small but significant early communications with my child. In those first few days, weeks, and months, he taught me about simple, joyous fascination. I hope I never forget his early teachings.

* * *

Bonnie: I learned to slow down. I've always been a planner, but with my daughter I couldn't plan my day, because when I did, I ended up being frustrated and it just wasn't worth it. For months, it seemed like every time I thought we had a routine, she'd change it. A few times, I almost wished I could impose a feeding or sleeping schedule on her so things could be more stable. But then I'd look at her sweet face and know I'd rather change and become more flexible than have her crying until her needs were met.

I learned I had more choices than I ever imagined. If I didn't get the laundry done one day, there was always tomorrow. If the house was messy, oh well. If dinner wasn't cooked, we'd get take-out food. The one thing I could guarantee was, when I was able to shed my expectations, I'd have a great (although possibly exhausting) day with my daughter. Without plans, I left myself time to adore her and revel in her infant antics when she was awake. When she was asleep, I could look at her peaceful face before falling asleep myself or take the time to get something accomplished around the house.

Games You Can Play

There are fun ways you can play with your infant. All infant play is a way to interact with your infant as you help your infant form valuable attachment bonds with you. By interacting with your infant and focusing on her as you play, you're encouraging your infant's social, emotional and cognitive development. Using an accessory like the award-winning Boppy pillow, which gently and ergonomically cradles your infant in a sitting position so your hands can be free to interact with your infant, will make playtime easier and even more fun for both of you.

- Touch hands, watch your infant's hand movements, then imitate them. Try clapping and seeing how your infant responds: some infants don't like the noise and others do.
- While sitting with your knees up to provide a back for your infant, and keeping your hands on your infant for support, look into your infant's face and make a sound he likes.
- In this same position, repeat sounds your infant makes and have a conversation in her language.
- Hand him a small, easy-to-hold object (that he can't choke on).
- Fetch something she drops.
- Make tongue movements while looking and smiling at each other.
- Blow bubble kisses.
- Share simple toys. The first ones can be black and white, then move up to primary colors.
- Sit and look out a window together holding your infant on your lap. Point to things and explain them. A window is a slower moving form of visual stimulation and easier to cope with than television.

Parenting High-Need Infants

When my child was in child care and I was nursing or visiting I often noticed a little five-month-old girl who cried throughout the day despite being held and talked to quite often. One day, I asked an experienced infant care provider if it was ever difficult for her to keep providing hugs and soothing talk, because they often didn't seem to have much impact. She wisely responded, "Oh no, not at all. I know this baby is trying to tell us something. It seems, for some reason, that her little world doesn't feel too good to her. We may figure it out one day. Or who knows, maybe she'll always be the squeaky wheel and get herself heard. But, for whatever reason, she needs more loving and understanding than the quieter infants. If we keep giving her cuddles and understanding hugs, she'll sense our love and acceptance, and it'll all catch up with her one day."

It took a long while. This child didn't smile freely or easily for about a year and a half. But she didn't cry all the time either. From about seven to eighteen months, she took her surroundings in carefully and participated with other children at times, but she often sat back, intently watching what was happening around her. A few months later, I noticed a tiny little girl looking up at me with a radiant smile. I almost didn't recognize her. It was the little girl who used to cry so much. The loving had paid off. The last time I was there, she was three years old, still smiling, and had formed playful relationships with several of the other children. She was not a "squeaky wheel." The caregiver had been right. All that extra loving and acceptance (rather than frustration and anger) had caught up with her.

Sometimes, nothing seems to work the way you want it to. One mother, after hearing examples other mothers had given me, said, "I don't have a lot of those wonderfully wide-eyed awesome stories to tell you. Mine are more like: 'How can this be happening?' in a surprised and shocked how-do-I-deal-with-this vein."

As we talked, it became evident that mothers and fathers of high-need, intense infants and babies often have a difficult time getting support. When these parents tell friends stories about their infant, their friends wonder what they could possibly be doing (wrong) to cause or exacerbate such behaviors. Some friends are sure the parents are exaggerating. Other friends often have advice and suggestions they're certain will work. If the problems persist, then these friends assume the parents were not following their good advice. As a result, parents of high-need infants and babies often become isolated. They begin to fear judgment or more ill-fated advice.

The mother I was speaking to made the point that she had done everything she had read to do, everything she believed in her heart she ought to do to calm her baby, but her baby didn't stay calm for long. I reminded her that Dr. Sears did not write his book on the high-need child for just one set of parents, and I encouraged her to keep doing what she was doing, because her child would feel better from her efforts even if it wasn't happening right away. This mother's input reminded me that most of the examples in this book are about children who respond fairly easily to Respectful Parenting techniques. In real life, families have high-need children or children with special needs. Therefore, it's important to have examples of really difficult times as well. The following parent's story reflects that practicing Respectful Parenting with some infants can be more challenging, takes a great deal more effort on the parents' part, has fewer immediate rewards, but the extra efforts will eventually bring positive results.

Cindy: With my first daughter, I did all the right things, and the result? I had an uncalm baby and intermittent self-doubt. This child was nursing or in a sling—on me in some way—almost twenty-four hours a day. Why? Because if I put her down, she'd start screaming in a second. Not only would she scream, but she'd quickly proceed to turn purple and throw up. Rarely could her father or anyone else comfort her; it usually had to be me. Lots of people offered their advice: "Put her down. It won't take too long, and then she'll get used to it." I just couldn't. The few times I did try, she'd be in such obvious distress, needing to be held, that I couldn't let her scream. I just didn't have it in me.

At first we thought it was because she had been separated from me right after her birth. She had been born at home, in a quiet loving environment, just as we had planned and dreamed, but as soon as she was born I sensed something was wrong. I finally convinced my husband to take her to the hospital. I couldn't go along because I hemorrhaged after her birth, and our midwife said I had to stay put and rest. For the next two days, I wasn't allowed to stay with her and could hold her only occasionally. She finally did come home, after five days, but she had to be hooked up to oxygen for another eight weeks, and she had some other health problems through her first birthday.

We kept thinking her unusual need to be held was due to her post-birth trauma, her hospital stay, and her health problems...you know, her body was so out of control, hooked up to machines, deprived of my closeness, the long-term oxygen...but over time she never seemed to get enough. No matter how much holding and rocking I gave her, she still needed more. She would calm down; she just wouldn't stay that way for long. I finally figured this level of upset is what she came into this world with, and as her mother, I needed to address it as best and as lovingly as I could.

So what did I learn from my infant? You can have a mellow home birth, be loving parents, understand your infant's need to be held, nurse on demand, and you can still have a high-need infant who screams in a way that causes people to look at you and say or think, "What is going on with that infant?" or "What is that parent doing to that infant?" I realized that if being loving and understanding was resulting in such vocalizing, I had to keep reassuring her, with continued closeness and attachment, that I still loved her, that I would be there, and it was okay. It would be okay. I knew that in my head, and mostly in my heart, but sometimes my self-confidence wavered. It's difficult, frustrating, and scary to do what you believe is right, yet not get the results you know you ought to be getting.

Our daughter cried—no, she screamed, bloodcurdling screams—when she was hungry, and that was about every hour and a half, around the clock. So we brought her into our bed for easier nursing. Still, in our bed, with me right next to her, when she was ready to nurse—no, when she needed to nurse—she'd still cry out in that incredibly intense way.

My mother-in-law visited when my daughter was ten weeks old. She saw us holding her, seemingly unwilling to put her down, and most of the time walking or rocking her as we held her. My mother-in-law thought we were being absurd; clearly we were spoiling her. She repeatedly advised, "Just put her down and she'll cry her way through it once or twice and then you'll be past it."

On one of the first days of her visit, we had gone to the supermarket. I had my infant strapped to me in her Snuggli as we shopped. When we got back to the car, and I started to put her in her car seat, she began to fuss. Ordinarily, I would have spent a few minutes comforting her or seeing if she wanted to nurse before putting her into her car seat. But my mother-in-law said, "Come on, we'll be home in five minutes." So instead of taking the five or ten minutes in the parking lot to comfort and nurse her, I acquiesced and plopped her into her car seat. Within two seconds my daughter had gone from 0 to 100. Crying, screaming, turning purple in the face, and then throwing up all over herself. At that point I had had enough; I took her out, cleaned her off and comforted her. "Oh, I see," my mother-in-law said, "I hadn't realized . . ."

How do you explain that to someone who hasn't seen it? People just don't want to believe that you can't, as parents, prevent such behavior. But you can't. I quickly learned that I needed to love my daughter with all her unique qualities. I knew, really knew in my heart, she needed our love even more than if she had been a mellow, easier infant. And at times, yes, I was exhausted, and it was hard to maintain such an accepting stance. But thankfully, I could always talk to myself and intellectually understand, and from somewhere I'd be able to come up with a reserve of love and acceptance to give her.

We knew we had to keep doing what we were doing even if, at that point in time, we weren't getting the results we wanted. Intuitively, and from all we had read, we believed that later in our daughter's life our continual love, support, and attempts to make her more comfortable would be important and healthy for her development. And it's been true. Now, at five years old, she's intelligent, sharp, intense, loving, and creative. She is still often a challenge to parent, but also a great kid to be around.

Eliminating Old-Style Parenting Patterns

The lesson here is that high-need infants and babies need extra love and respect so they can become happy, well-adjusted children and adults. This extra effort can be particularly difficult if you were raised by gruff parents. Your inner tapes will tell you things like, "Why won't this baby shut up? I'm holding her!" or "I just fed him a half hour ago. He should be asleep by now!" Perhaps your infant needs you to think about her needs rather than your expectations. At times like these, try to remember that your parents didn't know any better. They may have misinterpreted your fussiness to be malicious attempts on your part to annoy them. If you can reframe your thoughts, and accept the fact that your infant's personal discomfort has nothing to do with you, remind yourself that you're there to soothe your infant and understand she's having a hard day, then you don't have to continue their legacy. You can hear those old, angry tapes and stop yourself from repeating them. Sometimes it helps to let the old tapes play through and then say, "Thank you for sharing, but that doesn't apply to my life today" and then go on with what you really want to do. By acknowledging your old tapes, you don't waste time fighting your personal history, and your energy is free to do something different today. You'll be able to give your child the gifts of love, understanding, and acceptance by embracing your infant heartily, and accepting her needs, even when she challenges you.

Postpartum Depression

Although giving birth and becoming a family is usually a positive, even magical transition, there are sometimes complications. The overwhelming experience of giving birth, the new things mom and baby must learn together, and the worry of what can go wrong can leave many new moms feeling overwhelmed with emotions. It's not unusual to experience fleeting or more persistent mood swings during the first few weeks after giving birth. This short-term vulnerability is often referred to as "the blues" or "mom's blues." If you find yourself crying more than usual, being irritable, looking at your baby and not being sure you can or want to take care of him, then you're probably experiencing "the blues." Most women feel better within a couple of weeks but, while they last, those odd and unexpected feelings can be upsetting. If you can relax with them and know that most women have some emotional ups and downs and unexpected feelings after giving birth, your feelings will probably go away faster. You don't need to feel guilty or wonder if you've lost you mind. You didn't. The accepted explanation for these blues is a combination of hormonal changes and lack of sleep.

If you find your feelings are persistent and seem to be getting worse over time, you may have postpartum depression (PPD). Between 10 and 15 percent of new moms experience postpartum depression. This type of depression usually sets in later than the blues, and may build gradually over the first few weeks and continue for quite a few months. Postpartum depression seems to be caused by a combination of hormonal changes, sleep deprivation, and real-life stressors. If you believe you have PPD, the best antidotes are emotional support and help around the house so you are not overwhelmed. Sometimes a doctor will prescribe medication to help you shift out of the depressive cycle and back to normal. Because your moods are more than you're able to comfortably deal with and are affecting your family, it's better to acknowledge that "something's not right here." Then you can get the help you need, rather than struggling and pretending everything's fine when it's not. Postpartum depression can be treated. The sooner you recognize that it's affecting you, the sooner you can get some relief.

Symptoms of Postpartum Depression

The symptoms of postpartum depression overlap with the symptoms of depression: moodiness, irritability, not enjoying things you usually enjoy, too much sleep, too little sleep, and changes in your appetite. In addition to the "usual" depression symptoms you may experience a whole set of discombobulating thoughts and feelings such as: 'I don't want this baby'; 'I don't want to take care of this baby'; 'What did I get myself into?' 'What was I thinking?' 'This is too much for me'; 'I just want to run away and disappear from all the added responsibilities.' These kinds of thoughts and the feelings that come along with them seem real because they are real to you at the time you're experiencing them. Sometimes women feel ashamed or guilty and try to fight those unwanted thoughts and feelings. They try to keep them hidden and suffer silently. You may think you're the only one who ever felt this way. Or you may begin to think, "What's wrong with me? I wanted this baby. Now that I have it, I couldn't care less." You can easily be confused and frightened by your thoughts and feelings, but they are exactly what define postpartum depression. They won't last forever, but while you're in the middle of it you won't realize that. You need to share your upsetting feelings and thoughts, or you may suffer alone for longer than is necessary.

SYMPTOMS OF POSTPARTUM DEPRESSION—YOU CAN GET HELP

- Low mood.
- Feelings of inadequacy.
- Feeling like a failure as a mom.
- Feeling hopeless and/or helpless.
- Being consumed with guilt, shame, or worthlessness.
- Confusion, difficulty concentrating.
- Trouble making decisions.
- Anxiety and/or panic.
- Not enjoying what you normally would enjoy.
- Insomnia or excessive sleep.
- Changes in appetite.
- Not caring about how you look.
- Inability to cope with normal routines.
- Crying for no good reason.
- Thoughts of harming yourself or your baby.
- Uncontrollable anger.
- Fear of being alone.
- Frightening thoughts or feelings.
- Obsessive, weird thoughts that keep coming back or won't go away.
- Hatred of husband, self, or baby.
- Withdrawing from family and friends.
- Overwhelming thoughts of wanting your old life back.
- Feeling like there's a dark cloud or a big hole surrounding you.
- A desire to leave your new family and run away.
- Thinking maybe they're better off without you.

What To Do

If you're having these thoughts and feelings it's important to ask for help. Sometimes talking and finding understanding help and support in your husband, family, and friends is enough. When you do seek help, either from family, friends, or a professional, look for someone who will listen to you, honor your feelings, reassure you, and support you as long as your postpartum depression lasts.

When you're not fighting the reality of having postpartum depression, you free up more resources to deal with it effectively. Here are some simple and important things you can do.

- Join a support group.
- Get out of the house and see friends, especially sympathetic, caring friends
- Reach out to other moms with young children.
- Sleep or rest when your baby sleeps.
- Get some help in the house and forgo housework.
- Exercise.
- Spend special time with your husband or loved one.
- Take a baby break (leave your baby with a responsible, caring person).
- Forget about having a perfect house or apartment.
- Eat well-balanced meals.
- Be kind and generous to yourself.
- Use the Internet to find support groups and information about PPD.
- Remind yourself that you have a sense of humor and you know how to use it.
- Remember, "This too shall pass."
- Call a doctor—a physician, a therapist or a psychiatrist.
- Consider taking anti-depressants if the feelings persist and interfere with your life too much.

If you try these ideas, but your moods still feel out of control, you may want to talk to a therapist who understands postpartum depression. A consultation with a doctor may also be important because the hormone imbalance can set off a more complex neuro-chemical imbalance that may need to be treated with anti-depressant medication. Most women who have PPD only need anti-depressants for a relatively short time period to correct the imbalance. Some anti-depressants are safe to take while nursing, but you'll need to consult with a knowledgeable physician or psychiatrist first.

Experiencing postpartum depression, especially when you were ready to be thrilled with your new baby, can be a scary time for dads too. Your emotional distress can and will affect your husband. He may be concerned about what you're going through, he may feel helpless, and he probably will wonder how long it's going to last. You both may worry about whether Mom's depression and distance will affect your baby. It's important for both of you to get reassurance about the transitory nature of PPD and help with the household tasks so that you will be less stressed and free to connect with your baby as best you can.

WHEN YOUR WIFE HAS POSTPARTUM DEPRESSION

- Give your wife lots of support.
- Consider seeing a therapist with your wife.
- Make sure your wife's therapist knows about PPD.
- Recognize PPD is an illness and not your wife's fault.
- Remember that PPD will pass with patience and support.
- Get support for yourself from family, friends, PPD websites, and your wife (if she can).
- Remember to do nice things for yourself—such as exercise, get a massage, meditate, talk with friends, or do something fun.
- Keep interacting with your infant and your wife.
- Help around the house.
- Let your wife know you love and support her.
- Be patient and reassure her that you're sticking by her.
- Have special husband-wife time by arranging for a caring, responsible babysitter.
- Remember your sense of humor.

Postpartum depression is real even though you didn't want to get it and you weren't expecting to have it. The age old wisdom, "This too shall pass" truly applies to postpartum depression. You will feel crummy (at best) while you're experiencing PPD. But when it passes, you'll be able to look at your baby and smile lovingly, feeling attached, bonded, and secure in your love for your child. You'll be in awe of your infant or baby and her ability to relate to the world. You'll feel awe with your infant or baby as she learns new things. You'll feel joy when you see and hold your baby. These newer, more positive feelings will last a lot longer than your postpartum depression lasted.

Eight
You and Your Baby

*I*T'S DIFFICULT TO IMPOSE a distinct time delineation between infancy and babyhood. Where does one stop and the next stage of development begin? When it seems to you that your infant has turned a corner, becoming significantly more responsive and social, then she has left infancy and become a baby. I went back recently and reread some journal entries I wrote about my own child. The following entries clarified my thinking about the distinction. The first was written when my son was one week shy of three months old, "Today I realized you definitely don't look like an infant anymore. You're so alert and responsive. I can see your brain going. Your disposition remains light and sunny." By the end of that next week I wrote, "What a month. Every day, every hour, every minute is so full of new things. . . . You communicate your needs so well, like coming off my breast repeatedly or raising your hands up straight when you need burping. You squeal with delight. Your smile lights up your face and mine. Just the other day you looked at me, smiled, and lifted your right eyebrow. What a face! You've definitely changed this month from an infant to a baby."

Being a baby starts right after infancy and continues until your child is beginning to toddle around. Some babies begin toddling at nine months, others wait until they're eighteen months or older. The ages can vary quite a bit, but it's during this early baby stage that you'll begin to get clues about the pace your baby will take in dealing with life. His frustration level begins to be apparent. You can see evidence of how he will tolerate discomfort. You can learn what makes him laugh. He'll show you his level of curiosity. You'll begin to see how he moves his body and you'll see his own particular brand of grace. He'll even begin to tell you he wants things or wants to know about things. You have to watch and listen carefully to pick up the nuances that are essential in deciphering your baby's emerging character development.

The following strategies will help you get in tune with your baby's unique development. You'll be learning from your baby, learning with your baby, and teaching your baby when you follow these simple strategies:

- Focus on your child
- Slow down
- Listen carefully, using all your senses
- Be spontaneous
- Begin reading to your baby
- Talk with your baby
- Enjoy your baby
- Be in awe with your baby and in awe of your baby as you watch him respond to the world around him

Communicating with Your Baby

At a few months old babies are responsive to different language stimuli. You can encourage your baby's sounds by making the same intonations back to her. If your baby says, "ba," you can say "ba" back. Before you try to get your baby to say a real English word, encourage her in her own language. After saying "ba" a few times together, you could say a few familiar words that have a "ba" sound, like ball, baby, banana, or stretch it to book. But always repeat your baby's sounds first so she feels heard and then suggest yours. Watch your baby's face light up with glee as she hears you repeat her sounds. When you do that, you're validating her reality, and that feels good to any human being at any age.

The more you talk with your baby, the faster your baby will catch on to language and start to make all kinds of sounds on her own. When you interact with your baby in ways that show you're as interested in her form of conversation as you would be with any interesting, engaging human being, you'll encourage her social and emotional development. It's fun to challenge yourself, and work really hard if necessary, to discover what she means with her gestures and tone of voice. It's fun for both of you. On an intuitive level, your baby will feel understood, safe, and good. You can have full jabber conversations or add real words and sentences here and there. You'll build your child's self-esteem and teach her valuable early language skills and the social skills of give and take.

Recognizing your baby as an intelligent small human being—who is taking in a lot more than you may think—can remind you to follow your baby's lead, build on her interests, respond to her curiosity, and go at her pace.

Stimulating Your Baby

Babies want to learn. They're hungry for information and stimulation (when they're not sleeping.) Babies are self-motivated little beings. They only seem to lose motivation when they aren't encouraged. Traditionally, parenting experts thought small babies should be kept at home, but today parents are encouraged to take their babies with them, to stimulate them by exposing them to different places and things. When they learn that the world is full of different stimuli, while surrounded by the safety and comfort of Mommy and Daddy, they may be less timid and, therefore, more self-assured about venturing out and doing things when they're older.

Parents need to respect their baby's individual ability to take in stimuli. If your baby seems to have a low tolerance for stimulation or noise, then you need to respond by cutting down the amount of stimulation your baby is exposed to. It's a balancing act of finding enough stimulation combined with enough rest, quiet time, and individual attention. When a baby is trying to tell his parents, "I've had enough," but the parents are repeatedly not addressing his needs then the baby will get more upset and stressed. Over time, the baby may associate noise and activity with discomfort. This could lead him to dislike and withdraw from noise and people later in life, recalling on an unconscious level his initial discomfort and trying to alleviate that early unresolved discomfort and pain.

There isn't one correct mix for every baby. But if you follow your baby's lead and respect the cues you get, you'll find the correct mix for *your* baby. That mixture will allow him to interact with you and the world in a relatively stress free manner, which in turn is good for his developing brain. Babies' comfort levels change over time, depending on their previous experiences, what they've learned about the world around them, and how they're feeling at any given moment. As a parent, you need to respond to today's ideal mixture with spontaneity and appreciation.

The most common cue your baby will give when he has had enough (or too much) stimulation is a cry of discomfort. If your baby's crying stops when you take him out of the immediate environment to a place where you can soothe and comfort him, you know your baby has reached his limit, and he needed less of what was happening. Sometimes your baby can be adversely affected by people around him, sometimes by noise, sometimes by temperature, and sometimes by smells. Your child's discomfort can also stem from internal factors such as fatigue, hunger, or a combination of any of these factors. If you encounter crying on your first few excursions, try to vary the type of setting and time of day before giving up and staying home.

Parents who expect too much, too soon can create problems for their babies because their babies cannot perform to their parents' expectations and they can sense their parents' disappointment. They may interpret parental disappointment as their own personal failure. Parents who expect too little can also inadvertently create problems for their children by not stimulating them enough. Lack of stimulation and inadequate nurturing can lead to developmental delays and emotional problems as babies grow up. This type of problem can be seen in children who have been adopted in foreign countries from orphanages where they did not receive adequate nurturing or holding during infancy. Children who have been passed from foster home to foster home, never staying long enough to get the attention, love, and understanding they needed also display a potential for developmental and emotional problems. As a result they sometimes have a great deal of trouble bonding or maintaining close relationships throughout life. The term *attachment disorder* encompasses a baby's extreme reactions to not enough closeness in early life and what happens later on. At either extreme, getting too much stimulation or not getting enough, a baby's self-esteem can be damaged and his mental and emotional developmental processes can be affected.

A baby isn't able to make sense of all the things he is experiencing, but his little brain is soaking up the stimuli every time he turns and observes another angle of the world. He will process some of the stored information later, when he has more building blocks and experiences to match with previous experiences. Still other information will remain lodged in his unconscious mind, affecting behavior and emotions in years to come in ways he won't understand.

The following list of strategies can be used with your baby during playtime to help you continue to respectfully parent your baby.

- **Play.** Sounds simple—but it can be difficult to leave behind your adult responsibilities and thoughts and get down on the floor to play, following your child's lead. It's an activity that you can learn by watching your child carefully (in case you've forgotten how to play or have long considered it too immature for you). Playing with soft blocks for thirty minutes is certainly different from playing a couple of holes of golf. Kid play is much freer than adult play. You'll need to be spontaneous and set your adult agenda aside if you're going to share a respectful playtime with your baby.
- **Follow your baby's lead whenever possible,** rather than imposing your own agenda.
- **Be in awe with your baby.** Share your baby's sense of awe if you begin to feel bored. Rediscover the world through his eyes rather than changing to a new activity when your baby is still satisfied and engaged with what he is doing.
- **Be in awe of your baby.** Sit back and watch your baby's brain working as he puts things together. Be in awe of all he is learning and how much he has added to your life in such a short time.
- **Watch for signs of stimulation overload.** Slow down or discontinue the play. Provide your baby with a calm environment where you can help her soothe herself back to a more comfortable place.

Sometimes while parents are playing with their baby, they forget to follow their baby's lead. For instance, one baby was watching fascinated as her mother was holding and showing her a small, stuffed-animal rocking horse. Finally, the baby reached for it, grabbed it, and was looking at it, when the mother said, "Jenny, look what else Mommy has for you." What hidden messages are in that mother's action? The mother meant well; she was just showing Jenny another toy. But Jenny was still involved and had just engaged with the first toy. Unconsciously is Jenny being told to hurry up with things? Or that she takes too long at things? That she should be interested in the things someone else is interested in? That she should put her interests aside? All those messages are being unconsciously received, along with, "Stop what you're doing and look at this," or, "I'm more important than you." Such messages discount the baby's interests and the baby's developing sense of self.

I think parents often do that kind of thing out of their own boredom. They're tired of looking at the stuffed-animal rocking horse (in this case); they're ready for another toy. But was their baby? Whose needs and interests are they there to stimulate? Their own or their baby's? You may say both, and that's true. If a parent is bored, he won't be a good play companion with his baby. But if the parents' needs usually come first, then they're forgetting to keep pace with their baby, and they're not respecting their baby's natural curiosity or intellectual functioning.

The solution in Respectful Parenting terms is to get interested in your baby's interest. Of course you may tire of a toy before your baby, but stop looking at the toy as the object of stimulation and shift your focus to your baby and how she's interacting with the toy. What is your baby discovering? Shapes? Textures? Colors? Movements? Observing your baby's interactions with things and her awe will stimulate your awe, and will keep your interest a lot longer than any toy will. Baby games can be simple, focused interactions between you and your baby which also end up stimulating her social, emotional, and cognitive development while you're both having fun.

BABY GAMES

- Build a little tower of soft blocks or toys and let him knock them down or move it around.
- Lay her under a tripod with hanging toys and help him make them move, sharing in his delight. Quite a few companies make this kind of toy.
- Converse with him in a mixture of baby sounds and adult speech.
- Comment on what your baby is doing; give her a running description of her playful accomplishments.
- Find things to giggle about: run a clean feather across his skin, watch a block falling off the top of a pile, tickle, watch an animal at the zoo.
- Put things in a container and let your baby help. Transfer small play items or shapes from one container to another.
- Play drums to music using pots, pans, wooden spoons, chopsticks, and other safe kitchen utensils.

- Dance around the room with your baby safely in your arms or in a soft carrier.
- Listen to music that appeals to young ears. There are lots of musicians who cater to young children, including Raffi, Tom Knight, and Tom Paxton.
- Big, pop-together beads can be fun for teaching colors and small motor coordination.
- Take walks and talk about what you see.
- See and point—your baby points to things and you explain them.

Watch your baby learn, discover, enjoy, and see how he fills his cup of knowledge. Look for cues that tell you he's ready for something new. Let him ask in his own way before you offer or take over and introduce something new. Ideally, you want your baby to enjoy exploring and learning about new things as much as possible. You could be discouraging just such a thoughtful process by presenting too many toys in too short a time. Again, follow your baby's lead by presenting stimulating things at your baby's pace, not yours.

The Benefits of Being in Awe

Being in awe with your baby will bring you a rich source of pure joy and excitement. As an adult, you often wear blinders that leave you oblivious to a lot of what's happening around you. The end result: like a horse on a racetrack, you function with the tasks at hand, focusing on one thing, and ignoring the beauty and richness of the world around you. Your baby's enthusiastic eyes can break through your blinders and bring you endless hours of wonder and awe.

Being in awe of your children will open your senses to being in awe with them, which in turn will expose you to endless, simple pleasures of experiencing the world through their senses. You'll be able to communicate with them and truly be there with them, experiencing what they are experiencing, appreciating their discoveries, their accomplishments, and feeling as warm and excited inside as they do.

You can give them such incredible gifts by understanding and appreciating their discoveries. They will be giving you the incredible gift of rekindling your innocent appreciation of the world and everything that catches their eye. Perhaps you'll even notice things you've ignored or never seen before and be able to bring it to their attention if they haven't noticed it first. Being in awe will (re)awaken your senses. What better basis for establishing a respectful relationship can there be?

Carl: My baby has this plastic rattle with a piece that spins on it. He likes the rattle a lot. I used to show him how the piece spun by taking my index finger and making it move. He'd stare in complete fascination as the little wheel spun. One day recently, I saw him crawling toward the rattle on the floor, pick it up, and actually take his tiny index finger and twirl the spinner. He had the most serious look on his face as he watched the part spin. As it slowed, he made it go again, watching seriously until I came up, interrupting his interactions by congratulating him. I was so excited to see him doing that all on his own. He even used the same finger I did to spin it. Incredible!

* * *

Laurel: When our baby was about six months old, my husband bought one of those trailers for babies that hooks onto a bicycle. It's incredible to see this little baby get very excited each time he sees his dad take out the trailer. He knows he's going too. Actually, I don't know which one is more excited, my son or my husband. My husband can't get the thing attached fast enough. And my son waves his arms as if to say, "Hurry up, where's my helmet? Let's go." As they drive off, I can see their faces, beaming with delight. I love seeing them like that.

* * *

Bonnie: Sometimes the associations my daughter makes just amaze me. She has this beautiful fish mobile in her room made out of bright, woven ribbons. She loves to see them "swim" when we blow on them. Recently, we went to visit my parents who have a real fish aquarium in their house. I said, "Oh look, fish" to her, and she immediately toddled over and blew at the fish tank. My mother didn't understand that at all until I told her about the mobile. When we got home and my mother called us, I asked my daughter if she wanted to talk to her and she got on the phone and immediately blew into the phone. Her association was just amazing.

Safety Concerns

When a baby's curiosity has taken her to places and things you would rather not have her encounter, it's important to remember that her curiosity is capable of motivating her to wander and reach delicate, favorite, breakable, irreplaceable, and dangerous objects. She's still a baby and doesn't deserve blame or shame for interfering with something she "should know better about." That kind of response is old-style parenting. Instead, you as the respectful parent should know better than to leave it within your baby's reach. It's *your* responsibility to know better, not your baby's.

Instead of an old-fashioned admonishment or spanking, stop her movement with a gentle hug-hold, followed by an effective and respectful explanation: "I can see you're curious, but Daddy knows that's dangerous for you. I'm sorry it's within your reach. Let me take that out of your hands so you're safe." Or you could say, "Let's wait a second while I help you," followed by an explanation. Either approach is a loving way to set a limit with your baby. These approaches can calm your fears about a favorite object being broken and teach your child that you're available to help when a situation is beyond her ability to handle safely.

Your baby's actions won't instill anger in you if you remember that she, like all babies, is a naturally curious little human being. She wants to explore everything that invites her by simply being in her world. You might comfort yourself by knowing that the more curious she is, the more intelligent she is. Her interest needs to be stimulated, not curbed. This natural curiosity can be safely managed if you childproof your house. You'll probably need to continue to childproof your house as your baby grows and is able to reach different levels. Otherwise you'll find yourself lunging to save precious objects from your baby's curious hands and to save your baby from accidents with heavy, breakable, or otherwise dangerous objects as she grows and explores.

You may find yourself daydreaming about constructing shelves around your house about five feet off the floor, so you can have access to things you want while your baby stays safe. An easier solution is cabinet and drawer latches. You can always try the "scarcity model" of knickknacks: put them away until your child is old enough to have developed better dexterity and can handle them carefully. It makes life easier and more relaxing.

Got the Baby, Where's the Manual?!?

By employing these simple safety procedures, you'll know that when your baby grabs for an object, it's something she can handle. You won't be sitting on the edge of your seat, watching every move she makes. She's free to roam and explore. You might leave a kitchen cabinet unlatched and full of light, unbreakable plastic containers. This treasure chest may prove to be your baby's favorite destination . . . crawling to that cabinet, opening the door, and pulling every plastic container and lid out of the cabinet until it's completely empty. Babies who enjoy doing that usually smile proudly at their parents as they sit amidst the array of containers strewn around the kitchen floor. It looks like absolute glee on their faces as they behold their ability to empty the entire cabinet. Maybe it's a little bit of role modeling, doing what they see Mommy and Daddy doing.

The positive side is that you get to watch how your baby's mind works and what triggers her interests and subsequent actions. It can be awesome and such fun to watch a baby play and explore!

What Parents Say

Sarah: When our baby was three-and-a-half months old, my husband and I left him with my parents for a few hours while we went out to dinner. When we came back, my parents were chuckling. I asked them why. They said that our baby had spent the better part of two hours entertaining them. They had wanted to watch a program on TV, so they had propped him in his infant seat facing them. They had been talking and interacting with him, but when the program began, they started to ignore him. He began with my mother, staring at her intensely until she felt his gaze. When she looked at him, he started smiling. Then he turned his gaze to my father. Apparently, my mother's attention hadn't been enough. He wanted both of them watching him. My father, like my mother, felt his gaze and looked down at him. He, too, got a big smile. Well, my son played that game over and over, graduating from a smile to a giggle with both of them. They ended up taping the program and playing his game for a long time.

* * *

John: It's difficult to say, but I know my wife was more enthralled with our baby than I was when he was tiny. I think it was his first winter, so my son would have been about ten months old when I saw him do something that just struck me, and probably changed our relationship quite a bit. It certainly changed the way I saw him. I mean, this kid had a definite sense of humor. I was sitting opposite him as he was maneuvering pieces of banana from his high chair tray into his mouth. He kind of cooed and smiled as he ate. Then, out of the blue, he picked up a piece and held it out toward me, as if he was going to share. Well, my heart just melted. He wanted to share with me, his daddy. So, I of course reached out to take the banana he was offering. As I was about to take it, he pulled his hand back quickly and smiled, his eyes sparkling. At first I wasn't sure if he had changed his mind about sharing, but when he did it again, I realized: it wasn't that he didn't want to share or had changed his mind. No, this kid was teasing me. Here was my son, ten months old, and he had gotten me. I looked at him with more respect and awe that day, realizing he was indeed becoming his own little person. And what a cutie.

* * *

Linda: You can just see them learning sometimes. It's fascinating. Like the morning my daughter maneuvered herself over to the coffee table, pulled herself up holding onto it, then pulled the drawer open, grabbed out the boxes full of coasters and happily spilled the coasters all over the floor. What joy and accomplishment were reflected on her face. I loved seeing her mind connect with her body and do all that.

* * *

Annie: I'm really in the throes of deciding how much to push her to grow and how much I should accept her messages. I started an exercise class two or three weeks ago, and my ten-month-old daughter is having a hard time adjusting to the on-site babysitter. The first few times she cried so much the woman in charge came and got me after ten minutes. I had asked her to get me if she was still crying after ten minutes.

The second week she did better, crying intermittently throughout the hour, but the rest of the day she was so clingy, she didn't want me out of her sight. This week, she's doing a little better, but she's beginning to wake up more at night (although she had actually started doing that before I began the exercise class). I'm trying to figure out if I should just give up on the idea of exercising for a while. I'm not sure. There's steady improvement, but . . . I hate to see her upset. The last time I picked her up she had fallen asleep in the swing, but her face didn't look peaceful, she looked upset in her sleep, which I've seen every once in a while, but not often . . . I wonder . . .

This mother and I talked for a while and decided that before she gave up, there were two things she could try: leaving her daughter for less than the hour, since she seemed to be doing fine for thirty minutes or so, and gradually leaving her a little longer until Mom could take the whole class. The second thing she was going to try was talking to her daughter about how important the class was to her and showing her some of what she'd be doing while she was away from her. That way, the mother would be sharing the process and reasons why she was leaving her daughter for an hour, three days a week. When I ran into this woman a few months later, she told me that she had tried both things we had talked about and they had worked really well.

Nine

Toddler Lessons

*T*HE BEGINNING OF TODDLERHOOD can vary by as much as one year. Some babies walk before they crawl, others run before they walk. Whenever they begin, walking is a great accomplishment for a baby. You can see the delight all over his face. In fact, sometimes it looks like a toddler's whole body is smiling with pride and excitement as he takes his beginning steps. Toddlers have a whole new view of their world because they're standing and their eyes can see things from a higher perspective than when they were crawling. A nine-month-old really hasn't experienced the world and its limits as much as a twelve-, fourteen-, or even eighteen-month-old. Therefore, it may be easier for older babies to begin to toddle because they may be more prepared emotionally and intellectually for the consequences of walking: it's farther to fall, the bumps hurt more, and their legs can carry them places they don't belong (ledges, precipices, or away from Mommy and Daddy). Of course these changes mean it's necessary to childproof differently once your child can walk and climb.

Right after walking comes more proficient climbing, with its share of ups and downs. As a result of this wonderful new set of skills, parents need to watch toddlers extra carefully. Their freedom is heady, and they usually don't have a firmly entrenched sense of danger, limits, space, distance, or fear. When toddlers exhibit pure excitement and pride in themselves, the purity comes from not having the socialized sense of fear and limits that parents need to provide. Parents are faced with a balancing act: provide necessary safety limits without taking too much away from your toddler's newfound sense of confidence, self-esteem, and adventure.

This age brings about a whole new set of questions and challenges for the parent. How do you learn to calmly say, "Wait a second honey. You're getting very close to those stairs. I'm not sure you know how to get down them safely by yourself. Wait for me and I'll help you learn," instead of being startled and screaming, "Oh, my God, don't go near those—you could fall and crack your head open!" How do you acknowledge that your toddler has just entered another developmental period and yet keep in mind that he is still a baby? His maturity and life experiences haven't changed, just his motor skills. Once you see your toddler motoring around on his own legs rather than crawling, it's so easy to forget that he's still basically a nubile, inexperienced little human being who needs just as much love, understanding, respect, and support as he needed the day before he started walking. In fact, he may need more because his world has just gotten a lot bigger as his visual perspective has changed with his newfound physical talents.

His world has exploded wide open, leaving him excited about exploring all he can reach now that he's standing upright. Your world has become scarier as you realize he is completely unaware of the imminent perils and dangers in his path. What is the solution? One woman humorously suggested head-to-toe padding and a helmet. Your goals are to instill caution without undue fear, and encouragement without overestimating his physical abilities while still providing lots of loving attention.

One child I know skipped walking and took off running. He had been crawling for a few months. One day, he pulled himself to a standing position by hanging onto a lawn chair, looked around, and then took off running after his two older brothers who were playing basketball on the street. He had an unsteady, seemingly about-to-fall-over gait, but he was running. I ran inside to tell his mother, who came out laughing at the sight. I was sure he must have been walking for a few weeks and I had just not seen it, but no, she said, this was it. His transition went from crawling straight to running—no need to walk for him. Do you think it was any coincidence that that little boy started running track when he was nine years old?

Setting Limits

It's fascinating to watch a group of toddlers and see which seem to instinctively know certain things are not to be done, no matter how tempting they may look and which ones have no sense of restraint or personal danger. Some cling to their parents or don't venture more than a few feet away. Other toddlers are perfectly content to just sit on mom's lap and watch other children walk around a room, bouncing off each other as they perfect their balance, while others are in the lead, careening around with everyone else following behind. When you observe these differences, you realize how unique children are, even at this young age, and how much personality, enthusiasm, and curiosity each little toddler possesses.

It's important at this stage to begin setting reasonable limits that take into account your toddler's personality. You should base the limits you set on how much freedom is safe for your child. Telling your child what the limit is once usually won't be enough. Sometimes parents lose their tempers with toddlers because they expect that if they've told them to stay off the coffee table once, they should listen and remember. When parents find their toddler climbing on the table again and looking down through the clear glass to their toys underneath they can get angry if they forget that once is not enough. An old-style father might come over, sweep the child up into his arms and say angrily, "I heard your mother tell you not to climb on that table. What's the matter with you? Can't you listen? You're going to have to go to your room because you didn't obey your mother!"

This response would be an unnecessary overreaction. If your child could talk and felt safe enough to respond, she might say, "But I never see my toys from up here; I want to see what they look like through the glass table," an innocent and curious perspective. So often, toddlers are just following their brain's questions and curiosity. They don't have the ability to practice forethought. Toddlers aren't able to think through a situation before they act. They can't consider all the ramifications of their actions prior to doing something. It's up to parents to teach them how to think things through over time. A Respectful Parent might say, "Climbing on the glass table does allow you to see your toys underneath. But it's also dangerous, because the glass can break and hurt you. Tables are not for climbing. We go to the park for climbing. Thank you for listening."

I remember one mother tearfully telling me about a visit to her in-laws. Upon their arrival, her toddler immediately began to play with several objects within his reach. He was being gentle, but his grandfather said "No" to him. He looked confused and picked up one of the objects again. This time his grandpa said "No" more angrily and slapped his hand. The mother picked up her son to comfort him. Her father-in-law said, "You're going to spoil him rotten. He needs to learn the meaning of 'No.'" The mother said, "Yes, he does, but at our house everything he can reach is a 'Yes.' We try to reserve 'No' for dangerous things so it isn't a constant admonishment. Her father-in-law replied, "That's ridiculous!" The mom said at that point she was already wanting to leave but knew she was stuck there for the weekend.

She and her husband talked that night and decided they would try to explain some of the differences between old-style parenting and Respectful Parenting to his parents in the morning. If they seemed responsive, they would ask them to play along and see how well Respectful Parenting worked. If they were not responsive, the young parents would try to do what they thought was right, quietly, with their son, and hope to avoid arguments with the grandparents.

The next morning, just as the grandfather was about to admonish their child, the father took his son into his arms and said, "Grandpa and Grandma do things differently here than at home. That's something Grandpa says is not for playing. It's not a toy for you. Let's put it up here where it won't catch your eye as much." The grandfather looked on disapprovingly. At breakfast they broached the subject of different parenting philosophies, found the grandparents disinterested, and dropped further attempts to share their method of parenting.

By Monday the mom was frazzled by repeated examples of old-style (grand)parenting and entered my office grateful to see someone who agreed with her and who would respond empathetically to the punitive nature of her weekend's encounters.

Using the Strategies

The following are the basic Respectful Parenting strategies for life with a toddler.

- **Focus on your child's growing world.**
- **Teach your child to slow down and learn about new things.**
- **Childproof your house** to your child's new height.

- **Learn how your child processes information,** by watching carefully, so you can be a more effective guide as you play.
- **Play, but begin teaching more and explaining more complex concepts** such as safety and thinking before doing.
- **Listen.** Be willing to change or compromise your ideas if your child suggests something you hadn't considered.
- **When you're feeling stuck** and you can't think of how to handle a situation in a respectful way, give yourself a time-out and ask yourself, "What do I, *(name),* as a *(age)*-year-old adult on *(today's date, including year)* want to do?" By reminding yourself of your age and today's date, including the year, you'll be more likely to access a mature, healthy, creative part of yourself and avoid any old tapes that would repeat your parents' responses.
- **As you begin to set limits, remember that repetition is the key.** Once is seldom enough.
- **Remember most of what motivates your toddler is spontaneous curiosity.** Old-style parents would misinterpret this by thinking, 'malicious intent,' or 'disobeying.' Respectful Parenting sees opportunities to teach children about safety, limits, and the beginnings of how to think things through.

When your toddler is doing something you asked her not to, it is time to calmly take her into your arms and explain what you want her to refrain from doing, why you want that (for her safety, what might happen, etc.), and ask her if she understands. Toddlers, in spite of their own limited vocabulary, understand much more than they can speak. Thus, you can often reason with your toddler. After that conversation, it's important to keep watching carefully to make sure your toddler doesn't forget. If she repeats the action, remind her, "Remember, we stay off the table because I want you to be safe." If your child doesn't listen and is about to climb again or continues to climb, then you can give her a reasonable consequence: "I guess we'll have to give you and the living room a time-out because you can't seem to remember about staying off the table. We'll just leave the room for a while and see if you can remember better in a few minutes. While we're in the other room, I'd like you to try and remember that tables are not climbing structures."

With this kind of explanation, you begin to lead your child through a process she needs to learn. She will begin thinking things through to their end before making a decision and acting. This skill will take years to fully develop but you can begin to help her by teaching the basic building bocks for sound decision making with these kinds of explanations. Sound decision making is a difficult set of lessons to learn. Adults sometimes have trouble thinking things through before acting. Parents need to be patient with their toddlers. The more you do this with a toddler, the less frustrating the next stage, "the terrific twos," will be because your young child will be a little more used to looking at situations and asking for help or figuring them out rather than being instantly frustrated. By giving longer, logical explanations you'll also help avoid power struggles. Your harder parental work during this toddler stage sets the groundwork for easier stages to come.

Let's look at another scenario: how something that was previously high enough to be out of reach can become a curiosity, a desire, and then a mess, and how you could react. Your toddler climbs on a couch and reaches for a pretty red plate, which drops and breaks. From the toddler's perspective, she is delighted with her new ability to climb, she is looking at a plate that she's seen before, but she no longer has to be held up to look at it and touch that pretty color. Now she can get it all on her own. She reaches for it, she has it, but then it goes away. When the plate falls and makes a big noise, the toddler begins to cry. Mom hears her daughter crying in the living room and runs in to see what's wrong. She sees her daughter on the couch, looking over the side at all the pieces on the floor.

That's how easily a curious desire becomes a big mess. Mom has a choice about how to react—angrily or with the patience to teach a valuable lesson. "Oh, that's too bad. I liked that plate a lot. I guess I should have put it away when you started climbing around. Did you want to see it up close like when I'd hold you to look at it?" Child nods.

"I can understand that. It was pretty. You know what honey? When you want to see things and they aren't your toys, you need to come and get me to help, especially things that are heavy or that can break. Did you know that could break into so many pieces?"

"No."

"I didn't think so. Now you've learned. That was sad, huh?"

Child nods tearfully again.

"You know how sometimes Mommy has you help clean up? Well, this time I just want you to watch because these kinds of pieces can cut you. You can help carry over the dust pan and I'll get the broom, come on."

An old-style parent would have said something like, "Oh, no! I can't believe you broke my plate! What were you doing over there? Why did you touch it? Don't you know better than to touch my things? What's wrong with you?" This second reaction instills shame and blame in your child. It's not good for her self-esteem, and it doesn't acknowledge your responsibility in the situation. The child has learned nothing except that she did something wrong and now feels bad about her independent adventure. The new feeling she's experiencing, which may not have a name in her vocabulary, is probably the beginnings of shame. Parents should remember there's nothing wrong with curiosity, a child just needs to learn how to deal with her curiosity so it doesn't lead to an unwanted consequence. A child needs that curiosity in order to learn. You don't want to squelch curiosity at a young age; you want to teach your toddler how to begin to manage her curiosity by making different decisions like asking for help.

Wants Versus Needs

A different but overlapping concept to begin teaching your toddler is the difference between wants and needs. This is another one of those life-long lessons that should begin in toddlerhood. Earlier in this book, I discussed not being able to spoil an infant or a baby because they only had needs not wants. I suggested that needs should be addressed immediately. Well, at this age you want to begin explaining the differences to your toddler. Toddlers now have wants that feel as intense to them as their needs used to feel. They are used to you taking care of their needs so they begin toddlerhood assuming you'll take care of all their newly discovered wants. Toddlers, whose world has expanded dramatically due to their increased range of vision, have gone from crying because they need more food to crying because they want something that looks interesting but they can't have it because it's not a toy. The difference between needs and wants and the artful game of waiting for the appropriate time is a big lesson to learn. People of all ages are very used to instant gratification or "I want what I want when I want it." You may be able to relate to that statement. If your credit card comes in regularly with a higher balance than you can pay, you probably haven't learned this lesson very well. You too can learn, with and through your toddler that sometimes you have to wait.

Let's say you ask your toddler what he wants to eat and he happily responds, "Ice cream."

"Now there is an interesting idea. Ice cream for breakfast. I'm sorry. I should have given you a choice of cereal or eggs because that's what I meant for you to choose from. Would you like cereal or eggs for breakfast."

"Ice cream, ice cream. I want ice cream!"

"I know you want ice cream but you need to eat something better for breakfast so you can play all you want today. Again, your choices are eggs or cereal. Which do you want, because ice cream is not an option. "

"Egg."

"Thanks. You've got it. I'll fix an egg for you."

In this conversation, the parent has apologized for leaving the choice too open-ended and has offered acceptable choices with an explanation of why the child can't have the desired ice cream. The child will feel respected because his parent did take his choice seriously, but there was a good explanation for why that was not possible. This lesson is instrumental for your toddler to learn the difference between "I want" and "I need." By using this technique you can help your child prepare for later developmental stages. The better your child learns the differences between needs and wants, and that wants often have to wait or may never even happen, the easier your child will experience being two, three, four years old, and beyond.

What Parents Say

Linda: When my daughter started toddling, a whole new world opened up to her and to me. I had to often remind myself to ignore my first instinct. For instance, if we were walking along and I wanted to get someplace, but she had noticed an ant, and she wanted to stop and watch it move, my first instinct could be to brush her off and say, "Yeah, that's an ant." But if I ignored that, and crouched down with her, we'd have just the greatest time watching that ant, how he moved, what he could carry, and then we'd notice more ants and watch them too. We'd talk about them and watch them . . . maybe even recount the incident to Daddy that night. If I hadn't ignored my first "so what?" response, I would have missed out on seeing the ants. . . . And when was the last time I watched ants?

Bonnie: Sometimes it seems a little harder as my daughter gets older. I have to remember to look at things differently, and there's more things to look at as she's more active and asserts herself. Like when she wants to read a book for the hundredth time. And of course at thirteen months if she wants to read a book it usually involves Mommy reading it to her. At those times, I have to consciously remember that as a young child repetition is important to her, she enjoys the familiarity she feels with a favorite book. But I also have to honor my needs. How can I always do that and still be there for her? I reframe the situation, I get in awe of her enjoyment, and I get my needs met, not from the hundredth reading of her current favorite book, but from watching her as she sits there on my lap, cuddling into me as I read to her. That's pretty special. Enough to make up for the perceived boredom of a hundredth reading.

Sometimes, when my thirteen-month-old daughter needs my attention and I need a break, I try to find something that will interest her, like a book or crayons and paper. I tell her she's resourceful and resilient, that I'm just going to take a break for a few minutes and then come back to her. I let her know where I'm going and she can call me if she really needs me. I try to let her know she'll be fine. She usually responds really well when I leave, because she's focused on something that doesn't involve me. Then I run to the next room where I can still keep an eye on her, and make a quick phone call to a friend just for the adult conversation. I can go back to her refreshed and start playing with her again. It just takes a few minutes, but it's so important to me and to her. I want to role model taking care of myself so she doesn't grow up being self-sacrificing.

* * *

Sarah: When my son was about fifteen months old and still rather nonverbal, I saw him exhibit such compassion with one of his child care buddies; I was really touched. We had just arrived at child care and one of his teachers was standing outside his room, holding one of the other little boys he often played with. The other little boy (we'll call him David) was crying hard. My son indicated by pointing and saying "Eh! Eh!" that he wanted to go over there. I carried him over to David and the teacher. As I asked what had happened and why David was crying (he had woken from a bad dream screaming and crying), my son started patting him on the back and made cooing and "Ah, ah" sounds.

I needed to get to work, so after letting my son comfort David for a little while, I started walking away with my son still in my arms. I was going to take him to the room where the children would be playing who had napped already (he had napped at home with me). As I walked away, he protested loudly, "Eh! Eh!" and pointed back to David and his teacher. He wanted to go back.

When I brought him back, he comforted David some more. I soothingly said to my son, "Honey, we have to leave David and your teacher now. She's going to comfort him. He just woke up from a scary dream. He'll be okay. That was really nice and so sweet how comforting you were. Unfortunately I have to go to work now, so I need to bring you into the other room, otherwise I'd stay with you and David. I think your teacher will take good care of David. We should go in the other room."

He listened as I talked and seemed to understand. How did I know he understood? He didn't protest anymore or point to David; he just hugged me as I carried him to the playroom.

After dropping him off, as I drove to my office I was amazed at his compassion and interest in David. I didn't know toddlers could be so involved in someone else's emotions, or want to be so sweet and caring. It was a scene I'll never forget. I just loved that he was so compassionate and caring. I hope he gets to keep it as he grows up.

Ten

Good-Bye Terrible Twos, Hello Terrific Twos

WHY NOT BANISH THE CONCEPT of "the terrible twos" and replace it with "the terrific twos"? We know from educational research that labels are powerful. What you are called is often what you become. Remember hearing the words, "You're a naughty child!"? Did those words often result in you acting "naughty?" Perhaps, from stubborn pride, you decided at some level that you'd be good at something—you'd do naughty well. Or maybe you thought you wouldn't disappoint them by giving them the naughty behavior they expected. You might have believed *you* were naughty rather than naughty being a description of your behavior. Borrowing this idea from educational and developmental research, doesn't it make sense that if you perceive and verbally label your child's behavior as "oppositional," "acting out," rebellious," "bad," or "annoying," you'll encourage the very behavior you've labeled, even though that's exactly what you want your child to stop doing?

The following are basic strategies for Respectfully Parenting two-year-olds.

- **Listen with the intent to validate your two-year-old's experiences and feelings.** Then, if it's necessary, introduce a more appropriate way to handle her feelings.
- **Listen. Be willing to change or compromise your ideas if your child suggests something you hadn't considered.**
- **If you don't like how you're viewing your child's behavior, refo-**

cus your view. Look for another, more positive angle to view the current situation.

- **Focus on your child's curiosity, natural interest in learning, and desire to please.** Then talk to your child, providing information and choices so she can more easily behave in a way that is pleasing to you and society at large.
- **Monitor your child's frustration and stress levels and help her set her own limits.**
- **Avoid power struggles** by using time-outs, humor, or cuddles to defuse the situation.
- **Two year olds love to please and love to copy what Mom and Dad do.** To "teach" manners simply use the expressions with your child that you'd like your child to use; such as "please" and "thank you." No lectures are necessary.

Temper Tantrums

Oh, those terrible twos: characterized by temper tantrums, whiny days, and struggling through what ought to be simple tasks like dressing or bathing. In truth, haven't you had moments as an adult when you wished you could cry, scream, and throw something across the room? Especially when you're trying to learn something new and it isn't happening as easily as you would like? What about when something emotional happens in your life? You want to handle it differently, but you can't seem to calm down? During those times, do you feel your emotions rumbling around inside? You might even want to let out a frustrated roar, but you're probably too mature, or you realize it's not the appropriate time or place to be loud. So you don't. You end up stuffing your feelings down until there's a safe place and time to express them. Sometimes your feelings dissipate while you're waiting for that safe place.

Are you ever secretly envious of your two-year-old's ability to let it all out and not care about the consequences? But then, of course, when he does let it all out, you probably have to shift back into the parent role. How you were parented can play a large part in how you deal with your two-year-old's behavior. "Stop that nonsense!" is a common refrain in old-style parenting. If you think about it, what's nonsensical about letting out your frustration, anger, or exhaustion, especially if you're at your limit, you have a limited vocabulary, and you don't know *how* to keep a lid on things yet?

Don't adults spend a lot of energy, therapy dollars, work-out time, or time sitting in seminars trying to learn how to get in touch with their emotions and express themselves more freely? Maybe some lessons from a two-year-old would help. They have the "let-it-out system" down pat. They haven't been socialized into an emotionally constricted stance. Let's look at it yet another way. When a person can't make sense of two or more intellectual ideas and feels confused because he can't resolve the conflicting notions, psychologists call it "cognitive dissonance." "Emotional dissonance" is when a person feels all jumbled up inside and can't express herself in a rational manner. A two-year-old caught up in the throes of emotion and having a classic temper tantrum is probably in the middle of experiencing emotional and/or cognitive dissonance. His insides feel horrible and completely out of control, perhaps from his head all the way down to his toes. Even worse, he doesn't have enough words to explain all that's going on inside.

How can adults relate to what a two-year-old may be feeling when he's out of control? Imagine yourself in this scenario: You're in the process of looking for a house. You find yourself involuntarily waking up in the middle of the night with an unending series of questions in your head: "Which house should I choose?" "Which would be the best investment?" "What if I get a lemon?" "Do I want to go for potential?" You want the questions to stop, but they won't. Night after night you wake up with the committees going at it in your head. You want to sleep but you can't. After a few stressful nights where you can't control your own thought patterns, do you notice how raw you feel inside? That's when small things can set you off. You're barely holding on to some degree of calmness.

Think about how nerve racking, scary, and frustrating looking for and purchasing a house is. Yet as an adult you have the emotional and intellectual wherewithal to cope with complicated situations. Try to remember those jumbled feelings when you're dealing with your two-year-old, who has only a two-year pool of life experience to dip into and a two-year-old vocabulary for expressing himself. The example of buying a house is a reasonable facsimile of what your two-year-old feels inside when he's having a temper tantrum or stubbornly struggling over something that is simple to you. It's not simple to him.

Frustration also leads to temper tantrums in children while adults often express their frustration by yelling, withdrawing, giving up, drinking, headaches, resentment, a nervous stomach, high blood pressure, heart attacks, and ulcers. Can you imagine an adult having a temper tantrum in a New York subway car because it was too crowded, too hot, and they were going to be late for an appointment? I don't advocate encouraging your two-year-old to have temper tantrums or having temper tantrums yourself, but when your child does lose his composure, stand back a minute and think, "Do I want to teach my child to suppress these feelings, or do I want to sympathize, listen, and teach him to express them differently?" Always begin by listening closely enough to be able to validate his feelings before asking him about other ways he could express himself or providing him with different options. If you're in a hurry you can do this quickly by offering concrete suggestions. If you have the time, ideally you can guide him by asking a series of questions until you two identify different options or alternative ways of behaving.

Dealing with Temper Tantrums

Let's say your child is in such emotional pain that she's yelling, kicking her feet, and flailing her arms. What if your heart went out to your child and you thought something like, "She must be feeling so bad inside her body and mind right now. She deserves my love, not my admonishments to calm down." Thinking that way will lead you into a different way of behaving than how you might have experienced as a child.

If your child could deal with whatever is happening calmly, don't you think she would? What if you hugged her instead of being angry, but then she refused your hugs and indicated she needed a bit of distance? You could try soothing talk: "I understand you're upset, and it looks like you don't want me close right now. I'm going to leave you for a minute. When you have the words, let me know why you're upset, or show me how I can help."

What happens when you role model anger, disgust, irritation, and annoyance with stressed out two-year-olds? They tantrum more, because they're being taught the verbal part of temper tantrums. Since they don't have sophisticated language skills, they're substituting flailing arms, kicking feet, and throwing themselves or objects around the room for a verbal expression of annoyance, anger, or pent-up and overflowing feelings. Instead of role modeling the behaviors you don't want to see, try to respect your child's emotional pain, which is as real as if she had been hit by a car and was in the hospital with injuries. You'd stand by her there; you'd sit at her bedside until she came to if she was unconscious. She needs you when she's in emotional pain as much as she does when she's in physical pain. Remember, you may receive the brunt of the barrage, but she isn't doing it *to* you. She's just doing it, period.

In fact, if you are the object of her attack or acting out, it's probably because she trusts you enough to be able to handle what is too much for her to keep inside. She believes you'll know what to do. She wouldn't be putting it out there if she didn't need your responses to her on some level. Her body, mind, and guts are doing it to her, and she's just expressing the extra stuff that's overflowing as best she can.

When you grow up in a family where there are two choices—you're right or you're wrong—you never learn that there are actually many different options in most situations. If you've internalized a two-option system, you're going to have a lot of trouble with your children as they're turning two because they're experiencing the world in a very different way. Black and white just won't work because it does not have room for the wonderfully blossoming world of a two-year-old with so much to see, try out, and learn! Thinking in black or white will block out the amorphous gray areas where all the fun and subtle learning is hiding. You'll probably feel like you're hitting your head against a brick wall if you try to impose such a constrained system on your two-year-old. Her world is opening up at such an incredible pace. Her mind shouldn't be constrained by such a finite system as bad or good, right or wrong, this way or that way. You'll feel a lot better the more flexible you can be.

A good example here would be flexibility in avoiding a temper tantrum by listening carefully to the pre-tantrum whininess that often occurs before a full blown tantrum, being willing to stop what you're doing, and taking your child out of the situation that's causing her distress, thereby avoiding a tantrum entirely. Or, if the tantrum has started, instead of reacting in anger or frustration, be calm, look at your child compassionately, and say something like, "I'm sorry you're feeling so bad. Let's figure out a way for you to feel better. How about starting with some cuddles outside. I'll carry you if you'll stop kicking. Then we can talk and see what we do next." When you take your child out of the situation that stimulated the tantrum, you are in a more conducive environment where you can talk *with* your child and listen carefully to what she's saying. She'll often tell you what was too much for her. Then you'll know you're child's stimulation overload limits better and it'll be easier to avoid a frustrating situation next time.

Being flexible involves including your child as a full-fledged partner in a lot of decisions, negotiations, and options affecting your child's life, rather than dictating and dishing out judgments and edicts. When people use a Respectful Parenting approach with their children, they experience few full-blown, embarrassing, in-public, down on the floor, kicking and screaming temper tantrums. Their children don't need to express themselves in this way because they usually don't get to that level of frustration. Their parents see what's happening and intervene in a loving way before their child's emotional dissonance has mounted to an overwhelming level.

AVOIDING TEMPER TANTRUMS

- Be aware of building tension.
- Introduce something else to distract your child from the tension.
- Talk about the tension; ask him how his tummy feels and if he'd like to do something to make his tummy feel better.
- Sympathize.
- Let your child know that you don't like what's happening either and suggest you put your heads together to figure out how else you can both act and feel so you both have an easier time.
- Provide words to describe the situation.
- Tell your child that it's okay to stop.
- Offer alternatives such as a time-out to calm down or a less stressful alternate behavior.
- Lead him to other options through questions.
- Give your child hugs and cuddles if he wants closeness.

What Parents Say

Cindy: You know what they say about two-year-olds and temper tantrums? Well, my daughter hasn't had those. I mean, maybe a few times she's laid on the floor and cried, but she hasn't had any of those lie-down, scream, kick your feet, flail your arms out of control ones I'd been warned about—you know, the reason most people refer to a child's second year as "the terrible twos." She's two-and-a-half now, and with me being pregnant and all, I just don't think we're going to get those. I think maybe because I watch her so carefully and can see frustration building . . . we always deal with that by talking or changing activities. So maybe her tension just doesn't get to that boiling point because we lower it or lighten it along the way.

* * *

A story from my practice: I worked with a mother who came in saying her two-year-old was driving her crazy. I asked her if she could be more specific. She said, "Whenever we go someplace and Jason is enjoying himself, he throws a fit when it's time to leave, and I'm embarrassed. I mean, it's to the point where I don't want to go anywhere." I asked if she ever gave her son a warning before trying to get him to leave, or if she ever sympathized with him about how difficult it is to stop playing and shift gears. She said she hadn't tried that. We talked some more and she decided to try it.

The next week she came in and said, "I was at my friend's house and our children were playing so nicely. I figured it would be hard when it was time to go, but I tried what we talked about. First I went over and said, 'Jason, I'm glad you're having so much fun. You're playing really nicely with Scott. I want you to know we'll be leaving soon, and I'll give you one more warning before we go.' He looked up at me and kept playing.

"Then a little while later, when I went over for the second warning, I said, 'Jason, this is the second warning I told you about. Now we're going to help clean up and then we'll be going home. I hope you can cooperate so we can come back again soon. It's clean-up time now. Let's see how quickly we can pick everything up. Should we sing a song as we clean up?' He was distracted by the song, and he left happily in my arms as we waved to our friends."

Maybe if children are listened to, respected, validated, and helped through difficult times, they won't have the kinds of frustrations that lead to temper tantrums. If tensions are eased with understanding hugs, soothing words, or creative options maybe the children won't need to tantrum.

Teaching Manners by Doing Rather Than Lecturing

If you've always said, "Would you please _____" or "Thank you for _____" to your child, then your child will automatically start using these words in the same contexts you do. The same goes for other polite expressions or actions you'd like your child to use or do. You can't really expect them to incorporate these kinds of expressions into their natural conversations if you don't use them often. When you're all using polite or caring talk then you avoid lectures because you don't have to teach manners in a didactic way. Your children learn by following your example, just as they are learning most of their communication patterns by listening to and watching yours.

Linda: You know how some kids are taught to be artificially polite ... "Yes sir," "Yes ma'am," "Please," and "Thank you" for everything? I've always hated that artificiality. That's why I was so surprised when I started hearing my two-year-old daughter say "thank you" to things. I had never sat her down and taught her to say "thank you." But I guess my husband and I both would say "thank you" when she'd bring us things or give us things. She just picked up those words and their correct context and started using them, as if they were just part of her everyday language.

Eliminating Old-Style Parenting Patterns

You'll probably need to disconnect from your old tapes so you can respect children by validating them and being there for them. Taking time outs always helps you disconnect and reconsider what you want to do today. You'll need to move a few giant steps away from your personal history if you were scolded when you were "bad." You were probably never really **bad** in a truly malicious way. Perhaps you broke something by accident and got blamed as if you did it on purpose. Perhaps you broke something on purpose because you weren't getting any kind of response from your parents and you had to do something to get them to notice you. But were you morally bad? No, you were being creative in thinking of something you could do to get their attention, which you so desperately needed but weren't getting so you could survive.

When I work with people, I often point out that what they did when they were small children was necessary to cope with an unhealthy situation. I congratulate them for finding a way to cope, even if it didn't bring them the kind of loving attention they really wanted. They couldn't have survived in their family of origin without some of what they did. Yet, their attempts to cope often backfired because they didn't get the love and respectful, gentle attention they intuitively knew they needed. Instead, they often got yelled at, spanked, or worse. But at least they tried to get something. They tried, in their own creative way, to break through the emotional vacuum their parents presented. It can be empowering for adults to see their childhood efforts, which they had viewed for years as ineffective or futile, as necessary and creative coping strategies that they came up with on their own and that indeed helped them survive in their dysfunctional homes. If this sounds familiar from your childhood, please remember you don't have to set your child up to break through a vacuum of emotional distance. You can be close right from the start. You can respect this little human being's basic right to be loved, understood, held, and cuddled.

Power Struggles

Through careful, attentive interactions, parents are able to guide their children through potentially frustrating experiences. When children do start to lose it, Respectful Parents don't lay additional trips on their children by being angry, annoyed, or judgmental about their behavior. Instead they feel and express sympathy for their child's emotional discomfort and the children feel understood by their parents' attention and compassion, which in turn helps ease their discomfort. You can usually avoid a power struggle where you want one thing to happen and your child adamantly wants something else by using kindness, creativity, caring listening skills, and compassionate responses. Limits are set but not in an overly rigid, or angry way.

This is not to say that your children will never have temper tantrums or power struggles if you follow these suggestions. They will. Even the best use of Respectful Parenting strategies cannot prevent those kinds of tense human interactions from occurring sometimes. But often parents can diffuse a power struggle by asking themselves, "How important is this right now?" "What will really happen if he doesn't get his shoes on in two, five, or ten minutes? Do I need to insist and go at it head on when he's not quite ready, or can I role model flexibility by saying, 'It looks like you're not ready to put your shoes on right now. I think that'll be okay. I can go for the flexibility. Why don't you play with that truck a little longer and then we can try getting your shoes on again? How about if I come back in two minutes?'" The child gets to play a little more. He also gets a sense of being able to impact and manipulate his world (in a positive sense). The parent is teaching the child about negotiating, patience, flexibility, and understanding. Nine times out of ten, two minutes later the child is willing to cooperate.

DEFUSING POWER STRUGGLES

- Be aware of building tension and back off.
- Sympathize with your child's feelings.
- Give yourself a time-out and ask yourself if this is really important.
- Ask your child if there's a different way he'd rather be behaving.
- If he's unsure, ask him if he'd like some suggestions from you.
- Encourage him, now that he's heard your ideas to think of a few himself.
- Discuss the ideas you each come up with.
- Back off for thirty seconds to two minutes.
- Calm down together.
- Try the new option(s).
- Tell your child you don't like what's happening either and you want to put your heads together and figure out how to do it differently so you both can go back to having fun together.
- Have a good laugh with your child about the whole situation.
- Thank your child for helping to calm things down.

Power struggles can often be sidetracked or avoided with a little creative thinking and questioning by parents. Some parents do this in their head, while other parents find it helpful to hear themselves ask out loud, "Is this really so important that we have to struggle about it?" Somehow, hearing the words often helps them realize that it isn't so important, and they can figure out another way of handling the situation. In old-style parenting, if parents gave in it was considered capitulating, losing ground, or spoiling, and was thought to be the cause of the child losing respect for the authority in the household. In Respectful Parenting there's no such notion as giving in. Instead, flexibility is seen as a means to an end: your needs and your child's needs and wants can be met in the most peaceful and loving way possible.

Who says you're the only one who should be respected (as in old-style parenting)? How about giving your child dignity and respect? Giving children dignity and respect leads to less acting-out behavior. They don't have to resort to inappropriate behaviors. By practicing respect and flexibility you circumvent the potential problem, head it off at the pass, and avoid the child's need to act out by providing loving guidance or assistance at the first indication that it's needed.

Budding Independence

After working through your old parenting issues and incorporating Respectful Parenting ideas into your daily life with your two-year-old, the next task is to support and encourage your child's independence and not push him too hard when he's not really ready, even though he may look and act ready at first, or not hold him back too much when he's ready and you're not quite ready. If he starts crying after trying new things (like running farther away from you than he ever did before), he may be telling you, "I thought I could do it, but now that I'm trying, I'm not so sure I'm ready. Hold me a while, so I know you're still there and I'm still safe."

Another source of power struggles or ways to help your child become more confident and independent is when your child wants to do something you're not sure he's ready to do. You explain why you don't want him to and he argues why he can do it. How do you compromise on that one and help him begin to make his own decisions and take those important independent steps safely? This is another opportunity to help your child learn how to make effective decisions. You can set it up as a "scientific experiment" where you try it his way (as long as it's safe), you look at the results together, and see if he was indeed ready. If it works well, you can tell your child you learned from him that he really was ready and you hadn't known that before you saw him do it. You can thank your child for allowing you to set up the situation in a way that he could try what he wanted and you were assured he'd be safe in his attempts. If it doesn't work out well, you can talk about what didn't go so well, and he'll learn how to thoroughly assess a situation. This will help him learn more about sound decision making and learn more about what he was or was not ready to tackle. By doing this, you're helping your child become an effective, independent thinker and decision maker. These are important skills he'll need throughout his life.

Here is one mother's experience side stepping a power struggle.

Amy: One day, when my son was about a month shy of three years old, I arrived at day care to pick him up and found a little plastic baggy in his cubby with a little rock inside and a note, "Dan's rock." I thought, "Oh, how cute. He found a special treasure rock and the teachers set it aside for him." When I went to thank the teachers for their extra effort and get the story behind the rock, I got a different picture. Apparently my son had stuck this little rock up his nose. He was brought to the office and, luckily, another mother, who was a nurse, was able to get it out with tweezers. I was more than a little surprised.

As my child and I were walking toward our car, I talked to him about the seriousness of putting things in his nose, how dangerous it was, and how I didn't want him to do it again. As I finished, I looked at him, expecting his usual response of "Okay Mommy." Instead, he looked at me and said, "Well, I will if I want to." I was about to crack up, but I knew he was serious. So I repeated my explanation, adding at the end, "And if you do that again I'll just have to ask your teacher to give you a consequence." His eyes opened wider as he said, "Okay, Mommy." He hates consequences, and the threat of one was enough to get his attention.

After he was in his car seat, I was thinking, as I drove away, that this was the first evidence of a changing child. He had always been a compliant, reasonable, easy kid. But here he was growing up. I wasn't sure I was up for this one. It had been hard not to laugh, but I sensed that this first act of defiance had to be dealt with "right," or at least seriously. But it was pretty funny. Of all things for him to get independent about, the "right" to stick a rock up his nose?

Pacifiers

I think some of the biggest power struggles ensue when parents decide it's time to give up the pacifier. Remember, that's a parental decision, and if you make it categorically without consulting your young child, unless you happen to arrive at that decision at the same time as your child, you may be in for some trouble. Pacifiers are one of those primitive pleasures of early life. You allow your infant and baby to have one so she can feel secure, so she will feel comfortable, and so she can soothe herself. Even though you've given her that privilege, you can't just snatch it away. Be gradual and use the sophisticated techniques of distraction and communication. Talk to her about how big she is getting and how she may not need it anymore. Ask your child if she's ready to try not having the pacifier for a few minutes. You could even set a kitchen timer for periods of time. Ensure success by first getting a sense of how long she can go without it when she's engaged in another activity, and begin the timer with a time you know she can handle already. Gradually ask her if she wants to see how long she can go. Reinforce her progress rather than rushing her too quickly.

Pacifiers are a very personal thing. You might ask her if she'd like a special stuffed animal now that she doesn't need her pacifier at night anymore. Take it slowly and if there are a few slips back to wanting it again, make sure you respond kindly and respectfully to that too. One step forward and a half-step back is still progress. Remember, you will get there. Your child will not enter kindergarten with a pacifier in her mouth. Don't get anxious if your child doesn't meet your initial suggestions enthusiastically. It's another one of those times when you want to suggest and lead but not force, and then follow your child's natural pace once she knows where you're heading. Work with your child and make it a mutual effort. You want your child to know that you want to help her so it's a comfortable, good experience for both of you.

If your child is really adamant about not giving up her pacifier and you've tried everything in this book, consider what else is going on in her life. Think about what other changes are happening and why she might still need it. See if there's anything you can do to make her world a safer place so she can feel comfortable and soothed in other ways. If necessary, consult with a professional who can help you assess the situation and see why your child needs the extra soothing she gets from her pacifier. A professional might see where you can make her world a little safer so you can again pursue retiring the pacifier. Or, when in doubt, wait and try again a few weeks or months later. If this is done on a mutually agreed upon time frame, it should be a relatively easy process.

I've certainly encountered a number of families where the pacifier has mysteriously disappeared. The child is told that it was lost or "I can't find it," and requests for purchasing another are met with evasions. Children do survive that kind of transition. I still prefer the more thoughtful and mutually agreed upon transition where everyone is honest and open. I think it's important to set the precedent of, "I'll be honest and respectful with you, and I'd like the same in return." It's not a valid excuse that you get to lie for convenience. If you lie for convenience, watch as your children learn to lie for convenience to keep themselves out of trouble.

No More Diapers

A common source of developmental frustration for parents and children is potty training; especially when parents try hard to potty train a child, instead of having it happen more naturally. In this situation, a child's frustration often stems from the parents' impatience and frustration. Parents are ready to live without diapers, so they introduce the potty seat. If the child is not as ready as the parent, the child won't be able to do what the parents want. It's a very simple developmental impossibility.

When that reality isn't accepted, parents may become disappointed, frustrated, angry, or even disgusted at the prospect of endless diapers. If parents express or ooze these feelings and their young child feels them, the child can get upset and stressed. A stressed young child won't be able to perform successfully in the potty department. What a great setup for a vicious cycle of a child holding his poop and pee because he's picking up on his parents' tension. The parents, in turn, are tense because the child is not accomplishing what they want him to accomplish, namely using the potty. It's a great example of how parents' and children's tensions feed off each other. Potty training is often a stress-filled, frustrating situation that ultimately, results in success. But like most frustrating situations, there are easier ways to reach a goal if you take the time to explore alternatives with your child.

Throwing out the expression *potty training* may be a helpful first move. Why think about *training* a toddler or two-year-old? He's not ready for regimented training of any kind. He learns better by experimentation, modeling, and sensing. If you can leave him naked in the summer, around the time you think he may be ready, he'll be able to feel his own body sensations better than if he's encased in a big diaper. If a little potty seat is left in the bathroom next to or near Mommy and Daddy's potty, then he may get the idea on his own and go running for his potty when it's time.

Talking to your child about the possibility of using a potty that's a special fit for him may be a great place to start. You can even go on a special shopping trip so he can pick out his very own potty seat and his own big boy padded underpants for when he doesn't need his diapers anymore. You can talk about when he'd like to unpack his potty from the box, when he'd like to see what it might be like to sit on it, and, later, what it's like to maybe use it. No pressure. Sometimes it's easier for children to feel an urge to go if they're undressed and the bath water is running. They can even let the faucet water trickle over their fingers. With the potty right there in the room, and the water running at a comfortable temperature, your child may be successful and want more of those experiences.

Accidents are bound to happen. They can be dealt with lovingly and in a nonjudgmental manner. Not getting to the potty in time or forgetting about the potty entirely is part of the process of learning how the body works. If no fuss is made and if the child is developmentally ready, then he will go back to the potty fairly easily. On the other hand, if you want him to use the potty, and he's not ready to give up the security and ease of diapers, he'll let you know by having frequent accidents. You have a choice to make: either you continue to frustrate yourself and him, or you decide to calmly say, "I seem to have made a mistake. It's not time for the little potty yet. That's okay. We'll try it again in a while, and maybe then you'll want to use it."

If you say you made a mistake, you won't feel like your child failed and your child won't feel like he failed you. Putting off using the potty does not become a blow to his self-esteem. In addition, you have modeled being human, making mistakes, taking responsibility for your mistakes by admitting them, and changing your course of action. By doing so, you all learn valuable lessons.

The examples from this chapter and others will go a long way toward helping you experience the wonders of the Terrific Twos with your child. Enjoy!

Eleven

Respectful Limits, Consequences, and Boundaries

HISTORICALLY PARENTS THOUGHT they had to discipline or punish a child, "to teach him a lesson," "for disobeying," "for being lazy," or because "he was being disrespectful." Parents have traditionally used physical, emotional, and verbal forms of punishment and discipline. Parents justified whatever form of discipline they used by saying it was necessary for the child's own good. Verbal discipline was often shame-based along the lines of, "You should have known better," "What's wrong with you," and "How could you be so stupid?" They didn't consider, or know, how those particular forms of discipline would affect a child's sense of confidence or self-esteem. Those kinds of punitive, shame-based methods became the basis for old-style parenting. Old-style parenting instilled poor self-esteem in many children who then grew up to become insecure adults.

Children need limits, consequences, and boundaries to feel safe, to grow up well-balanced, to understand how they fit into the world around them, to help them remember what's acceptable and what isn't acceptable, and to help them feel emotionally and physically safe. Limits prepare a child for the real world. In old-style parenting, parents doled out discipline according to their own level of frustration, anger, and confusion, rather than looking at the child's behavior and rationally deciding how to best deal with it. Parents can fly off the handle when their emotions are triggered. If a parent has a short fuse, and engages in old-style parenting, the child will probably be disciplined more frequently and more harshly than a calmer, more creative parent who is tolerant of challenges and more willing to take the time needed to think of an approach that fits the particular situation at hand.

When we look at how parents have disciplined their children in the past it seems to be more about an angry parent doing something to make themselves feel better than teaching a child how to behave. Let's look at this in detail. A parent blows up at their young child for an indiscretion. The small child will remember the level of emotion and perhaps some of the words that were yelled at her in the heat of the moment. If a parent repeatedly yells put-downs or shameful things, the child will feel bad about herself, assume that at least some of what's been yelled is true, and her self-esteem will suffer over time. But will the parent have taught the child how to handle things differently so the same thing doesn't happen again? No. What has the young child learned? "When Mommy or Daddy is angry with me, they have a big tantrum and act mean. I don't want them to do that. It's scary." The child is stressed, but doesn't have the skills to prevent another adult tantrum in the name of discipline.

Respecting Your Child's Mistakes

Respectful Parenting offers many "discipline" options but considers many of the alternatives used on previous generations to be unnecessary and often unacceptable. If you start with the premises that: a) everybody makes mistakes and b) mistakes are opportunities to learn, you'll react to your child's mistakes differently. You won't have to blow-up. You will know that when you have limited life experiences, as little children do, you're likely to make more mistakes because you don't know much about cause and effect. Babies and toddlers don't do things wrong out of an inherent malicious nature. Usually they're following their curiosity. They're exploring the world and unexpected things happen. That does not make them naughty or bad. It makes them curious learners.

If you throw in the knowledge that children do not hone their analytical skills until at least eight years old (and even then they still have limited life experiences to help them thoroughly analyze a situation) a parent can begin to see herself as a patient guide rather than a harsh, know-it-all disciplinarian. Your young child needs to learn about himself and the world around him; his limits, how he fits into the family; you, your limits, your sense of values; right and wrong; how he fits into the community; how he fits into his preschool; and how to think things through and anticipate.

"If I do this, such and such will happen." There's so much to learn, so many opportunities to make mistakes—that's where you and Respectful Parenting come in.

Mistakes are often triggered by a combination of curiosity and excitement; a kind of enthusiasm that creates a result your child didn't know was going to happen. In Respectful Parenting, when limits are set, when consequences are given, when boundaries are kept, the purpose is to respectfully teach children skills that will help them cope in life. It is *not* about the old-style parenting philosophy that a "punishment has to fit the crime" or that a child should be shamed into doing something different. When children are treated respectfully they rarely commit crimes, so they don't need punishment—especially babies, toddlers, and two-year-olds. All they need is respectful guidance when their behaviors result in something they need to learn more about.

When your child makes mistakes you can talk with him and help him learn from them by guiding him through a series of questions designed to see what happened and why, and what he could have done differently to get a better result. As he becomes more verbal this questioning becomes easier. You can ask him to come up with some other options and discuss what might have happened if he had done things differently. That way he will have other acceptable options to do if the situation comes up again. You can offer other alternatives and discuss the possible outcomes from your suggestions as well. This process provides your child with new ways of doing things that are acceptable to you. Your child will also be learning how to think things through (how to assess a situation) and how to handle a situation (make a sound decision) without making the same mistake he made the first time. It's about learning together rather than accumulating shame for not already knowing better before the lesson presented itself.

Setting Appropriate Limits

Setting limits, consequences, and boundaries, and talking and learning from mistakes is a modern twist on the old concept of discipline. It's a respectful approach that teaches rather than reprimands. Skills are offered and limits are kept. Self-esteem is honored. Limits are important for your baby's and young child's physical safety, physical health, and mental health. They need consequences to help them remember that certain behaviors or words are not acceptable in their home. All this can usually be done consciously, calmly, and gently but firmly. Children learn you mean what you say, and they don't have to test the limit as much. They're guided respectfully rather than shamed into acting a certain way or complying out of fear. Their self-confidence is built up rather than torn down. They learn and feel good about themselves. You teach, you protect, and you get to feel good about your efforts.

Limit setting is done through the perspective of, "What's in my baby's best interests?" and taking your baby's individual needs into account. An early limit you set is not giving your baby anything to play with that can fit into her mouth, so she doesn't choke. That limit protects her physical safety. When she cries, instead of saying, "Stop crying or I'll give you something to cry about," you check to see if she's hungry, if her diaper is dirty, if she needs to be held, or if she's tired and needs to be taken to a quiet place to sleep. You take care of her needs instead of setting unrealistic or inappropriate limits that would be damaging to her emerging mental health and sense of self-esteem. If she needs holding, but you need to do something else, you can use a soft baby carrier like the Weego so your baby gets the closeness she needs and you get to do what you need to do.

As your infant grows into toddlerhood and beyond different kinds of limits and consequences will need to be imposed so your child continues to be safe and to grow up with confidence and independence. When a toddler is walking, her intellectual curiosity will lead her to new things, shiny things, things that move, and things that make noise—you want her to exercise this curiosity and intellect. Your job is to childproof the house so her natural curiosity is safe to explore somewhat freely without being told "No" and "Stop" all the time. You'll want to use opportunities presented when you least expect them to help your child learn about the environment around her and how she can keep herself safe.

A mind needs room to safely grow, explore, expand, and learn by making connections to previous lessons. Here's an example of how a child's thoughts and actions can provide you with a great opportunity for your child to learn rather than for you to reprimand in a shame-based way. Your child's thought: "I have a red ball. What's this red thing Mommy put on the table?" So the child starts pulling on it. It's a tablecloth. You go over to the child and talk to her about the tablecloth and lift her so she can see the dishes on top of it. Show her that by pulling on the cloth things move. Then let her know she can safely look at the cloth, she can feel the cloth, but she can't pull on it, because then the dishes could fall on her, hurt her, and even break. Kindly let her know that you don't want that to happen. You love her and you want her to be safe.

STRATEGIES FOR SETTING RESPECTFUL LIMITS

- **Give your child positive messages.** Rather than saying, "Don't spill your milk," or "Be careful not to spill your milk, " say, "You're doing a nice job of holding your sippy cup," or "I like how carefully you're drinking your milk." Wording messages positively helps ensure the response you want.

- **Look for the positive intent in your child's behavior.** Ask yourself, "What could my child possibly be telling me?" You can also look at what's happening within a broader context. By looking at the context (e.g. is she hungry, tired, overstimulated) you'll see things you hadn't thought of before you react. Additional information will enable you to be more understanding with your child.

- **If you don't like how you're viewing your child's behavior, refocus your view.** By refocusing your view, you're looking for another, more positive angle to view the current situation. When you see the situation in a more positive light, you'll feel differently about it and you can respond in a more caring way. It's like putting a new, wider angle lens on your camera and seeing a more complete picture than you saw with a finely-focused lens.

- **When you're in a power struggle with your child, back off for at least thirty seconds.** By backing off, you'll clear your mind a little. Remind yourself that you're the adult and you need to give the situation another look before getting caught in a power struggle with an eighteen-month-old. There's always a different way to handle a situation than head on. Backing off gives you the breathing room to figure out a more creative solution to the dilemma at hand.

- **Take time-outs for yourself and have your child take time-outs whenever either of you needs to calm down and think rationally so you can change your mood and/or behavior.** A time out is a cool-out time in a safe place; a time to reconsider what's happening and what you want to do to change it. When you take time-outs for yourself and come back in a better mood, your child will be more willing to take one when it's her turn to calm down. You'll probably take more time-outs than you give your toddler and two-year-old because your child usually reacts to your energy. If you're tense and stressed, your child will probably be tense and stressed. When you calm down, the world feels safer to your child, and your child usually calms down too.

- **Set reasonable limits and be willing to repeat them as your child's curiosity tests those limits.** You need to verbally repeat limits with small children over and over again because children honestly and easily forget when they're playing, having fun, or being driven by their curiosity to explore things around them.
- **Pick the important stuff to make your points.** Don't struggle or teach all day long. Take breaks and enjoy each other, let the little stuff slide.
- **Make sure your limits are appropriate and reasonable.**
- **Instead of lecturing, ask leading questions so your child can figure out what you want them to learn.** "What do you think mommy will do if you keep doing _____ when you've been asked to please stop?" or "Would you like to have a fun afternoon? What can we do to make that happen?"

Creative Boundaries, Limits, and Consequences

Young children need encouragement to express themselves. They need safe boundaries so they don't hurt themselves. Safety, limits, and consequences can be established without telling them they are bad for touching something that has come within their reach. They are not bad; they are simply exploring, using their curiosity and intelligence. Perhaps their explorations are challenging to you, as a parent, making it difficult to keep them and your valuables safe, but that's your responsibility in being a parent. If you aren't doing your job well, they shouldn't be punished for their curiosity. The following strategies will help you practice Respectful Parenting and refocus how you view your child's actions as you set appropriate limits and boundaries.

See Your Child in a New Way

When your child tells you he's had enough (in his own way), rather than seeing his actions as aimed against you, you could see your small child communicating as best as he can (even if it's through a temper tantrum or crying fit in the middle of your shopping trip). Other times, if he touches too many things or wants to wander off, you can see him as a naturally curious human being. You can stand back in awe of where his mind is taking him and his confidence in wanting to explore more of the world around him.

One woman I was working with came in around Christmas time obviously frustrated. When I asked her what was upsetting her, she told me about her eleven-month-old daughter who kept crawling over to the Christmas tree and pulling on the branches and ornaments. The child had unwittingly shaken off and broken her favorite ornament. The mother was frustrated because she had told her daughter repeatedly not to touch, yet the small girl insisted on crawling over to the "No-no tree." After talking for a while she admitted that she was angry because her baby wasn't listening to her. Her anger was heightened because, as a result of her baby not listening, her favorite ornament had been broken. Her emotions were understandable, and I empathized with her.

But after some empathy, I said, "Let's look at your daughter's side now. Can you imagine yourself as your daughter? Okay, you're crawling along, minding your own business, checking out the living room, where you know you have a lot of toys, and during your regular routine you come across a new, large, glittering, beautiful object. It appears to be a tree, and indeed, upon closer inspection, you find it is a tree. But this tree is different—it's inside the house (in your domain) and it has pretty things you can just about grab onto if you reach and reach. And you do. But *oops*, here comes Mommy and she doesn't look happy."

"Why is she looking at you like that? Her voice sounds sharp and she's saying 'No! No!' Then she's picking you up and carrying you away from that beautiful tree. Usually she encourages you to explore new things and points out pretty things to look at or gives you nice things to touch. But now she's taking you away and saying 'No! No!' Why? When it's so big and so beautiful and so obviously there for the . . . what? Just to sit? Couldn't be . . . and back you crawl again. Your curiosity is captured. You're enthralled. It's so big! You look at its texture, the decorations, their colors, shapes, sheen. They dance when you touch the tree. How could you, as an excited baby, be expected to leave it alone? *Oops!* One broke. You didn't maliciously decide to break what turned out to be Mommy's favorite ornament. You don't even posess the concepts of malicious, or favorite, or even that what you touch may hurt you (the tree could fall?) or hurt something else (the ornament?).

Respectful Limits, Consequences, and Boundaries

Once the mother heard that perspective, her anger disappeared and she started laughing, "I expected too much from her. Of course she didn't listen to me. I see it now. But what do I do? I still want to have Christmas."

Together, we worked out some compromises. The Christmas tree was put inside the portable crib so her daughter could see it but not touch it. We also decided the mother should take down any ornaments she wouldn't want broken and not use them for a couple of years. Although she had been about to put some presents under the tree, she decided to wait until her daughter was asleep on Christmas Eve. We also talked about how she could talk to her child about how exciting and enchanting all the colors were, and how special having a tree inside was. I encouraged the mother to tell her daughter about early memories she had about Christmas and to share her daughter's fascination and excitement instead of squelching it.

Plan Ahead

A different way of dealing with potentially unacceptable behavior is to plan around it so you can avoid difficult situations. When parents anticipate their child's abilities to deal with an event, they can make plans that fit their child's abilities rather than pushing their child into handling more than she can—which usually results in an overtired, overstimulated, or overanxious child. Make sure you figure naps, snacks, and down-time into your day at the rate your child needs them.

Put It Away

Another basic preventive idea is to remember that anything within your child's reach or climbing sphere is fair play. If he can get it, he can play with it. You should accept that part of your job is to childproof the house. As your baby toddles, and as his world gets larger because of his climbing abilities, you'll have more to move. Many parents find it easier to put mementos or breakable objects away for a couple of years. Then the baby is completely free to let his imagination and curiosity be his guide in exploring his world. You are free to enjoy his explorations rather than fearing for a memento's safety or wondering how to refocus your anger as he reaches for yet another breakable object.

Give Your Child More Time or Space

An alternative method that works well with young children is to stand back from the situation and give them a little time or space. For instance, if you're trying to get your child ready to go to child care and she wants to play, you can either get into a power struggle or you can say, "I can see you want to play right now, and I was hoping we could get you dressed. You can play for a few more minutes, but as soon as I come back I'll need you to cooperate and get ready to go, okay?" Reach an agreement before you leave. Another tactic is to say, "Here's your warning that it's almost time to get dressed. You can play for just a little longer, and then we'll be ready to get you dressed." Another line you can use is, "I'll give you a minute to finish and then I'll come get you or you can come get me so we can move on to the next step." Invariably, within thirty seconds, having handed control to your child, she'll come back and say she's ready.

If your child still isn't ready to cooperate, it's important to remind her of the agreement and let her know that for you to be a good mom or dad you have to stick to your part of the agreement so she knows she can trust what you say. Tell her you understand she wants to play more, but playtime is up, and it's time to move on. At that point you want to gently but firmly move her to the next task, such as dressing or getting into the car.

Children are struggling for mastery and control over their environment. Providing them with opportunities for some independence within your timeframe helps both of you get what you want: the task done and a sense of accomplishment. A simple but sincere "thank you" when your child cooperates makes the next time easier because your child remembers how nice it felt to be appreciated.

Give Your Child Choices

Another idea is to say, "We need to brush your teeth and get dressed now. Which would you like to do first?"

"Brush teeth first."

"Okay, let's do it in the order you suggested, we'll brush your teeth and then we'll get dressed." In this example the child was able to talk, but these same ideas can be used with preverbal children. As long as they can point, they can express their desires. Just watch where their little finger points, and you'll have the answer to your question.

Whenever possible respect your child's desire to have a say in what you do. Give him acceptable options and ask him what he'd like to do first, or how he'd like to accomplish the necessary tasks. It helps to repeat what you understand you'll both be doing to make sure you understood him correctly, to make sure he knows what he said, and to make sure you two have an agreement. By repeating his suggestion, you make sure he still wants to do what he blurted out because that can change too. It's a human prerogative, we're fickle beings. Remember that children are also entitled to fickle moments. When you allow them to sometimes change their mind, they'll be more flexible when you change yours.

Admit You Don't Have All the Answers

Sometimes rather than imposing a rigid rule with your young child, try admitting you don't know how to handle something. Tell your child you want to think about it. For instance, "I'm not sure what to do right now so I'm going to think about this and let you know what I come up with." Consider your options. And when you're ready, come back with a workable alternative and explain it to your child. Using this thoughtful method can often prevent a power struggle.

Be Creative and Flexible

Being a healthy and loving parent is one of the most intellectually and creatively challenging tasks in life. You have to come up with new ideas as your child grows, questions, and tests your limits. Children don't wait for adolescence to test boundaries, they're actively rehearsing in their first few years of life. Be creative, not rigid. Follow through and be consistent so your child knows you mean what you say. When you're feeling challenged by her behavior, sometimes soothing talk and cuddling helps. Sometimes, tell a child you care, but you've tried everything you can think of and now you're going to leave her for a few minutes—but when she thinks you can help she should come and let you know. Then stand close by, maybe right outside the doorway, so you can monitor her while you give her some space to work through her feelings. In most cases she'll quickly come find you and be delighted to see you again.

What Parents Say

Cindy: My two-and-a-half-year-old daughter has a strong will. Once she gets on something it's sometimes difficult to get her off it. One day, as I was cooking dinner, she started in with "I want to paint, I want to paint," so I took the time to get her paints out and went back to dinner. Almost immediately, she started saying, "I want water, I want water." I said, "I'm in the middle of cooking, please give me a minute and I'll get you the water." But that wasn't fast enough for her. She continued with, "I want water, I want water," louder and louder, switching to "WANT IT NOW! WANT IT NOW!" In the middle of that, just when I was going to get angry, I saw her father coming up the driveway and said cheerily, "Oh look, Daddy's outside, let's go see him." We went outside, and she forgot about painting. I came back in and cooked dinner, and he took over with her. Sometimes diversion is necessary, especially when you have a few children and the task at hand needs to get done. I suppose if I hadn't forgotten the water for the paints, part of that episode could have been avoided. I did the best I could.

Thinking Outside the Box

When my son was about two and a half I noticed that one of the most difficult times we experienced was when I needed to prepare dinner and he wanted to play. I wasn't making fancy meals. I was usually taking only about fifteen to twenty minutes to prepare the meals. But invariably, he'd want my attention and hoped we'd play.

First I tried to bring toys into our small kitchen and have him play near me so I could interact with him as I was getting dinner together. That worked fairly well but didn't quite solve the problem. I felt stretched between what I needed to concentrate on and what he was doing. Plus, I was forced to look down as I walked around the kitchen so I didn't stumble on him or his toys. One day at the grocery store I saw an empty box. I told him how much fun I used to have with empty boxes when I was little and we decided to bring the box home. The next few days were easier as he played car or boat in his empty box while I prepared lunch or dinner. His playing so close to me in the box triggered wonderful old memories of when I was a kid. So for a few days we were fine, except that I wanted to be little enough to play in his box too. But after a while he was back to wanting more attention.

I think the first real brainstorm was to ask him if he wanted to cook with me. Now that wasn't such a novel idea except for the fact that he was only two-and-a-half, and we were talking real food not Play Dough. I pulled a chair over to the counter, lifted him onto the chair, and we began. I was making salad and he had fun tearing the lettuce. I opened a can of tuna, drained the water, and took the top off as he watched. Then he helped take the tuna out of the can with a spoon as I held onto the can. He even mixed in mayonnaise I had spooned into the bowl. We had a blast except for one thing: I was worried he'd accidentally step off the chair.

When I saw how much my son liked making the salad I tried to think of a safer solution than standing on the chair. The empty box sparked my creativity. We went back to the grocery store and got a large, square, empty box. And then we had a major art project in the making. We covered the box with white poster board. He helped press the white pieces of paper onto the box after we put glue on them. Then I cut out "burners" from black colored paper. We pasted them on top of the box. Our "stove" was taking form. In order to be able to work on it and clean it off, we bought clear contact paper and put that over the white poster board and black paper burners. It needed one more thing for authenticity. We went to the local hardware store and found four simple, black, wooden knobs. I screwed the wooden knobs in the front of our box just where the knobs were on my big stove. *Voila,* we had a stove.

The first thing we prepared on his stove was meatballs. First I washed his hands. Then we put the chopped meat in a bowl. I held his hands on the spices as he sprinkled them onto the meat. We giggled as we mixed it all up with our hands. The next step was even more fun as we formed the meatballs. He caught on right away. After all, he had experience already with Play Dough. When I had filled the pasta pot at the sink and put it on the real stove to boil, I brought a bowl over to his stove. He and I broke up the spaghetti that would go into the pot once the water boiled. Later, when we were all eating dinner together, he proudly told his daddy about how he made dinner with me. He was quite excited.

For the next couple of years almost all our meals were prepared on his stove. Meals might have taken a little longer to prepare, but it was such fun that it never mattered. The solution to interacting with my child while I prepared food was found. The preparation became the play. Whatever needed to be seasoned we'd place on his stove. At first I guided his hand on the spices as he sprinkled them on the surface. But later he was so good at seasoning, he did it himself. We'd break up green beans and put them in the pot. I'd break the eggs; he'd scramble them. It was amazing how much food preparation we could do on that box. We became a dynamic duo in the kitchen.

Eventually he grew out of the stove and showed me that he could use his little step stool and cook with me at the counter. That was fine, because if he accidentally stepped off, it was only about six inches to the floor. Soon he was tall enough that he didn't need a step stool at all. Now he's taller than I am, and he's a great cook.

My solution for the cooking bother was to involve him at a very young age rather than setting daily verbal limits and facing lots of potential power struggles. In solving a problem without old-fashioned discipline my son learned valuable cooking skills, and I gained a helpful and fun partner preparing meals.

Thinking "outside the box" solved a daily annoying problem. When he was tall enough to be at the counter with me, and the box could have been retired, he thought outside the box and came up with a creative idea. We ended up making a play kitchen in the basement. The stove was the first item. From there we went on to create a sink with a plastic basin in another cardboard box. The sink even had a "wooden" counter thanks to wood-like contact paper. Then we built a box refrigerator with knobs for the freezer and refrigerator compartments. It had shelves inside, too. We had box cabinets with cardboard shelves for play dishes and pots. We had box counters with wood-like contact-paper tops.

We saved empty boxes from all kinds of things including eggs, tea, pasta, and crackers so that he had a fully-stocked kitchen to play in, which also could be converted into a store. He'd use a Little Tikes shopping cart he had from when he was learning to walk to shop the shelves. A box would be put on its side and a toy cash register would sit on the store counter. We had hours of fun making the kitchen (and store). We had many more hours of fun playing in it when we weren't busy preparing real food in our real kitchen upstairs.

Eventually, he was done with the play kitchen and we talked about what to do with it. We carried most of the box appliances to the curb for the garbage men to take away. He suggested we keep the refrigerator and stove. They had too many good memories to throw out. A few years later he was ready to throw out the refrigerator but still wanted to keep the stove. Now, when I come across the stove in a basement closet, I'm surprised by how little it is, especially when I think about how many good meals were prepared on it. He felt ten feet tall because he was helping to prepare the meals that we all enjoyed eating. We giggled and had fun every day instead of dealing with power struggles and negotiating time away from each other.

When You're Angry

No matter how well you parent, no matter how calm you intend to be, there will be times when you'll get angry. It's a human emotion, often, as we're about to see, anger is a defense to protect yourself or cover up when you're really feeling sad, afraid, or hurt about something. I can assure you, that no matter what, at times you will experience a negative emotional charge. When you feel that surge of anger, welling up or overflowing, here are some things you can do.

Time-Outs

When big and little people feel backed into a corner or they're stuck in a power struggle, some breathing space almost always helps. I call that space a "time-out" or "cool-out time." Asking your child to take a time-out or giving yourself a time-out is not punishment! It's simply a time to calm down and get a different perspective and come up with solutions that will allow you to get unstuck and continue the day peacefully. Grown-ups need time-outs at least as much as children because children are usually reacting to their parents' emotional energy.

Time-outs are not meant to last long. Sometimes just saying, "I need a time-out" is enough to cool yourself down. Sometimes anywhere from thirty seconds to three minutes are needed. All it takes is enough time to change your mood and your behavior, including your tone of voice, and to come back with an explanation of what happened and an effective plan to avoid it in the future.

You need a time-out when your emotions are being triggered and you're concerned you'll be disrespectful with your child. When you're in that charged place the limbic area, or the automatic fight or flight brain-stem part of your brain is firing away, and you're probably not going to be very pleasant with your baby. You're likely to start yelling, screaming, or being unreasonable. A time-out can help you get back to the front part of your brain (cortex) where rational thought takes place so it's easier to be calm and respectful with your child. If you're trying to teach your child to be respectful, you need to role model how to do that, even when your emotions are firing off. Your first step is to calm down and figure things out. Easier said than done, I know. Here's a technique that will help a great deal.

Mirror, Mirror on the Wall. When you take a time-out it's helpful to stand in front of a mirror and look at yourself. Parents have sometimes said that when they're *really* angry or upset, they have trouble focusing and seeing themselves in the mirror. It's as if they're temporarily blinded by their emotions. They need to look in the mirror for a few seconds until their image comes into view. I suggest that when you can see yourself in the mirror clearly, remind yourself how old you are today and begin to ask yourself some questions. The answers to the following questions help you get a healthier perspective on the situation than your emotional response was allowing you to see.

- "How important is *this* (what's happening and challenging me) in the greater scheme of things?"
- "Am I really angry or am I covering up fear, hurt, or sadness with anger? And if I am afraid of something right now, or scared, or hurt, what am I hurt/sad/fearful about?" Sometimes when you're having a particularly challenging day with your child it's difficult to keep the perspective that it's a challenging *day.* A parent can get scared that this is how it's going to be from now on. "My child was such a sweet baby, but now he's becoming a 'monster.' How am I going to deal with the next sixteen years if this is what he's going to be like?" When you face your fear for what it is you can laugh at yourself and realize that unless you begin parenting differently and creating a "monster" with your anger and energy, your sweet child is still a sweet child, he's simply having a challenging few hours. You can leave your time-out, feeling more confident that you can face today's challenges without fear that this is a dress rehearsal for every day to come.
- "How do I [name] on [today's date] at [age] want to handle this?" When you remind yourself of today's date and your age, it often brings you out of old emotional patterns left over from when you were young and didn't have the coping skills you've learned since then.
- "How would _____ handle this?" (Put in the name of someone you admire.)

Respectful Limits, Consequences, and Boundaries   153

- "Why is this bothering me so much?
- "Is this saying more about me right now or more about my baby?"
- "How do I really want to handle this; not how would my parent handle this, but how do *I* want to handle this today with my child."

You'll be pleasantly surprised to see where these simple questions can lead. You'll like the rational answers you come up with. You'll enjoy being able to alter your emotional perspective to a much more rational, respectful approach. You can break the mounting tension between you and your baby and walk away from the mirror with a lighthearted, loving attitude.

What Parents Say

Sylvia: My son, (he's two-and-a-half) seems to appreciate time-outs. Like the other day, he was having a temper tantrum for no reason that I could tell. Nothing was wrong. I said, "Maybe you need a time-out?" He went over to the couch (that's his time-out place), climbed up, and sat quietly for less than a minute. He came back over to me saying, "I'm okay now." It was all over. He just needed a way to get out of it himself, and the nonstimulation in time-out did the trick.

Another day, he was getting upset with a toy, and he said, "Mommy, think I need time-out," and over he went for a minute or so. When he came back he had a big smile on his face. I think he was feeling good because he had been able to get himself in a better mood.

Shield of Anger

People often express anger and think they're angry, when, if they question themselves, they realize they were really sad, afraid, disappointed, frustrated, or hurt about something. I don't think there's a lot of *pure* anger; I think most of it's a cover up for vulnerable feelings people don't feel safe expressing. Thinking of anger as similar to the shield ancient warriors used increases your options as a parent (see pages 16–17).

When a person feels vulnerable feelings such as sadness, hurt, or fear, they quickly pull out what I call "the shield of anger" in order to defend themselves from the pain associated with those softer feelings. When a person is feeling vulnerable he or she wants to defend themselves against further hurt by "attacking" with anger. By attacking, a person is showing the *enemy* that he or she is strong. When you think about it, how much does that dynamic of feel-anger-defend-against-it truly apply to parent-infant, parent-baby, parent-toddler, or parent-two-year-old relationships?

When you feel anger being triggered, if you think of it as a cover up, a defense, or a shield against more vulnerable feelings, the first thing you can do is get honest with yourself and look behind your defensive, angry reaction. Take a time-out if you need to calm down. Look at what emotion is really being triggered. For instance, when your infant wakes up for the fifth time in a night, you couldn't possibly be *really* angry. You know your infant has a tiny tummy. You know infants need to eat often. Nursing every two hours around the clock is expected from an infant. So why would you be angry? You might feel sad that you have to get up and do something when you want to sleep. You might be frustrated that you're the only one who can nurse the baby (but this will pass quickly). And if you get very rational, you might feel good that your baby trusts you to wake up and nurse her. You might appreciate the fact that you can provide such wonderful nutrition to your infant, but anger? How could you possibly feel *real* anger?

How about when your two year old is over stimulated and having a tantrum in a department store? Parents often react with anger by yelling, "Stop this nonsense right now. I said *stop it!*" But what would that parent really be feeling if he were honest with himself, maybe embarrassed? Or the parent could realize his baby had been whining for a while. She had been trying to tell you she had enough, but you were pushing her limits. Your baby tried to go along with your program, but when she couldn't hold it together anymore, she had a tantrum.

If you had listened sooner, the tantrum could have been averted. You might feel sad that you didn't listen and recognize your child's earlier communications. In this situation is being angry an appropriate response to your child's tantrum? Instead you might try to apologize and say, "I think we'll leave now and go to a quieter place. I didn't realize you were getting overwhelmed. I guess I didn't listen to you earlier. I'm sorry. I understand now. Let's go to a quieter place."

Ask for Your Child's Input

You can also ask for your child's input. "I'm not sure how to handle this, do you have any ideas?" Another approach is to say, "I don't like what's happening right now. Do you?" Then say something like, "Let's figure out how we can have a more peaceful afternoon," or "I really want to have fun with you right now but my tummy's hurting. How is yours? Let's stop what we're doing (being in a power struggle) and figure out how to do this differently so we both get to feel better. Okay?" Then listen closely and consider your young child's alternatives. Try them out if they make sense. When the power struggle is over, thank your child for her good ideas.

Look at Your Baby

Sometimes a wonderful alternative to letting frustrations build and anger get out of hand is to simply look at your baby. Really see your baby's face. Look into your baby's innocent eyes. Focus on this little miracle in front of you. Yes, she may be a challenging miracle, but she's still a miracle. And if that isn't enough to cool you out, give her a big hug, tell her you love her (to remind her and to remind you) and snuggle for a while. Essence of "baby in arms" can often calm even the most fried nerves.

Have Signals With Your Baby

My son and I used to have a signal. When things got tense or he was really tired, he'd look at me and say, "Mommy, I need some lovings." That would be our "stop action" signal. Whatever was happening, we'd stop. He'd climb into my lap, or into my arms, and we'd snuggle together for a while, feeling each others' love. That would calm him down if he needed it, or, it could calm both of us down if we needed it. Whatever was causing the tension seemed to shift as we snuggled. After some "lovings" we could talk about whatever it was and easily come to a resolution that worked for both of us.

Take Short Breaks

You can call a friend on the phone as a short break from tensions with your child. Talking, sharing and brainstorming with another adult can help you release your emotions. Your friend may have some good ideas you can try. You can ask your spouse for some ideas or ask him or her to take over so you can get a break.

Giving In

Some parents opt for an approach to discipline that's easier in the short run, but much harder in the long run: they give-in to a child's whining or tantrum. That does stop the whining or the tantrum, but it also creates a longer-term no-win situation. The young child learns, from his parents' behavior, that he can get what he wants if he yells, whines, or tantrums long enough. It is an unhappy place for a child to be and an unhappy place for the parent. The child "gets something" but loses valuable life lessons such as learning to wait, being dealt with in a more realistic way, learning there are limits and the world does not revolve around him, and learning that you don't and shouldn't always get what you want.

Children whose parents cave in a lot often have trouble when peers and teachers don't respond the way a parent does; they're difficult to be around, figuring if their methods work at home they'll work at school. They're in for a rude awakening when a teacher sets an appropriate limit, and when peers don't want to be friends because they only want the play to go their way. Parents can be hooked into this pattern of giving in throughout the growing up years; with the situation getting worse over time as the child demands more. He doesn't learn how to self-soothe or to set limits for himself because limits haven't been used on him.

Previously I encouraged you to watch and listen to your young child's input and seriously consider it, but if you're always (or almost always) doing it his way your child will come to believe the world revolves around him. He'll become too empowered as he expects to get his way and he won't develop a healthy sense of frustration, tolerance, or compassion that other people have their own needs. He won't be able to handle, "You know, that's a good idea, but we won't be able to do it right now because _____." Young children who expect everything to go their way grow into what I call, "Entitlement Monsters" who can't take "No" for an answer. Children are not born as Entitlement Monsters, they're created by parents afraid to set appropriate limits. You can avoid that situation by creating a healthy balance of limits and encouragement so your child learns that you're taking care of him *and* he won't always get his way.

The faster you can tell your child, "I made a mistake, I've been giving into you too often and that needs to change for me to be a good parent," the faster your demanding child will turn into a delightful child again. It's up to you. You need to react differently and more consistently in a respectful way instead of giving in and giving up your responsibility as parent, guide, and limit setter.

Alternatives to Giving In

You need a number of alternatives to getting angry and letting your frustrations get the better of you. You also need a number of alternatives ready so you don't give in when times get tough. Each situation and each child within each situation is different. To further complicate matters, the first three years are so chock full of change and development that what was useful a few weeks ago may not work right now, but it may work again at a later date. Rotating options and always being open to new suggestions helps you parent creatively and respectfully.

Here's an example. In a calm tone of voice, you describe in specific terms what happened: "I just went into your room to shut off the light and saw your trucks and stuffed animals on the floor. I thought we had agreed that you'd put them away."

Your child just looks at you.

Then you tell your child how you feel without blaming or judging. You could also ask for help in understanding what happened, so you don't jump to your own conclusions. "I was a little surprised to see them still there. I wonder what happened?"

"I don't know."

A small child often doesn't know. He's not saying that to get you angry, so you could suggest something non threatening and see what happens. "Well, since you had agreed before, could you pick them up now?"

"Okay," or maybe, "Will you help?"

You have the choice of helping or letting your child do it himself. Helping will assure the task gets done and will reestablish the two of you as a team rather than adversaries. Letting your child do it himself allows him an opportunity to be proud of his accomplishments, but it also allows him an opportunity to be distracted by the toys as he cleans and that may lead to him playing again instead of focusing on cleaning up.

Creating Consequences

Respectful Parenting advocates boundaries and consequences. Whenever possible, they ought to be prearranged so your child knows they're coming. One example is an adult's work schedule. If there's a time when a parent must be at work, then flexibility in the morning has a natural limit. One parent didn't know how to handle her two-year-old daughter's power struggle about getting dressed in the morning. She had tried talking, cajoling, yelling, and threatening, but she was still often late for work, and her boss was beginning to give her a hard time.

We talked about it and she recognized that dressing had become a power struggle with her daughter and wondered if perhaps it was a way for her daughter to have Mom for a few extra minutes. We came up with the following plan. The next day she was going to talk to her daughter before dressing time arrived so she had time to adjust to the next thing on her morning's agenda. At that time, the mother was also going to talk to her about how Mommy has to go to work, and it would be nice if she could cooperate so they could both start their days cheerfully instead of being sad, angry, and frustrated. She would point out to her daughter that she really had some power to make the choice of a fun morning or an unhappy one.

If talking didn't do the trick, then the mother was not going to struggle. Instead, she would calmly tell her daughter the consequence of not cooperating and that if she didn't get dressed easily, the mother was going to carry through with her consequence. The consequence was that Mom would calmly pick out an outfit, take her child to child care in her pajamas, and have her get dressed there when she was ready, if the child care people had time to help her get dressed, or she'd have to stay in her pajamas while all the other children were in their clothes.

At our next session, the mother reported that her talk did not work the first day. As she was putting her daughter in her car seat in her pajamas her daughter said, "Ready. Get dressed now." The mom told her daughter she was sorry that she had not decided sooner, but that Mom needed to follow through on what she had said so her daughter would learn to trust that her mother meant what she said. Then she calmly drove to the child care center. The next day, when the mother again started talking to her about the upcoming getting-dressed time, and reminded her daughter that she hoped she'd make the choice to dress at home rather than at the child care center, her daughter said, "I pick out," and her mother said "Fine." Since then, they have had smooth mornings taking turns picking out her clothes.

When children are given choices, they have a sense of control, such as the little girl in the last example. Children will often choose to stay within reasonable boundaries and limits. They will also develop a sense of pride from being involved in decisions. Whereas, when children are expected or forced through coercion and punishment to meekly submit, their self-esteem is shot down each time.

Setting Limits

Limits are important in Respectful Parenting. Without limits, respectful parenting backfires because you give too much, and you become depleted, flat, impatient, and irritable. Your child can become a taker instead of a taker and a giver. Just the way you want to respect your child and not bombard his system with too much stimuli so he can't think straight or feel rational, you also need to do the same with yourself.

You have to respect your own limits and teach your child how to respect your limits so you have energy to spare, especially for those random sleepless nights that come along. Your brain needs to recognize its own limits. It's okay to say to your toddler, "Daddy is so tired tonight, we need to just play quietly and cuddle so Daddy can be patient with you." Sharing your limits teaches your child there are choices. When you're tired, you can push yourself to a point where you get stimulation overload. Then you're irritable and it's no fun for you or anyone around you. Or you can recognize you've had enough, slow down, be peaceful, and the evening will be pleasant for all of you.

Respectful Parenting is a two-way street. Mutual respect for yourself and others encourages gentleness and peace in your household. It also encourages flexible and logical thinking, listening to your feelings, and looking at a situation and all its parts before jumping to conclusions. It encourages everyone in your house to feel, listen, see, and think things through thoroughly so they can make sound, effective decisions. Sharing these skills with your child are life-long gifts they can use on a daily basis, and they don't cost a cent. Taking the time to do this kind of parenting guides you into setting reasonable limits, which will replace the need for traditional old style parenting "discipline."

Eliminating Old-Style Parenting Patterns

When children are loved and respected, they will love and respect others. Certainly they will test the limits you lovingly set. They will not always follow through with something you negotiated with them, and you will get frustrated, disappointed, and angry at times. Just the way it's important for you to follow through on your commitments, children need to know it's important for them to be consistent and do what they said they would do.

A lot of potentially volatile situations can be defused depending upon your attitude. If you begin feeling angry and say to yourself (hopefully, not out loud), "Damn it, why didn't he put his toys away! We talked about it, and he agreed. Now we have to leave and all his trucks and stuffed animals are on the floor. Why didn't that (bad?) boy listen!?" From there you might yell, yank, and criticize your child for not behaving or listening. An unpleasant scene would follow. Or, you could take a one-minute time-out to calm yourself down.

Ask yourself why you're getting so angry. Are you doing what your parents did to you? Do you want to? If your answers to the last two questions are yes and no, and you want to handle this relatively minor infraction differently, then before approaching your child directly, figure out exactly what he did or did not do in behaviorally specific terms. No value judgments; just specifics. Try to refocus on your child's behavior using the most positive light.

You might come up with this: your child said he would put his toys away and he didn't. That part is simple. But why didn't he? Was he testing your limits, and if so was he trying to get you mad? Was he trying to find out how his little world operates? When you're calm, you'll realize your child probably didn't do this to get to you. If he did, there was probably good reason. Maybe you were preoccupied and ignoring him for a long time. This might have been the only way he could get your attention. If it wasn't that, what was it?

Perhaps he forgot or got so caught up in handling the toys although he intended to put them away, somehow the cleaning task got lost in his spontaneous play. Or there might be something else you haven't thought of. At that point, your curiosity could be piqued, you could tell your child how you were feeling, and ask him what happened. Together you could figure out how to deal with it.

A short time-out allows you to figure out behaviorally what has happened and how you really feel about it. Perhaps your flare of anger is your own personal history from your parents' reactions. Often, as we've seen, anger is a symptom of other underlying more vulnerable feelings like hurt, sadness, fear, surprise, disappointment, or frustration. When you can look at your anger more objectively and think of ways you might get through a frustrating situation without an anger attack, you'll find that a lot of the "umph" in your emotional reaction dissipates.

Let's look at this same kind of phenomenon happening with a younger child. Let's say you just got up from the table to get something, and when you sit down you notice your baby pouring juice from her sippy cup onto the floor. You instantly get angry and yell at her to stop. You might grab the cup away. You might angrily say, "Don't do that!"

Instead, take the time to see why you're so upset and ask yourself if someone reacted to you that way in the past. Were you punished physically, through words, or tone of voice for exploring your environment, even when innocent curiosity caused a disturbance you hadn't planned? Respectful Parenting strategies allow you to look at the situation differently. If a baby takes her sippy cup and pours juice on the floor, she's not being bad. She may simply be exploring the world around her, seeing what happens when the cup is held upside down. She already knows what happens if it's right side up, or if it's tipped to her mouth, but she doesn't know what happens if it's upside down. If her action is met with a simple, "Now you know what happens when you put your cup upside down. I'll get a sponge and clean it up. If you want to drink your juice you'll need to hold it the other way." She probably won't do it again, because you haven't made it a big exciting thing by getting all upset about it. Babies and small children like to see they have an effect on the world.

When you blow up over small things, they see, feel, and hear the physical sensation of how they manipulated their little world. Your emotional reactions can be exciting to them. They're more likely to want to reproduce those exciting things again. When you stay calm, the situation loses its appeal and it's not likely to happen again. You can defuse a situation (including your reactions to the baby's actions) by looking at it, commenting on it for what it is, and getting on with your day, rather than becoming embroiled in an escalating power struggle.

Your parents probably disciplined you using a punishment that they felt fit the crime. What crime? The crime of being a curious baby? The crime of being an active toddler? The crime of being a questioning two-year-old? Unfortunately, discipline has often been coupled with shame. Parents can, unwittingly, through their tone of voice, portray a sense of shame. Messages like "You didn't pick up your toys" can be said with cutting sarcasm, venomous anger, or disgusted shamefulness by parents who are intolerant of age-appropriate forgetfulness. It can also be said angrily by parents who are caught up in their own personal histories and are about to repeat what was done to them.

After taking a few deep breaths or a short time-out (looking into a mirror if possible and asking yourself some questions) the words, "You didn't pick up your toys" can be said matter-of-factly, in a way that simply describes the behavior. A pleasant dialogue with problem solving, where you're both on the same team rather than in a one-up adversarial relationship, can follow. You actually invite a calm solution when you use a nonjudgmental approach.

Parents can use punishment as a shortcut to get something done fast. Talking takes longer. Examining where your reactions come from, asking yourself if you want to be stuck in old, automatic, unconsciously motivated behaviors that hurt you and your child takes longer. Asking yourself if your current behavior is what you want to be passing along to your children takes time and energy. So does coming up with new options, trying them out, refocusing and viewing your child's actions more positively, and behaving differently from your parents. Then, why do it? Because when you do, you feel better and so do your children.

Modeling

In past generations, parents often used hitting or spanking as their main form of discipline. If we think about it, isn't it ridiculous to assume we can teach children that a behavior is not acceptable by hitting or spanking them? A parent may hurt a child enough (by spanking them) to have them not do something out of fear, but that's learning fear, not learning acceptable options. When you remember that the most powerful way we learn is by copying what we've seen, a parent hitting is actually teaching her child a different lesson than she's setting out to teach. The lessons being taught are that hitting and intimidation, especially of those younger, smaller, and less able to defend themselves, are okay. Given this perspective, when a large adult hits a small child, that's about as disrespectful as you can be. The child can't hit you back. You're much too big. The child can't defend himself by telling the parent to go to his room or that he's out of control.

A so-called simple spanking can develop into a beating when a parent can't control her unleashed emotions. Abusive parents usually were abused themselves and find themselves operating on automatic pilot once certain remembered emotions are triggered. This time they may be on the giving instead of receiving end, but fury has its own path. It makes sense that hitting shouldn't be an option for parents.

Cindy: Somehow, we got into it one day. My daughter and I were just arguing. I don't even remember the specifics, but I know I was in her room. All of a sudden in the middle of "Yes, you will" and "No, I won't," I looked around. I mean, there I was at thirty-five, and there she was at two. Only her behavior made sense for her age, and mine . . . was the same as my mother's. I didn't like it when she did it to me when I was a kid, and I didn't like it when I saw myself doing it to my child.

I apologized and told my daughter there was really nothing wrong with what she was doing, but that I didn't like what I was doing or saying, so I was going to take a time-out, sit on my bed, and think for a couple of minutes. I asked her if she'd be okay and play safely for a few minutes while I went to my room. I left both doors open so I could hear her playing (our rooms were only about fifteen feet apart). She said okay.

A few seconds later, I heard the patter of her little feet as she walked down the hall to my room. I was thinking I could have used at least a full minute to myself, but there she was. She pulled over her stool, climbed onto the bed and stroked my back saying, "It's okay, Mommy."

She was comforting me, as I've comforted her so often. By loving my daughter, I had taught her how to love me. My anxiety instantly cleared. I gathered her in my arms and hugged her tightly. I thanked her for her comfort and told her I was feeling better. By the end of the hug we were ready to play and enjoy each other again.

* * *

Stephanie: When my daughter was eleven months old, something happened that could have been really bad. It was one of those nights where she was overtired and had been whining a lot, all through dinner. I guess my husband's nerves were shot because when she threw her fork on the floor, he reached over and slapped her hand. She looked up at him and said, "Daddy no hit. You hit, I hit." And she slapped him. He looked at me bewildered. He was silent for a while. I took over parenting as he got up from the table and excused himself.

I had been upset when I saw him hit her. It was the first time. We had talked about spanking quite a bit and couldn't agree on it. I kept saying no, under no circumstances, but he thought when a child was really acting up and had been for a while, and all else failed, that a spanking was perfectly fine. I didn't like it that we didn't agree, but I couldn't convince him. I guess I had been hoping, rather naively, that we'd never encounter the situation. So when it happened, and she was so young, I was pretty upset. But before I could even intervene she had stood up for herself.

When he and I talked about it later (after she was in bed) he said he had realized from her words and actions that she was right. If he could hit her, she could hit him. He said he had known, the second she responded to his slap, that it's wrong for a parent to hit a child, and he wouldn't be doing it again. The next morning, first thing, he talked to her and apologized for hitting her. He told her that he had learned from her that hitting wasn't okay for anybody. They agreed on a "no-hitting rule" for everyone in our family.

Being Real

Another feature of Respectful Parenting involves being real with your children, which means being honest, caring, and straightforward. Some of the examples you have just read illustrate this point. For instance, a parent can say to a child, "I'm confused. I'm not sure how to handle this. Give me a few minutes." Or a parent can say, "I don't like what I'm doing right now. I need a time-out." This kind of behavior teaches your children honesty. They learn all people make mistakes, and it's better to admit mistakes than to carry through with behaviors or words that don't feel comfortable. Your children are also learning how to assess and reevaluate what they're doing and saying, and if necessary, change midway. These are the basic building blocks of solid decision making.

Remember that old expression, "To err is human"? But how often do we see people stuck in behaviors they don't like because their false pride won't let them backtrack and say "I'm sorry, I've made a mistake" and change. Children of parents who are real see their parents with authentic pride, rather than false save-face pride. Being human isn't so scary to these children. Rather than feeling insecure about changing their minds, children learn that they can make mistakes and learn from them. They know they need time to consider their options and make healthy choices, they also know if things aren't working out well they can reconsider and do things differently. When children receive respectful limits, consequences, and boundaries they feel more confident in their abilities to cope with difficult situations.

Summary

Children need and crave limits. Historically, limits were imposed from a shame-based perspective that resulted in children feeling ashamed of themselves and unable to think things through because they lacked the skills and confidence to be able to do a thorough assessment and make sound decisions. Respectful Parenting advocates a humanistic, calm, thoughtful, negotiated approach with limits, consequences, and boundaries for children. The kinds of limits used with Respectful Parenting empower children by making them aware of consequences before they do something. As they get older they help decide their own consequences. They're able to make conscious choices rather than submitting out of fear and intimidation. Children know they can take a time-out to calm down and help them think clearly. They're encouraged to learn from their mistakes, knowing we all make them, we all want to learn from them, and it's okay to do things differently once you realize you don't like how things are going.

Twelve

Dealing with Your Child's Frustrations

YOUNG CHILDREN WORK so hard and at such an incredible pace to learn about the big world around them! Since learning something new is often frustrating, it makes sense that young children will often become frustrated. Your child will need your help to learn how to deal with her emotions and the situations that cause them. You can't prevent these feelings; they come along with the learning process called, "Life."

There seem to be eight basic situations that produce frustration for children between birth and age three:

1. A basic need not being filled, such as closeness, hunger, or the need to rest or sleep.
2. A baby or small child trying to accomplish something he can't physically or developmentally do yet.
3. Overstimulation.
4. Too much time engaged in adult activities without enough playtime or child-centered time.
5. The "I want it now" frustration, as a child begins to learn the difference between needs and wants.
6. Not understanding something and wanting to.
7. Wanting to say something but not having the words to express him- or herself.
8. Not being able to fill a parental expectation that is developmentally beyond the child's capacity.

Think about situations where you're feeling frustrated because you want something to be happening and it isn't. You have no control over the situation. You're looking for the best way to express yourself in front of your small child. You don't want to curse, scream, throw things, or shake someone, yet you're so frustrated you can't think straight. Crying might be a way to release feelings, but adults are often too socialized or adapted to allow themselves a healing cry. You may also worry about how your crying could affect others around you, so you hold back your tears. You're feeling all this pent up frustration, but you're not sure how to express it.

Small children can feel exactly the same way, and they still have to learn there are things that won't get addressed just as they would like all the time. In other words, they need to learn the art of waiting, and that can be frustrating for them just as it is for you. Long before your child has words for expressing her frustration, she has nonverbal ways of letting you know "I've had it!" The first and most universal expression infants and babies use is an all-purpose, slightly altered intonation of their basic cry. This chapter will address how to help your child deal with frustrations and will give you lots of examples of how other parents dealt with their children's and their own frustrations. It begins with the basic Respectful Parenting strategies.

- **Remember that teaching patience and the art of waiting takes time and practice.**
- **Look at difficult times as life lessons for you and your child.** You're learning her limits better, and she's communicating hers to you and trusting that you'll listen.
- **When your child is upset, try to think of reasons that explain the stress and ways that you can lessen the stress.** Try to help him out with words so he can talk about his stress. Don't blame or shame your child.
- **Plan your days around your child's schedule** so that activities occur during times she is normally energetic, and naps and meals can be taken at the usual times, even if food is eaten on the run and naps are taken during car rides.
- **Reassure your child.** When he's frustrated by a task he doesn't have the manual dexterity to perform let him know that it will come in time. Try and figure out a similar activity for your child that he can accomplish.

Unmet Needs

Infants and babies instinctively know that crying is a great release. Besides releasing their built-up tensions, crying often results in someone (often a parent) responding quickly, to check out what's happening, soothe the baby, and alleviate the situation. The end result? The baby is no longer feeling uncomfortable. In old-style parenting, the parent might come in and say loudly, "If you don't stop crying, I'll give you something to cry about. Now enough is enough!"

Babies raised with parents who are being respectful have much less cause for frustration. As soon as they express their needs, the needs are addressed and resolved. The result: happier babies and less stressed parents. When babies are mellow because their needs are being taken care of, they're genuinely happy and they feel safe and secure. Old-style parenting with regimented feedings and naptimes provided infants and babies with more opportunities to be frustrated because their basic needs for food, comfort, and security weren't being met.

Babies who are raised by people using Respectful Parenting techniques are freer with their expressions of love and appreciation than old-style parented babies. Old-style parenting considered adults who responded on demand to be creating spoiled children. Respectful Parenting views timely responses as *responding to a need* and creating good self-esteem. Responding lovingly to a need perpetuates the family's cycle of gentleness and love.

What Parents Say

Jeanne: So far, my baby is only nine months old, but I deal with his frustrations by picking him up, holding him, and nursing him. It's such an easy simple way to calm him down, and it works every time. So that's really all I've had to develop so far.

Bonnie: I recently had one of those days with my sixteen-month-old daughter where everything was going wrong for her. She couldn't quite communicate and when she seemed to want something, once she got it, she didn't really want it. You know, one of those days where I just couldn't please her or solve it or anything. I started getting frustrated too. All my attempts fell flat. Finally I brought her into my bedroom and started pounding on my mattress. She looked at me kind of funny, and then as I invited her to pound, she joined right in. At first we both just pounded away, but soon, it turned into a fun thing, as our frustration just kind of melted away. Since then, I've given her a tambourine to use when she's frustrated. And when I hear it going, although noise like that used to bother me, I know she's getting out some frustration, and I feel relieved for her.

Developmental Hurdles

Babies raised with respectful parents experience frustration when they begin to try to accomplish physical feats they can't yet perform, feats that need the practice of smaller steps leading up to the whole. Walking is a good example. For most babies, learning to walk is a months-long process that involves falling down and frustrating bumps and bruises. Parents can help them, but sometimes, developmentally, small children aren't quite ready for what they're tackling. That leads to frustration. Lots of talking and soothing hugs help when a child really wants to do something and can't yet accomplish the task.

What if your baby has crawled to a baby gate and wants to get past it? The baby can't crawl under the gate, can't go through the gate, and can't quite manage to climb over it. The baby is stuck, emotionally frustrated, and cries. If a parent is utilizing Respectful Parenting techniques, he will come over to his child immediately to find out what's wrong. What happens? He picks up his baby, so he can communicate with her more easily. By picking up his baby, Dad has lifted her over the gate, where she wanted to be. As her father soothingly asks what's wrong, she feels safe, loved, and secure. If she squirms in his arms, he knows that she was after something on the floor level, or perhaps she's pointing to something on a piece of furniture. By taking cues from his baby, the father is able to provide a satisfying end to her frustrating experience. Everyone is happy again.

Another example of an older child who wants to do something that he just can't physically accomplish comes to mind. It was a situation I encountered with my two-and-a-half-year-old. He really wanted to help me tie his shoes. (In truth, he wanted to tie his shoes all by himself, but he'd settle for helping.) When we tried to do it together, he was sometimes able get the first half-knot done, but often he got frustrated.

I'd take him in my arms and say something like, "It looks like being able to tie your shoes is important to you. I can see you're trying really hard to understand and do what I'm showing you. But you know what? It looks like you're not ready to tie them yet. I know you want to, but physically I don't think you can. And that's fine. There's lots of times where we want to do something we're not yet ready to do. Like you had to learn to crawl, pull yourself up on furniture, and walk along holding onto furniture for months before you could walk all by yourself. Tying shoes is one of those things that takes a while and practice. I hope you can have patience with yourself and wait a while till you're bigger."

I thought I had explained the situation well and hoped my son would understand he just couldn't be expected to tie shoes yet. He wasn't developmentally ready. But he was determined, and he responded with, "But I want to, please show me again, we'll practice." I thought a little and continued, "Even though tying shoes looks easy, because I've been doing it for years, it's really a hard thing to learn. I didn't learn till I was a lot older than you are now. I was almost in kindergarten, and even then it was hard for me to learn. There are some things you have to wait until you're bigger to be able to do. Tying shoes is one of them. We can try every once in a while to see if you're ready, but I don't want you to feel bad over something you're just not able to do yet. Can you understand that?"

"But I'm big now," he said.

"Yes, you are big now, and you'll be getting even bigger. And when you're quite a bit bigger, your fingers and your brain will be much better at tying shoes. I like the way you keep trying and wanting to. One day you'll be able to, but let's put off trying for a while, because it looks like you're getting frustrated and you don't have to. One day this will be much easier and you'll learn without too much frustration. Okay?"

In that situation, I wanted to validate his efforts. He was persistent, and I think persistence is a good quality to reinforce. But persistence in the face of a task that developmentally he can't master may lead to unnecessary frustration and feelings of failure. He didn't need that. I also wanted to tell him that he's not the only one who can't master tying shoes at two years of age. It's one of those things older kids get to do.

I used my memories as a reality mirror for him. The other thing I did, which I recommend, was to look for ways of alleviating the frustrating situation. Since he wanted to help, or be able to put his own shoes on, when it was time to get his next pair of shoes, we bought shoes with Velcro closures. With the Velcro closures he could be independent, get his shoes on, be developmentally just where he belonged, and feel good about himself and his accomplishments.

When your child is frustrated in other situations, look for creative solutions. For instance it often helps to take away the stimulus that's producing his discomfort and offer an explanation. Help him through it by talking about what's happening. Face reality and decide if he's ready for the situation he's facing. It's fine to shelve things for later. Life is a series of experiences. Sometimes the timing is right. Sometimes it's wrong.

When you explain to your child that the timing is wrong and that he's feeling frustrated for good reason, he'll feel relieved. When he's feeling better, try to explain that he was just challenging himself in a no-win situation. Assure him that you'll help him again when he has a chance of successfully accomplishing what he's attempting. You'll be modeling appropriate behaviors he can use later in life—when he's faced with situations where he needs more resources than he has on hand. Perhaps he'll learn how to ask for help when he's an adult rather than attempting the impossible, or being afraid to try because he's afraid of failure.

There's a link here between knowing your limits, learning to ask for help, putting things off until the timing is better, or waiting for the proper resources to accomplish a task and procrastination. People procrastinate when they assume, "I can't do that. It's just too hard. Why tackle it at all?" A Respectful Parent does not say, "We'll never do it," or "You'll never do it." A Respectful Parent says, "We'll do it when it's possible," and "We'll try periodically to see if you're ready." Respectful Parents teach their child how to cope with difficult tasks and frustrating situations.

What Parents Say

Bonnie: Our two-year-old daughter started saying, "No, no," when we offered her things, and when we withdrew the offer she'd say "Yes, yes." This could go on a few times until we were all confused and frustrated. We realized that with her, it wasn't about the thing itself; the no, no, yes, yes had become a power struggle and a vicious cycle. So when we got into it with her, and were on the merry-go-round of "No, no," "Yes, yes," instead of falling into frustration with her, we made up a "No, no. Yes, yes," song and made it fun. The song completely defused the power struggle and we all ended up laughing and going on to something else that was more fun.

When my daughter was about two-and-a-half, she was going through what my husband and I came to call the "I want it, I don't want it" frustration a lot. At first I kept trying to fix it for her. And the result? She just became more frustrated. Finally I found that after a couple of attempts at talking or fixing it, the best thing I could do was recognize that it was her frustration and know that sometimes it's okay for her to be frustrated. After all, frustration is one of those human emotions we all have from time to time. So I would recognize that the object she was venting her frustration on might have little to do with what she was really frustrated about. I'd let her be and let her work it through on her own. Amazingly "it" would just pass, and she'd calm herself down.

* * *

Cindy: My husband and I have always told our daughter stories. It seems to be a good way to help her "get" stuff. Direct input doesn't work well with her, but metaphors in story-form that go right into her unconscious seem to work really well. Here's one my husband told her one evening: There was a Momma bear, a Papa bear, and a little girl bear named (our daughter filled in the blank with *Barbara*). One day Barbara was playing with a big pair of scissors and Papa Bear took it away from her. Barbara was mad. She said mean things and cried. Papa Bear said, "This is our job. If we let you play with the big scissors, you could get hurt. Our job is to keep you safe. Your job is to play, but our job is to help you play with things that will be fun so that you don't get hurt." After a story like that, it would be easier for a while. We could remind her about the bears, and she had an easier time cooperating with our limits, which were designed to keep her safe.

Trying to Do Too Much

Toddlers and two-year-olds often get frustrated because their parents have planned too much in a day, and they develop a good case of stimulation overload coupled with exhaustion. That's not their fault. A mother who was learning about Respectful Parenting said, "I can't blame her when she starts acting up in a store after a couple hours of shopping. It's simply her way of telling me I overdid it for her." When children start losing it in public places, parents ought to tell their child, "Thank you for letting me know you've had enough. Let's go sit someplace quiet," or "Let's get a snack and give each other some good attention for a while," or "Let's just forget all this right now. I'll explain to the salesperson. You and I can go home and get a (nap, snack, quiet time, playtime, etc.), which you really seem to need right now." How different from old-style parenting where a parent would say, "Will you please just behave? What's wrong with you? You need to stop this nonsense right now or I'm going to _____!"

When you take time to look at the situation, you *can* understand. You probably created the situation by doing at least one of the following: over-exposed your child to adult stimuli without providing enough child-centered time, missed a nap, was late for a meal or missed a snack, didn't include enough cuddling, close, snuggle time, or ignored your child's pace and her needs. To ask her to "stop right now" is an unrealistic expectation that will only result in more unhappiness and frustration for everyone. She wants to please you, but can't. Calmly leaving the situation as quickly as possible and understanding her frustration are the first steps toward everyone being able to calm down.

This type of frustration can often be avoided with forethought and planning. Try to remember that your small child hasn't planned an over-stimulating day. She's just along for the ride. You planned the day. She's doing the best she can. If there are consequences you hadn't planned for, who gets to deal with them? You ought to, as understandably and lovingly as possible. Again, walking in your child's shoes for a few minutes, seeing and feeling what it must be like to be an overtired, overly hungry, or overly stimulated two-year-old will go a long way toward you being able to lovingly take your child out of the situation. Your other alternatives are to be annoyed, disappointed, angry, or furious. Which will it be?

Patience

Another source of frustration for some children in the older range of the birth to three-year age bracket comes when they're learning the art of waiting. As infants and babies, their needs were addressed immediately. As toddlers and two-year-olds, they are beginning to want some things they don't *need* to get as quickly. To them, their wants feel as urgent and as important as their needs felt. Since there's no difference to them in how it feels to *want* to stay at a park longer and to *need* to eat, they don't understand why, from their perspective, all of a sudden you're no longer readily responding. They hear their loving Mommy and Daddy say, "No, we're not going to stay. It's time to leave," or "I can see you really want to stay, but it's getting late and we really do have to go now." Even though wants may feel as important to them as needs always have, they're going to have to learn the subtle and not-so-subtle differences between needs and wants. It's a difficult lesson at any age, but being exposed to it for the first few times is particularly frustrating.

Children going through these lessons also have to get reassurance that Mommy and Daddy will still be there for all their basic needs: comfort, security, love, food, and sleep. Parents using Respectful Parenting techniques can help their children learn about these differences. Learning is a two-way street, with solutions, compromises, and limits. Parents need to offer solutions that address the child's wants directly, validate them, understand the immediacy behind them, explain why they can't be addressed right now, and then follow through with what the parent says has to happen at that point in time. Sometimes, a parent will listen to her child's wants, rethink her own agenda, and agree to be more flexible after explaining why (so the child doesn't get the idea that Mom is a total pushover).

In other situations, a parent can listen to the child, rethink the entire situation, and suggest a compromise. An example would be, "You're telling me you really want to stay at the park a little longer. Maybe I didn't give you enough time to get adjusted to the idea of having to leave. I'm going to give you that time now. Why don't you play for another five minutes, and then we'll go. When I tell you it's time to go after you have this extra time, I want you to agree and come willingly. Can you agree to that?" It's a compromise that holds both of you responsible for the new agreement.

When you're helping your child learn the art of waiting, it helps to really listen to her desires and really consider them before making a decision. Your child will sense whether you've taken the time to listen and consider her perspective. When she senses you have, she'll be more willing to listen to your perspective. Whatever happens after that, it's more likely to go smoothly when you've respected her by listening and considering her input, rather than simply sticking to your agenda.

What Parents Say

Steve: My two-and-a-half-year-old son sometimes gets almost frantic for some toy or thing he wants, but he's saying, "I need this, I need this!" I say to him, "No, you want it, and if you'll calm down, I'll get it for you because we do have time to play right now. It's okay to want this, but you don't really need it, like you'd need food if you were hungry, or something to drink if you were thirsty."

I'm trying to teach him the difference between needs and wants, and I figure if I can use the examples he gives me and use the right words, explaining the differences, he'll get it eventually. His mother and I have agreed from the beginning that we'd use the right words and concepts for things even if they were beyond his so-called capacity to know exactly what we were talking about, because one day he'd get it and we'd never know when that day was.

It feels like we're respecting his mind, his ability to know, by parenting the way we do. I'm glad it feels natural to both of us. He's a great listener. So far, we can reason with him on just about everything. Sometimes it's seemed like our talking alone has been soothing for him, even if he doesn't understand the words. I like what we're doing with him, and I just think he's the greatest kid.

The Art of Being Human

As you're teaching your child the art of waiting, keep in mind that for his whole life, he hasn't had to wait. Now you're beginning to change the rules he has come to know. He needs your patience and understanding while his world is changing in rather drastic ways. It's no wonder he's frustrated, scared, questioning, and testing.

As one mother said,

> I want to respect his attempts at independent thinking, but I'm not used to him saying "No" when I tell him something. He's always been so agreeable. I know he's feeling confident when he says no. I know he knows it's safe. He knows that I won't go away or get angry at him. That's terrific. I've worked hard these last two-and-a-half years so he can feel confident and good about himself. There are times when it's difficult to not get, or sound, angry, because I am angry, or at least annoyed when his wants conflict with mine, and with having to take the time and make the effort to try to get them in sync. It's a balancing act. We're both learning to sort through how we're feeling so we can be kind and gentle with each other.
>
> I want him to learn that he can say "No." I can get angry, and our world is still safe. He has to learn I still love him and I'll always be

there for him, even though I won't always agree with him. When I leave extra time for explanations and remember that's part of what I want to be doing as his parent, then I'm okay. But when I'm rushed or I forget it's worth the extra effort . . . then I can start sounding shrill as I say, 'I know you want to but we just can't right now. Let's go!' Actually, what I'm saying is that we both have to accept that we're both human.

There is real wisdom in this last quote. The more you can accept your own and your children's humanity, the more loving you'll find yourself being. The more loving you are, the more easily you'll respect and accept their human foibles, including their frustrations, the behaviors that result from their frustrations, and their attempts at independence, however ill-timed they may seem to you. Keep in mind that your frustration and theirs is interwoven. One builds on the other. It's also true that one can de-escalate the other.

What Parents Say

Sylvia: When my son was about two-and-a-half, he was having a rough time one morning. Nothing was right, and he started whining. Before he escalated any more I went over, bent down to his level and asked, "Do you need a Mommy hug?" "Yes," came his reply and we hugged and hugged. When we released each other, he was okay again. It feels so good to do those little loving things that can help him so much.

Thirteen

If You're Wondering About Your Child's Development

*W*HEN YOU'RE WITH A GROUP of parents and children do you find yourself wondering why your child seems to be *so* different? Do you find yourself thinking things like, "Will my child ever settle down, he's been going since I was about six months pregnant, doing cartwheels inside, and now I just can't keep up with him." Do you notice that her attention span seems to be much shorter or much longer than other children's? Do you see other young children running down the street, but your child is barely toddling? Do you feel at the end of your rope too often? Are you noticing that your child doesn't blend in with the crowd of babies you know? Do other toddlers seem much less aggressive than yours? Why is it always your child who's being given a time-out? Why is you're child the one biting when his peers seem to have grown out of that a long time ago?

Perhaps at first you thought you had a mellow baby, but now you're thinking this is going too far. She doesn't get excited about anything. It's hard to engage her. She doesn't want to play with other children. Or your baby gets scared too easily, then he begins to scream, people look at you as if you're mistreating him, when all you're trying to do is comfort him. But he won't be comforted. You may have tried the techniques in this book, but they just aren't working or aren't bringing you the results you can see other people getting. You have nagging, reoccurring worries when you think about your child's moods or behaviors. Friends and relatives try to reassure you, but when you see your child doing _____ you again think that you shouldn't ignore it because something may be wrong. Or maybe it's a different reaction from relatives and friends. Maybe they look at you and wonder what you're doing wrong with your baby and why you don't set limits and stop his _____ behavior. Are you getting lots of advice that *they* swear by, but that doesn't work when you try it with your child?

The "Wondering If" Stage

How do you know if there's really something *wrong* or if what you're seeing is just slightly outside the edge of the normal range of development? How do you decide if you just need more patience, and your baby just needs more time to get through a difficult stage? Most parents who wonder about their child go through a process before they can ask for professional help. Denial comes first—"No, I'm just being a worry wart." Or "Come on, give him a break, he's just a little energetic." Or "Not every child walks by fifteen months, he's just on his own schedule." Or "Okay, so his speech seems to be delayed, but look at how observant he is. He points so well, he doesn't have to say anything." Or "It can't be anything serious, his father and I don't have any of these kinds of problems. He'll be okay." And he may be okay. Sometimes parents feel too scared, too ashamed, too hopeless, or too alone to find out if their concerns are valid.

There are also parents who go the opposite direction: "There's something wrong, I know it, I just don't know what it is yet." Or "There's got to be something wrong, otherwise she'd be doing _____ by now." Other parents' expectations are too high, and their child is just developing along her own unique path. There are so many possibilities for how you may be feeling and what you're thinking as you try to reassure yourself yet deal with your nagging questions at the same time.

Sometimes you can lose patience with your young child and be angry that she's not doing what the other children are doing. You can feel insecure, wondering if your parenting skills are causing the problems. "Why can't I comfort her?" Or "Why does he arch his back when I try to hold and comfort him. He doesn't seem to want me near him at all. Is it me?" You can find your emotions ricocheting all over the map.

Here are several examples of what confused parents experience:

- **Fear:** "How can she cope with life if she continues to behave this way?" "Won't the kids tease her unmercifully?"
- **Worry:** "What if she never talks?" "How will she have friends if she doesn't want to be around these sweet little babies? What will she do when they get to be sassy three year olds if she's intimidated by sweet babies?"
- **Sadness:** "I wanted to be a parent so badly, but seeing him struggle just to tolerate a little noise . . . this is making me so sad. Will he ever fit in with 'normal' kids?"
- **Anger:** "I don't have the time between working and keeping up with the house to go to all these appointments. And where, tell me, where is the money going to come from to pay for all the therapies this kid needs? Why can't she just be like other kids?"
- **Disappointment:** "I waited so long for this baby. I dreamed about how it would be when we went from being a couple to having a family. This was never in any of my dreams. I didn't think I'd be comforting a child who couldn't accept my nurturing."
- **Hope:** "Maybe when we go see the next professional (occupational therapist, speech therapist, neurologist, child psychiatrist, or child development specialist) she'll be able to figure it out and help us. It'll be okay. We can cope. Someone will have the key to unlock the mystery box inside my child."
- **Bargaining:** "If I wait two months, he'll probably grow out of this. He's just going through a fussy stage."

All these feelings are normal. They're part of the process of coming to grips with knowing if you need to seek help for your baby. You're not an expert; you don't know how to interpret what you're experiencing. And you don't know what to do about what you and your baby are experiencing. You don't want to alter the picture you had in your mind of how things were supposed to be in your family. You ask yourself, "Wouldn't it be easier to accept people's reassurances?" But then there's one more incredible tantrum in public. There's one more aggressive incident. There's one more parent looking at your toddler oddly when your baby is off in the corner and the other toddlers are running around the room having fun.

Deciding to Seek an Outside Opinion

If your child continues to look, act, and feel outside the developmental guidelines you've read about in this and other books, and the differences are apparent in a variety of settings, you probably want to seek more information about what may be happening. Another way to decide if you should seek help is to consider your life. If you're spending a good deal of time trying to figure "it" out (what your child is doing that's disturbing you) and worrying, it's probably time to ask what trusted family members, a pediatrician, and/or a child development specialist think. Another criterion to consider is whether you find yourself reorganizing your life in order to help your child fit in or to accommodate your child's needs. If so, your concerns and questions may mean that you're in tune with your child and you're the first person to acknowledge that something needs attention. You know your child better than anybody else.

Questions You'll Want to Ask Yourself

You'll want to look at different areas of your child's life as you prepare to share your concerns with someone who may be able to help you figure out what's happening with your child. Does your baby have unusual patterns of interacting with people? Does your baby have unusual patterns when interacting with toys? Does he need to line trucks, cars, or blocks up in a row rather than engaging in more creative play with the toys? Does your baby want to play with only one or two toys all the time? Does your baby scream when other people come into the room? Is your child consistently in the corner while other toddlers are mingling during play dates? Does your baby have developmental delays or differences that exceed everything you've read and seen around you? Do you feel like you're able to do what you're reading about in this and other parenting books, but your baby isn't responding the way the books describe?

Do you see things that are worrisome about your young child's general behavior, her language and communication, or her social interactions? Is your child's temperament, mood, or behavior extreme? Is he chronically frustrated? Is she unbelievably irritated at anything that crosses her path, or for no reason at all? Take a close look at your baby's interactions with adults and with other babies. When is he comfortable in his skin? How does she communicate? Does he have trouble holding things? Is she a very slow crawler? These are all areas you'll want to consider. Take notes at home to detail your concerns so you can bring them with you and provide an accurate picture to the professionals you're consulting.

Stressful Cycles You Want to Avoid

As you begin to see patterns in your young child's moods or behaviors that don't match what you know they're supposed to be doing, you can get anxious and concerned, and for good reason. But you'll want to avoid common stressful cycles. When you're anxious, it can trigger a vicious cycle affecting you, your young child, and your spouse. If you're anxious when you're around your child, she'll probably feel your anxiety. She may interpret your anxiety as meaning the world is not a safe place for some reason. If your anxiety persists, she will react by being more stressed. When she reacts with more stress, her behavior and mood will change—probably not in a positive direction. You see her stressed behaviors and interpret them as the very problem you're worried about getting worse. You become more scared and anxious when you're around her, she gets more stressed, and so on. You can create a problem that didn't exist before your anxiety triggered it, or you can exacerbate a real problem when you have anxiety and let it build in both of you instead of seeking answers or solutions.

When you're anxious about your child's behaviors or moods and your spouse is not, that can create stress, friction, and distance between you two. Your spouse may be as convinced that what you're worried about is nothing, as *you* are that it *is* something. During discussions with your spouse, remember to be gentle, kind, respectful, and supportive of each other when you disagree. You two may decide to respectfully disagree and still move forward to seek an outside, knowledgeable opinion so you can get your questions answered. I will offer one caveat. Sometimes it can turn out that you're worried, your spouse is not, and your spouse agrees to seek a professional's advice so you can stop worrying. The professional says all is well but you still don't believe your child is developing as she should. Your spouse says, "See, I told you everything was fine, now can you just relax?" You may want to go home and relax a little. But, if you continue to see behaviors and moods that concern you, observe and take notes about what you're seeing that you think is out of the ordinary. If you find your child's developmental problems continue, you may want to seek a second opinion. Experts are not always right. If your baby is not developing (cognitively, socially, emotionally, language skills, or physically) as she should, you will need to become your child's advocate and seek a professional with more expertise in developmental problems.

First Steps

Your first step is probably going to be talking with your spouse or partner. What if he or she thinks you're worried for nothing? Do you pursue it? And if so, how do you pursue it? Sometimes it's really difficult for a parent to see the child, who they love and who they have high hopes for, as someone who might have something out of the ordinary to contend with. It can be a very emotionally charged issue for a parent to face. Do you have any friends who work with special needs children? You can ask them for their input, especially if your spouse has trouble seeing what you're seeing as a real problem.

If you have access to the Internet, you can begin to explore the symptoms you're seeing and are concerned about. Sometimes having the words in black and white helps parents talk about what they may be seeing in their own child. It's not unusual for the parent who spends more time with the baby to be the first to say, "Hey, we need to talk, I'm worried about this problem." And for the reasons we've just outlined, it's not unusual for the other parent to minimize at first. This is where some gentle, respectful discussions are needed. You're both feeling vulnerable and scared and possibly stubborn about your perspective. Slow down. Listen to each other well. Validate each other's perspective. And then decide on a course of action, which you can both live with.

When parents decide to seek explanations and answers they usually turn first to their pediatrician. It may be helpful to make an appointment with your pediatrician without your child so you and your partner (if possible) can talk about your concerns, give examples, and have your pediatrician's full attention. This may be an emotional meeting for you, so bring in your notes, they can remind you of everything you wanted to talk about. The more specific examples you can provide your pediatrician in terms of your baby's moods and behaviors, the easier time your physician will have developing an accurate picture of what you're dealing with. Your first visit with the pediatrician is your first step in an assessment to see if "it's" serious enough to pursue.

Your pediatrician will probably ask you to bring your child in for a follow-up visit so she can see what you're talking about. Sometimes during a brief office visit your pediatrician may not see the concerning behaviors that you encounter at home. You'll need to reinforce your concerns and describe how different things are at home. Remember you have your baby for hours at a time, the pediatrician is seeing your baby for just a few minutes.

If your pediatrician does see something that raises red flags or at least bright pink warning flags, she will probably refer you to a child development specialist who can narrow down the areas to be examined in more detail. If your pediatrician does not see a problem, you might try taking that perspective for a while. But if you're still convinced from continued careful observations that your child isn't developing as he should, then it may be prudent to trust your instincts and go for a second opinion, or even a third and fourth if necessary.

Unfortunately, in this age of managed care and rising health care costs, some professionals who are not child development or learning specialists may think the parent is making a mountain out of a molehill, and in an attempt to keep costs down, they may attempt to discourage you from seeking another opinion. They may misinterpret your concern and peg you as parent who wants his child to be super-smart or super-special and cannot be satisfied with normal. Remember that you know your child better than anybody else. One mother's story at the end of this chapter is an excellent example of an astute mother who identified a problem with her child only to be stymied by the system for quite a few years.

If you're concerned about your child, pursue your concerns. The advantage of early detection, early identification, and early intervention with the right mix of services is that your child will be more likely to maximize her potential by learning to deal with any differences early in life. Every state has an Early Intervention Program (EI), which serves young children up until the age of three. Once a child is three years old, then the federally-funded special-education preschool programs assess and provide necessary interventions. In addition, larger cities often have teaching hospitals with child development clinics or private clinics where a multi-disciplinary assessment can be done. Your pediatrician may refer you to one of these programs or you can refer yourself.

Early Intervention programs usually send someone (or a team) to your house to conduct a home visit so they can become familiar with your child's environment and provide an assessment from a developmental educator's perspective. The educator will look at a variety of things including your child's play skills, social interactions, and attachments with her parents and caregivers. After this initial screening, your child may be assessed by an occupational therapist, a speech and language therapist, or a physical therapist. They can provide services your child may need.

When you have some direction, try to find the right (set of) professional(s) to help your child if it's more than the EI team can provide. A variety of professionals help babies, toddlers, and two-year-old children with special problems including occupational therapists, speech and language pathologists, physical therapists, pediatric neurologists, pediatricians, developmental and behavioral pediatricians, early childhood educators, early intervention specialists, child development specialists, and child psychiatrists, psychologists, and social workers. Some parents also seek help from nutritionists, homeopaths, acupuncturists, and toxicologists. Choosing your team of specialists may be daunting or overwhelming at first, but breaking the process into small manageable steps will enable you to find your way through the maze of alternatives.

Finding Support for Your Family

Extended families can be wonderful sources of support or they may undermine your efforts until they understand you're not exaggerating your child's difficulties. When family members are interested and supportive, they can be a tremendous source of support for you and your family. Friends can also be supportive. You'll need to decide what to tell people and how to tell them. It's often helpful to tell friends and family what's happening in a descriptive way rather than throwing out a label or two. You can share what you're experiencing with your child by giving family members or good friends specific examples of your child's moods and behaviors.

For instance, if your child has trouble filtering out stimuli and gets very upset and inconsolable in situations with too much stimuli, you may want to share how you've learned to modify the environment to make it easier for your young child to function. For instance, "We've learned that when we're having dinner, it's easier for Hannah if we don't play music in the background." You might need to explain to a friend why you wouldn't bring him to a party even though twenty-five of your closest friends are anxious to meet your baby. "You know I'd love to bring him, but we're finding that Eric does a lot better with only one or two people around. He really has trouble in larger crowds or when there's a lot of stimulation. His little body just can't take it all in, and he gets very upset. We can't calm him down at times like that unless we leave. So we're learning to respect his limits and avoid situations that would make him so uncomfortable." You could decline the invitation completely; you could offer to come and bring pictures of Eric while your spouse stays home with the baby; or you could look for a babysitter so your spouse could come too.

Another explanation might sound like, "We've found that Caleb gets upset when his food isn't separated and it becomes mushed together on his plate. It's easier for him to stay calm when we can separate the different foods. So at Thanksgiving, you'll see Caleb eating from his special plate that we'll bring with us." Most people are unfamiliar with labels and diagnoses or they can bring up a stereotyped image that doesn't have much to do with your child. You want your child to be real, not a diagnosis, for the important people in your lives. Descriptions work better as a way to initially explain what's happening in your family.

A parent with a young child who has developmental differences to one degree or another doesn't have to feel isolated or alone. All kinds of parent support systems and groups are available through organizations, specialists, and on the Internet. A useful place to start may be www.firstsigns.org. This site is "dedicated to the early identification and intervention of children with developmental delays and disorders." The professionals you're working with will also be able to steer you to appropriate resources for you and your family.

You may have to actively advocate for your child once you've identified his unique issues. Don't be shy. Get right in there and insist that your pediatrician, your state-run early intervention program, and your school system (if your child is three or older) identify your child's developmental differences and address them early on. You may consider hiring someone who knows his or her way around your community and school system to be an advocate for you and your child.

Summary

It's better for everyone if you learn your child's unique way of operating within the world as early as possible, then you can do more to help your child and guide her unique way of being. We do know that early intervention is often much more effective than delayed interventions. You read about how flexible a baby's brain is in the first few years of life and how rapidly it's developing in the brain science research chapter. If possible, you want to begin interventions and therapies during a child's early development so there's more room for flexibility, new connections, and early learning to take place. Early interventions will also help address any situation before a child starts comparing him or herself to others and feeling inadequate, less than, or *too* different.

One mom said: "I noticed when my son was an infant that he was doing these funny things with his hands—clenching his fists and rolling them. I later found out this was called *stimming*. I thought maybe he was just playing with them or something . . . but when he was around one year old, he was doing it more intensely. Then I noticed he played differently—you know, when some kids play with cars they make sounds, make them crash, or pretend to go somewhere—well my son would line them up and stare at them; he didn't really *play* with them. I talked to my pediatrician who told me to relax. Yet I knew from experience as a teacher and motherly instinct that what I was seeing was odd.

Those first few years, people were telling me I should just relax would really bug me. They made me feel like I was looking for something to be wrong with my child. We took him to a few specialists and when they didn't see him do what we were describing, the doctors kept telling us it was okay. But my instincts were saying, "no it's not." They finally started taking us more seriously when I provided videotapes of his behavior. But still they couldn't identify what was happening.

After three years of no answers I talked to a good friend of mine who works with PPD—Persuasive Developmental Disorders. She guided me to the best doctors in the field and shared current research and connected me to other parents and professionals for support. It was through her direct intervention that we were able to see someone who could tell us what was happening. My child finally was diagnosed with Asperger's Syndrome.

They tell me it was difficult to diagnose because my son is so high functioning and only borderline symptomatic. He doesn't know how to initiate a conversation or how to continue one if it doesn't relate to his interests. Right now we're lucky because he's liked by his peers and they seem to compensate for his lack of social skills. But, if he doesn't get the help he needs, he'll be that odd kid—the one that can talk on and on about a subject he's interested in, but not be able to socialize properly, interact, and ask questions. He can spew out information if he's asked, but he can't read a face to know it's enough. As he gets older I worry that kids won't want to play with him—that he'll be one of the nerds.

He needs special help, and now we're fighting the schools. The saddest thing is that sometimes you have to be rich to get your kid help. We'll have to take a second mortgage on our home if we have to fight the school system in a legal battle to get the correct services the doctors and current research say he needs. Even to pay an expert advocate to fight for us with the school system costs a lot. I'm a teacher, and I can't get people to respond to me when I'm just on my own. I need an outside expert; a mother's instinct or quoting the law to a school system just isn't always enough. School budgets these days are tight, and they sometimes can't afford to give the latest services to all the kids that need them unless they are made to do so in a legal battle.

We started trying to figure this out when my son was one. We went through a state run program called Early Intervention. But it took almost four years to get the diagnosis—it was four years before we knew exactly what was wrong. What if I hadn't been so persistent? What if I hadn't believed my own instincts over the first few doctors' diagnoses of "no problem—the mother needs to relax?"

You have to fight for your kid if you know there's something wrong. Don't be afraid to ask questions and get outside opinions. It's been a nightmare for four years. At least we know what we're fighting for now, we know what our child needs to become a happy, socialized and productive part of society. I won't give up. This is my child's life. It's his future."

* * *

Another mom said: "My son couldn't keep up with other kids his age because of developmental delays. I didn't know that at first. I practiced patience and encouragement, and it brought him further each time there was a delay. He started walking at eighteen months, but I had to push him to try. My real confusion came when his speech was delayed. He wouldn't speak much at all. A word now and then, and then to my surprise a full sentence would come out of nowhere. So I thought with encouragement and patience this delay would be corrected too. He was walking, it had taken a while but he was doing it. I was shocked out of my denial by my stepmother telling me that I needed to face the fact that I had a retarded son. I still wasn't sure I wanted to face what she was saying, but because I wanted to do what was right for my son, I went to a pediatrician and followed his recommendations.

We started audio and speech assessments at Children's Hospital. My spouse supported my efforts. Different therapies, such as sign language, were used by Children's

Hospital to help my son. We then went to Head Start. We couldn't afford expensive therapy. Head Start was the best choice because they do all the testing for the public schools, and when my child began kindergarten he was already enrolled in special programs. I learned how to teach my son through his special education teachers and personal experiences. As a parent you often feel lost and confused.

My son is in his twenties now. I realize that I was his first teacher and I will always be a teacher for him as long as he needs me. I was able to teach him to do math on a calculator and then we went on to learning how to use a checkbook and how to keep a budget. It took a long time, but it happened. I also taught him to drive, and he passed his driver's test.

All children are different. We need to encourage them and understand the fear and stress they encounter when they learn something new. Patience, determination, and helping them to believe in themselves are very important elements. Never discount the human spirit. It's amazing what children with disabilities can do when they believe in themselves.

Fourteen

Helping Your Child with Transitions

TRANSITIONS ARE TIMES AND CIRCUMSTANCES that change your routines and your child's routines. Some children love change and find it exciting while others prefer things to stay the same. It often doesn't matter whether a first or second transition is a major transition or a minor one. How you handle the first few transitions with your child may set the stage for how he handles changes later in life. Transitions can include mom going from being home full-time to not home full-time; we have been living here, now we're going to live there; I used to nurse, now I'm not. Your child's first big transition may be that mommy and daddy used to live together, and now they're going to live in two houses. *That* is such a complex transition for everyone that the next chapter (15) is devoted to divorce and making the transition from parenting in one home to co-parenting in two loving, safe homes.

No matter what the nature or degree of the change, remember, you're anticipating and judging the experience from your adult perspective. To your child, who's learning to deal with the newness of life in general, a change may be taken in stride because she doesn't have any fears or anxieties built up from previous changes to impose on this one, or she can become very upset because her little psyche doesn't like changes and she needs stability to feel safe. You can help her by being as calm and understanding as possible, so some of her world feels stable. If you try to hide the change from her or shield her from it, she may be frightened because she perceives things being different, but no one is taking the time to introduce the new ideas to her. She may not feel safe unless you introduce her to the change and help her adjust to it. Children will often follow your lead. If you're calm and prepared, they will feel safer and often mirror your behavior in a transition. If you plan things well and make the necessary preparations, going through transitions smoothly is just another learning experience for both of you, no matter how old you are and no matter how old your child is.

Always keep your child's perspective in mind. To a very young child, if something is packed into a box (for an anticipated move), it doesn't exist anymore. She may mourn the loss of a favorite toy. As an adult you know it will get unpacked soon, but it's difficult for a child to get the concept of soon—she only knows now or never. Thus, if you're moving or changing rooms around in your house and your child begins to get agitated, you'll need to stop and reassure her that this is for now, not forever. If your family is moving, it's a good idea to pack your child's room last so that your child endures the fewest disruptions possible.

Sometimes parents forget, and think that because they have helped prepare a child for an imminent change, once they are into or through the change, everything should be fine. Then the parent gets frustrated or annoyed that their child isn't *fine,* or they second-guess themselves, wondering what they did wrong or what they could have done better to prepare their child. As the parent, you may not have done anything wrong. You may simply have a child who perceives change as difficult and scary rather than something else she does in a day. Until you're part-way through a large change in your child's routine, you really won't be able to predict how your child will relate to the change process. And change is a process. There are the preparations beforehand, the change itself, and then settling into a new routine.

For instance, if you've been a stay-at-home parent and you're returning to the work force, there will be a number of steps you'll take, which creates an environment full of change: you'll look for a job or talk to your employer about a return date; you'll mentally adjust yourself to going back and dealing with adults all day instead of a baby; you'll begin trying on clothes or taking your baby with you to buy work clothes; you'll begin hunting for suitable child care arrangements—in your home, in someone else's home, or at a child care center—which may include numerous telephone calls and personal visits; you'll bring your child to visit for a short time and gradually increase the time at the child care setting; and you'll eventually have your actual first day back at work. But the transition isn't over then.

You still have to deal with your reactions to the changes, your child's reactions, what will happen the first time your child is sick and needs to come home, and whether you or your partner will pick her up. Then there are often psychological struggles that you thought you'd sail through. They might include what you do with your guilt and anxiety about leaving your child; your guilt at enjoying your work; your trepidation that someone else can really provide your baby with the love you had been providing; or maybe the guilt that you're a little relieved to be among adults for part of your time; or resentment that you have to work when all that's important to you is being a full-time mother to your baby and you can't have that one wish because of economic realities.

Any larger transition in life will be similar, with a number of things taking place over a period of time before and after the actual change itself. You will need to be sensitive to yourself, your partner, and your child throughout the entire period. Helping your child through transitions is a lot like performing a balancing act with various shaped objects, because there are so many different factors involved. You have to take into account preparing yourself, preparing your child, timing, dealing with your own personal background about change, dealing with transitions as a family process—as well as how to give and get support throughout the process so you're not drained of your own creative energy. That's a lot to keep track of.

In preparing your child, you'll want to talk to her about the impending change, walk her through it as best you can, and then hope she makes the transition as smoothly as possible. It helps if you can stay physically and emotionally close and calm with your child during the change itself, so you can support your child through any rough spots she encounters along the way. The following are Respectful Parenting strategies for dealing with transitions.

- **Keep your child's ability to cope with change in mind when planning transitions.**
- **Slow down the process** so you can all be rational and decide things with a first-things-first strategy.
- **As you introduce the actual transition to your child, look, listen,**

and feel your child's reactions with a willingness to compromise if possible. If a job opportunity has you moving in two months and you know you can't pass up the opportunity, you can still let your young child in on certain aspects of the decision-making process.

- **Prepare your child for the transition by introducing your child slowly to new things.** Engage and encourage your child to participate however he can.
- **Remember that you are an adult and change may be difficult for you in spite of lots of coping tools you have.** Remember that your child doesn't have all the years of life experience that you have. Be gentle and bring him along with you rather than pulling him into place.

Easing Your Child Through Transitions

Something new can be experienced as anything along a spectrum from exciting and engaging to paralyzing depending upon the new thing itself and how a person reacts to it. You, your child, and your partner may have different strategies for moving though a transition. Be alert to your child's reactions, and offer support whenever it's needed. Easing through a transition patiently is usually better than pushing everyone to get through it as quickly as possible.

Communicate

Some people believe small children (under two or three years old) don't need to be included in the change process. They believe small children can't understand or don't notice changes happening around them. Respectful Parenting assumes children will pick up enough cues on their own—noticing that change is in the air—that they deserve, are entitled to, and need an explanation as soon as your behavior and attitudes concerning the change spill into their world.

If babies, toddlers, and especially two-year-olds aren't included in the process, they'll make their own interpretations based on their sense of your changed energies, attitudes, and attentions. They'll know something in their world is amiss. When they're left out, they're more likely to develop fear and anxiety about why their world is suddenly different and what the differences they're sensing might mean. If your pattern of coping is silence, they'll probably take their cues from you. Instead of asking,

"Mommy what's wrong?" or "Daddy's angry?" they're likely to not question you and instead may act out their uncertainties and fears.

During transitional times, you're often overworked and stressed from trying to cope with your normal responsibilities as well as the added tasks and emotional baggage involved with the change. So, when your child acts out, you may not be able to react in as patient and understanding a way as usual; couple that with any unresolved stuff you have about going through changes in your early life, as well as how your own parents dealt with it, and you have a potentially negative set-up. You get more upset. Your child gets scared. She acts out. You get angry at her. She is more stressed and scared. She acts out more . . . and a downward spiral can be set in motion.

On the other hand, if you are open and talk about what the whole family is experiencing and why, your child will learn that it's safe to ask questions and ask for support; communicating helps reduce stress from the unknown. Your child won't have to demand reassurance in an indirect way that might not get her the kind of loving energy she's really looking for.

Stay Calm

When you're respectfully parenting your child, you become very close. You're intuitively connected to each other. Your child will therefore be aware of what you feel. He'll pick up on your mood shifts and swings. In order to help your baby feel safe when you're with him, you need to be as much your old self as possible. This way your baby knows external changes may be happening, but his mom and dad are still the same, so he's safe. That will help your baby tremendously and will be an important lesson in the differences between inside and outside changes and how you can feel stable when changes are happening around you.

Time It Right

Along with advocating openness, you need to consider one qualifier: timing. Timing is extremely important. You'll need to remember that a child's time frame is different than an adult's time frame. If you tell your child too soon, she may have too much time to conjure up all kinds of anxious anticipation. Or she may get impatient and feel like it's never going to happen. If you tell her too late, then she's already picked up cues from your behavior that she hasn't been able to interpret, and her behavior and yours will be a mismatch. That can lead to mutual discomfort until you straighten out what she thinks is happening from what is happening.

There's no set rule for knowing exactly when to tell your child about upcoming events. It depends upon her developmental abilities, how she copes with change, and the upcoming change itself. The key is to let her know as much as she can handle as soon as you feel like your emotional or physical energy is changing and impacting your child. Share the process with her, so she's not reacting to perceived differences without an accurate context to understand what's happening in her world. Even if she doesn't understand all the concepts, she'll feel safer if secrets aren't in the air.

One mother was trying to decide when to tell her child that she was pregnant. She didn't want to tell him until she was showing because, even then, four months would be an eternity for a two-and-a-half-year-old. The parents decided to wait. Unfortunately, nature didn't cooperate. During her second month, this mom experienced a significant drop in her energy level. She often needed to rest and nap. Her son became anxious. "Mommy sick? Mommy get better? Why Mommy not play?" became his refrain.

After thinking about the pros and cons, this mother decided to tell her son that she was really quite healthy and that she had a baby seed growing inside her. She reminded him of all the seeds they had planted in the spring and how they had to wait a long time for the flowers to grow. Since this mother had had a couple of miscarriages already, she didn't want her son to have too much false hope, so she added a caveat to the metaphor. She reminded her son that a lot of the seeds they planted didn't grow into flowers and they couldn't be sure this baby seed would become a real live baby. Like with the plant seeds, they had to be patient.

Perhaps because this little boy had experienced beginning the garden and waiting, his mother's explanation sufficed. His anxiety lowered, and he was content to play near her when she was resting.

Sympathize

If you take the time to think and act using Respectful Parenting techniques when your child is acting out, you'll be able to gather your anxious child in your arms and reassure him that, "Yes, things feel different, but Mommy and Daddy are still here with you." You can remember to view your child's behavior as his attempt to get something from you that will make his world feel safe and stable again. He probably first tried a more subtle approach that you didn't notice. Now, in desperation, he's trying something that's more likely to get your attention. An understanding and supportive response, assuming a positive intent on his part, would be the Respectful Parenting way to cope. Old-style parents would assume a stance of anger toward the child for adding more of a burden to them by being oppositional.

If you are able to stay present with your children during these times, it will initially involve more emotional and physical energy, but it will smooth the transition—thus saving you energy in the long run. Yes, you have to take care of all the adult details involved in whatever change you're going through, but you have to be there with extra reassurance, love, and playtime for your child even when you're scared, anxious, and stressed yourself.

Perhaps the hardest part is accepting how powerless you may feel watching your children going through these transitions. You can help smooth a transition by preparing your children, but ultimately, it's your children who go through the transition themselves, making their own choices, which you'll react to as respectfully and honestly as possible. Their emotions can run the gamut from delight and excitement to dis-comfort and downright misery. Your children will definitely take cues from you, so if you validate and respect their feelings and show them how you're handling your own, they won't feel as lost. Your reactions will rub off on them. The more you respect their reactions, the more you validate their feelings, the faster life will settle down.

When Nothing Else Works

When this scenario doesn't work so smoothly, it will help if you realize that after properly preparing your child, after sympathizing until you're losing your patience, after hugs and loving hasn't worked, the best thing you can do is let your small child know that you have faith in her and her ability to cope. Reassure your child that the transitional bumpiness will smooth out and life will be okay again.

There's one exception to waiting until the transition works itself out: if your child's complaints center around her child care situation, visiting at a friend's house, or unusual things happening with someone you know and trust, before you blithely take the tact that everything really is okay, make sure your child's complaints or uncomfortable feelings are not based in reality. In other words, make sure there isn't something real going on in the situation that's causing your child's discomfort. Children do get physically abused, emotionally traumatized, and sexually molested. Unfortunately, you can't blindly rule out these possibilities. When you suspect that any of these things has happened, make several unannounced visits at various times. Talk over your fears with someone else who is more familiar with the situation. If you're still not feeling secure about your child's safety, please call in outside assistance to investigate.

If all seems to be going well, then you can breathe a sigh of relief. Try to remind yourself that all life transitions involve emotional changes. It's the degree that varies. See if you can view your child's first transition as the biggest of her life, because it's the only one she's experienced so far. For that matter, her first few changes may seem monumental and scary because she doesn't have previous experience to draw from. For instance, to you, a new babysitter may not be a big deal. You've interviewed the sitter. You feel comfortable. You've talked about it in advance with your small child, but not so far in advance as to cause too much anticipation on your child's part. You know the person is safe. You know you'll only be gone a few hours. You're okay—so why isn't your child?

Try to understand that you have put your own mind at ease. Your emotions are under control. You may be a little sad at leaving your baby for the first time, or the first time in a long time, but you know that's a natural response. Your child's perspective is different. She sees you leaving. She feels your different energy. She sees you leaving her with a stranger. She knows you've talked, but all of sudden you're leaving and she doesn't want you to go.

If you sympathize for a little while, but then get uncomfortable with her feelings because you can't make it better for her, give yourself a time-out. Consider the scenario from your child's perspective. Acknowledge her increasing discomfort and try to identify where it's coming from. You don't want to make the change uncomfortable or scary. Change is an integral part of life and if your child is conditioned at an early age to dislike changes, life is going to be difficult for her.

Take some deep breaths. Go back ready to be with your child, talk soothingly, and accept where she's at. She deserves your acceptance and respect for her feelings, even if it's inconvenient for you. You can't always make it better. Sometimes feelings have to stick around for a while, even uncomfortable ones. That's a real part of life.

Try to see the bigger picture. Instill a sense of delight with change through your words and actions. Don't be afraid of your children's emotions. Don't try to will them away. Guide them through the process, explaining, planning, looking at the brighter side, and acknowledging the not-so-bright side. Your goals during your children's transitions are to be encouraging, yet not pushy, validating their concerns and fears, without reinforcing their fears to a very scary place, and being hopeful, yet realistic, until whatever change they are dealing with is okay with them.

Some Common Transitions

In previous chapters, I have dealt with developmental milestones that are also transitions for children and parents, such as learning to use a potty or giving up a pacifier. The following sections discuss other common transitions in children's lives.

Beginning Child Care or Preschool

At some point, usually before kindergarten and often anywhere from six weeks to three years old, a child will begin spending time in child care or a preschool. It's difficult to predict how your child will react, especially if this is your child's first major transition. Planning and preparation for you and your child will go a long way. We looked at how to choose a child care setting in Chapter 6. Even though you've done a thorough job in choosing a child care setting, your child will still be going through major changes. Your child's transition begins with the first visit to the child care setting. Choose a time of day when your child is alert, aware, and interactive. Don't take him when he's hungry or tired. You could tell him that you've checked this place out, you really like it, and you're wondering how he likes it. Even if he's preverbal, your thoughtfulness will somehow come through. When you're there for your first visit, make it a short one—twenty to thirty minutes, tops; that way your child won't feel overwhelmed, especially if he's used to being home alone with you. Afterward, if your child is verbal, ask him what he liked about the place and if there was anything he didn't like. Take his concerns seriously and address them individually.

Go back a few more times before enrolling your child. You might extend each visit a little longer so your child gets used to being there for longer time periods. Make it a fun, exciting change. Talk about how proud you are of how beautifully your child is growing up and how much fun you know he'll have with the other children.

After beginning the program, continue to take your child's feelings seriously. Get the staff involved if necessary. It's also a good idea to make surprise visits to see what's happening when the program staff doesn't expect you to be around. You can do this even if your child isn't complaining about anything. If your child is having nightmares or reacting very differently than before you placed him in the program, it's especially important to check out the program at unexpected times to make sure your child is being treated well.

Some children may have a difficult time adjusting no matter what you do. I remember our child care center staff saying that if a child care center isn't introduced before a child is nine months old, an older child will have a much more difficult adjustment. Before nine months, it's a relatively easy transition, because he isn't experiencing "stranger anxiety" thus adjusting to new people is easier for a child and the child care setting becomes what the child knows, and it feels natural to him to be dropped off. Each child is a unique individual, however, and will react in his or her own way. If your time for child care is delayed and your child is a few years old, in addition to visiting the center, you can try to find some books where children go to child care and enjoy it. These would be very helpful to read to your child.

As with any transition, the more you prepare, the better idea your child has, the more familiar he is with the change, the easier it will be on him. In addition, if your child senses that you feel good, that you're comfortable with the place, that you believe it's safe, and that you've been careful in your decision making about the situation, your child will feel your ease and most probably copy it.

Moving

In our current, highly mobile society, many families will move at least once before their child is in kindergarten. Moves may be family motivated or job related. Regardless of the reason for such a move, many factors will be similar. You'll all be leaving the stability of a home and community you all know. You may be moving to a place where you don't have a support network. A good real estate agent can be surprisingly helpful. They can introduce you to organizations or activities in the new place that can make your transition easier. Many community churches sponsor "Mom's

Day Out" programs once or twice a week, so after you arrive you can take advantage of them for a couple of adult days to unpack or explore.

As soon as you know a move is imminent, before the "For Sale" sign goes up in your front yard, your child should to be brought into the picture. Age-appropriate books such as *Moving House* by A. Civardi are fun ways to introduce the change. If you're visiting a new town, spend part of the day looking at houses or apartments and spend part of the time in a park or children's museum so your child gets to see how much fun this new place will be.

Pictures of your new town or home will help during the packing phase. You can make a little photo album of your "moving adventure" from start to finish. The most important thing is to ask your child for input wherever possible, such as which house she likes the best (from the ones you want to choose), why she likes it, and which room she'd like as her bedroom. If you're eating out a lot during the process, ask your child what she wants to eat and go to a restaurant where she'll get her favorite (comfort) foods. Moving can be experienced as a family adventure.

In the following examples, parents dealt with changes as just another thing families were going to do together or as a fun family adventure. You'll see how small children take their parents' leads. Transitions were viewed as interesting, problem-solving situations rather than onerous tasks. They also provide wonderful opportunities to teach your child sound decision making skills.

What Parents Say

Sarah: The hardest transition with my child so far has been when I dropped him off at child care for the first time. He was four months old. He was only going to be there a few hours a day, four days a week. I was even going to be able to visit and nurse him halfway through his day, three of the four days. We had visited the child care center several times the week before for a few hours. I had talked to him about needing to go back to work and how he'd be at the child care center while I worked.

I thought I had accepted reality—I needed to work and he needed to be in child care. I knew in my heart and mind this was a good child care center and he'd get good, loving care from the caregivers. Yet, as I dropped him off, I had a lump in my throat as big as Mount Everest. He was fine. I hugged him and reassured him that I'd be back soon. Then one of the caregivers took him in her arms and crouched on the floor so he could become acquainted with the other infants. He raised his head and looked around with interest. As I said good-bye and walked away, I watched his reactions carefully. He tracked me with his eyes and he was still fine.

I stood outside the door for a couple of minutes to make sure he wasn't going to have a delayed reaction to me leaving. I swear I would have torn back in there and grabbed him if I had heard him crying. He didn't. I knew he was attached to me. I could see he had a healthy sense of security. I think he intuitively knew that he was safe and I'd be back. I felt pleased and proud that he was taking my leaving so well. Yet there I was, in the hallway, unable to leave, my eyes filling with tears, my chest tearing itself up. I was surprised by how strongly I felt.

I shed a few tears each of the four days that first week after I dropped him off. My office was only a mile from the child care center, so I didn't cry a lot because I had to be composed when I arrived at work. But each day, a few tears slipped slowly down my cheeks as I felt poignant pangs because I was missing being with my child full time.

He, on the other hand, was easy-going all week. He smiled and cooed when I came to nurse him, and he smiled when I left. One of the caregivers always took him from my arms into her arms to help him with the transition of my leaving and it always worked.

His first transition in life was a positive, easy experience for him, and rather positive for me as well. I learned that he's a pretty easy-going kid. He has a strong sense of himself and a strong sense of inner security. I'm assuming being nursed whenever he asked, being held whenever he asked, and being loved a lot by his mother and father during those first four months at home helped instill his inner sense of security and comfort. I'm sure some of it was a terrific mix of the best genes his father and I had to offer. And I had prepared him well.

I also learned that my son's transitions are transitions for me as well. I had known he'd need preparation, but I was so used to the idea that I go through changes well, I hadn't anticipated my own needs and upsetting reactions. I had definitely underestimated the power of our first major transition on me. From that experience, I learned to anticipate my needs better during times of change.

* * *

Cathy: When my son's caregiver had a baby, he was able to be gentle and responsive when she needed him to be. He would play quietly when she told him her baby was sleeping. I think she had always done such a good job of making him feel special, he was happy to do something for her. Because he was so close to her, I worried over our impending move to a town about forty minutes away; I knew he'd need new child care arrangements, I just didn't know how he would adjust to losing her.

I think it may have been a little easier for him because we were building a new home and we'd often go see how it was progressing. He started getting excited about it, so the move itself and the new house wasn't a surprise to him. I also think losing her was somewhat softened by our excitement about the move, his anticipation, and our talking about how different and fun life was going to be living in the mountains.

After a couple of weeks in the new house he said, "We should go see [the caregiver] and [her son]." Instead we called and she talked to my son. Sometimes that was enough for him. He felt like he had visited, and he'd drop his requests to actually go there. But other times he was more insistent, and we'd go and visit. She still made him feel really special, asking about his new house and new friends. I was glad it was only a forty-minute drive, so it hasn't had to be a clean break. He's kind of eased out of it.

I've taken time off from work, so he hasn't had to establish himself with a new child care provider. I'm also glad he feels comfortable enough to express himself and say he misses her and wants to talk or visit. I've encouraged him to express himself, and it's nice to see that he does; especially those softer feelings, like missing someone... So it's been a pretty easy transition. I don't know what it would have been like if we hadn't been able to visit her occasionally.

* * *

Sylvia: My older son was only a toddler when I found out I was pregnant again. As soon as I started talking about the new baby, I referred to it as his new baby instead of Mommy's new baby. I talked about other children he knew who had babies in their family and stressed how lucky they were. I talked about the new baby I had had when I was growing up, and how that baby grew up to be his aunt (whom he loves). I pointed out babies on the street and reminded him he'd have one of those soon. We liked looking at old baby pictures and videos of when he was a baby. I explained how babies at first can't do anything for themselves, they can't talk, walk, crawl, sit up, or hold toys, so it would be great if he wanted to hold a toy for the baby. I'd explain the different stages he went through as a baby when we were looking at the photo album. I wanted to establish for him how big he was and how much he could do, so he didn't feel like the new baby was taking his place. I had always told him how proud I was of him, but when I was pregnant I would say things about how proud I was about all he could do and tried to really zero in on any new accomplishments he was making.

I was lucky because we had friends who had babies we could spend time with, but if we hadn't, I think I would have rented one of those video baby care films to show him how he could help with the baby. I also tried to help him understand that babies don't stay babies forever, and soon enough they'd be able to play together.

I let my son help me pick out some new rattles and clothes for the baby. He really enjoyed helping me fix up a new room for the baby. He was given the choice of picking out some of his toys and stuffed animals to give to the baby, if he wanted, which he enjoyed doing.

We played with dolls and stuffed animals often, practicing giving them love and having them give him gentle hugs. I gave him lots of gentle love and hugs too, knowing I wanted to prepare him for being loving and tender without having to use words or needing to stop him once the baby arrived. In preparation for the birth itself, I brought him to the hospital where I'd deliver, and he was able to see other newborn babies in the nursery. We discussed over and over again, as the date approached, exactly what would be happening and where he'd stay while I was giving birth, and that he'd get to come visit as soon as the baby was born.

After our new baby's birth he was able to visit within an hour. When he held the baby with such delight, I was thrilled and told him so. I also added, "He's looking at you. I think he likes you." The nurse took a photo of him holding the baby. It's still one of his prized possessions. He was excited about taking the picture to child care and showing his friends and teachers.

When I brought the baby home, I explained that because babies can't talk, they cry when they need things, and together we'd try to figure out what the baby was telling us he needed. I also explained that it took a long time to feed the baby (when it was nursing) but it wouldn't take a long time forever, just until he got bigger. I tried to let my older son make as many decisions as possible, like what his baby brother was going to wear that day, or pick something out for him to look at. I continually tried to stress his abilities and his special place in our family as the oldest child. Sometimes it was a tight balancing act between stressing all he could do and also acknowledging how young he was too, and not expecting too much from him—he was barely out of toddlerhood himself.

One of the more subtle ways I did that was by letting him show people his new brother, instead of me always being the one to show my new baby. When the baby would gaze at him, I'd tell him the baby loved him and wanted to grow up to be like him. A few times he did do things that might have hurt the baby, like throwing toys at him instead of giving them to him. I'd explain it was my job to protect the baby, just like I had protected him when he was a baby, and just like I still protected him if I saw him doing something dangerous. And I told him when his behavior was just not acceptable, although I didn't have to do that often.

I'm glad I thought ahead, planned, and made sure my oldest son did not feel dislodged with the birth of his baby brother. He was so young, he easily could have felt forced out, instead he seemed to naturally take to his new role of being big brother. I do think it helped stressing all he could do, and involving him so much. It wasn't so much me with the baby and him being left out, it was us with the baby, us having fun, and when the baby was sleeping, he and I had our different fun with toys the baby couldn't play with.

Fifteen
When Divorce Becomes the Only Option

MORE THAN HALF of divorce cases being heard in U.S. courtrooms today involve children under the age of five. Unfortunately, some of you may be experiencing the pre-divorce stage of "why is being married so difficult?" You may even be seriously contemplating a divorce or already be in the middle of the divorce process. Perhaps reading this chapter may encourage you and your spouse to work harder on *your part* of what's not working in your marriage before you begin the divorce process. It's so easy to point the finger and see your spouse's shortcomings in a judgmental way and want him or her to change. If you shift the focus to you and ask yourself what you can do differently to make this relationship work better, you're more likely to see positive changes. You can ask your spouse to do the same thing; see if there's anything she can see herself doing differently to help the relationship grow. People generally react better when you're not pointing the finger and telling them what they have to do for you to be happy. If this doesn't work, if you've tried counseling, and you two truly have grown apart and find yourselves incompatible, then it's time to consider setting up two loving, safe homes for your children.

No matter how you do it, divorce is a difficult time for everyone involved. Adults grieve their lost dream of living in one home and raising a family together. They grieve the lost love they had been so sure would last. They often suffer from mistrust, anger, and hurt. Children feel the loss of having two parents in the same home and have to adjust to living in two homes. There are many logistical hurdles to be dealt with. The good news is that divorce doesn't have to be traumatic or devastating for you or your children. It doesn't have to result in long-term emotional damage to you or your children. The bad news is that divorce can be damaging and traumatic to you and your children both in the short run and the long run. The information contained in this chapter may help you avoid many of the possibly devastating effects of divorce so you and your family can move into the next stage of your family's life with relative ease.

When You're Contemplating Divorce

The most important goal for a divorcing couple is to do what's in the best interests of your child(ren) and set up a cooperative co-parenting relationship that works for you and your family. This can be accomplished if you set up two homes in which your child knows he or she is loved and safe and each parent sees the other as businesslike partners with a mutual goal of co-parenting your baby into healthy adulthood. As the two homes are being established, both parents need to grieve and heal their own pain. If you pretend it isn't there, you'll probably find yourself doing and saying things in mean, cutting ways, often when you least expect to. Your young child doesn't need to see his parents bicker, fight, and put each other down. Your young child needs to see Mommy and Daddy getting along and living in two different places where they both love him. Then he'll know that his life is going to be okay.

Probably the most important first step is to decide how to get divorced. With any method you choose, please keep in mind that the less conflict you have, the less emotional turbulence the parents are going through, the less emotional upheaval the children will go through. Your children will do better the calmer and more cooperative you can keep this process, no matter what method you choose. Basically there are four ways to get divorced: a) *pro se* (you do it yourself without an attorney), b) mediation, c) collaborative process, and d) litigation process (you each get your own lawyer). Let's look at each of these alternatives in detail:

Pro Se

You can represent yourself in court, appearing without an attorney (*pro se*) by obtaining the forms needed to divorce, filling them in, following the instructions for filing the legal papers, and paying your fees in the proper manner. Sometimes both parents represent themselves. Sometimes one chooses to appear pro se and the other hires an attorney. The court process can be intimidating for people representing themselves, but judges are used to this and can be accommodating to people who are not familiar with the court process. They can't give legal advice, but they can be somewhat understanding when you don't know your way around the court system.

If you are both pro se and can negotiate with each other, stay relatively calm, and come up with solutions that work well for your children, this is a great option. The benefits of appearing pro se are saving a lot of money and saving the heartache an adversarial system can stir up. The disadvantage is that you don't have a legal counselor who is familiar with the laws, your rights, and how to move through the divorce process representing your interests. The legal system can get confusing and end up being a slow, ineffective process. When you can't agree, one spouse often takes a more aggressive stand trying to coerce the other into agreements. Sometimes this increases the tension and conflict, which will negatively impact your children, and things can escalate out of control.

Mediation

This process works well for people who want or need outside intervention in negotiating with their partner. They want an objective outsider who can help each of them be cooperative and fairly calm as they negotiate, rather than simply sitting around the kitchen table talking together with no one to referee. A mediator is an objective professional who helps you two communicate about options you two come up with. A mediator can be a trained mental health professional, an attorney, or a person with special mediation training. You probably want to interview a number of mediators to learn more about how they work with couples. The mediator should not push one idea or another, rather it is up to the couple to come up with options that may work for their family and to decide which options they both can agree on.

Parents who choose this option know that if they make an agreement with their spouse, their spouse can be trusted to keep that agreement. People who choose mediation may feel like they need some support, so they don't feel like the other person is getting his or her way. The mediator (whether a trained mental health professional or an attorney) is a trained professional who remains neutral throughout the mediation process and helps both parents negotiate difficult issues in a calm, caring environment.

The mediator helps you learn how to listen to each other, consider what each of you wants, and negotiate civilly, responsibly, and respectfully. These are all skills you need to successfully co-parent your children. It's often easier for couples to negotiate issues later on because of what they learned from the mediator. Couples may continue using the services of a mediator after a divorce when issues come up and they find themselves deadlocked but want to avoid a costly court battle. It's recommended that once a mediation agreement has been reached, before signing it, each parent has an attorney go over the agreement to make sure you have covered all your legal bases.

The biggest advantage of a mediation process is you can come to peaceful agreements, which are good for you and your children, and you learn effective communication skills you can use throughout your children's lives. The more peaceful the process, the better you all do. Mediation can also be cost effective (avoiding thousands of dollars in legal fees) and emotionally prudent—your heart isn't torn from your chest in a gut-wrenching court battle. The disadvantage is that mediation doesn't always work. Sometimes one or both parties simply won't budge and an agreement or compromise can't be reached. Other times one parent cannot be trusted and mediation doesn't feel "safe" to the other parent who may be too fearful of being "manipulated" and thus is reluctant to agree to anything. Then you have to go to court. But mediation often resolves at least some of the issues; the more you can resolve before court the less costly (emotionally and financially) it will be.

Collaborative Process

The collaborative process is fairly new and varies from state to state. It's a team approach to a more peaceful divorce. The basic premise of the collaborative family process is that the parties will stay out of court, they will be supported through the divorce process with whatever professional services they need, and the divorce process will feel as humane as possible. Most parents who choose this model believe that the traditional, adversarial, legal process does not belong in the domestic court, as it tends to inflame the situation and then backfires on parents and children as the parents become embroiled in an escalating legal battle. Parents choose the collaborative model because they want to avoid that possibility.

There are several collaborative models in use across the country. In one model each parent has a collaborative attorney and other professionals are brought into the collaborative team as needed. In another model, which is growing in popularity, each parent has an attorney, a mental health professional in the role of divorce coach, and the couple shares a financial consultant (all professionals involved should have received special training in the collaborative model). If the couple is having trouble deciding how to deal with the children, the team can be enlarged to include a child specialist. Often, the divorce coaches can help the couple enough that a child specialist is not necessary. In some cases, both parents use the same divorce coach, although in some circumstances it appears more effective to have a divorce coach for each parent so the coach isn't pulled between the two parents if conflicts should escalate.

In whatever collaborative model you choose, each parent has his or her own attorney who has been trained in the collaborative process. You sign an agreement with your attorney and other team members saying that you are committed to settling all issues out of court. If it should go to court, anything accomplished during the collaborative process remains with the team and you have to begin with a new attorney. This provides a big incentive to stay on track and work through all issues. Attorneys and other team members work very hard to help the couple resolve issues in a way that is useful to that particular family.

In addition to an attorney, it's recommended that each parent have a divorce coach to help them personally and emotionally through the divorce process. The divorce coach offers support, helps you understand the divorce process, provides important information, teaches communication skills, helps you get past being stuck, and helps you through painful emotions so you can effectively negotiate and focus on what's in your children's best interests. Usually there's also an independent financial consultant on the team to deal with the economic and financial issues who can help the couple choose viable options to provide the children with two comfortable homes. Finally, if the situation involves complex issues with the child(ren), you may employ a child specialist. The child specialist educates the parents about child development and helps the parents reach resolution on the issues involving their children.

All the professionals are members of your family's collaborative team. It is one team working for the benefit of your whole family. It's not you and your attorney and divorce coach against the other attorney and divorce coach. The entire professional team is focused on helping your family move from a tense situation in one home to two loving, safe homes for your children. The team strives to help you make divorce a life-enhancing experience.

It may sound like a costly, complex option, but it usually is less costly (emotionally and financially) than a traditional litigated divorce because the divorce coaches spend more hours with the parents than the attorneys, and they charge less than an attorney charges per hour. In addition, the financial consultant (who has specific training in divorce and the collaborative process) charges less than most attorneys. The financial consultant's work is more cost effective than using the attorneys to develop the financial piece of your divorce. When the collaborative process works, it is definitely less costly (financially and emotionally) than a contentious, long, drawn-out court battle, and it can be less expensive than a regular two party, two attorney divorce. All team members have specialized training, so they are particularly helpful in de-escalating complex situations and sending you to the right professionals who can give you the information or skills you need to keep the situation relatively calm.

Each Spouse Has His or Her Own Attorney

This can be an efficient, inexpensive experience, or it can be incredibly inefficient and costly in terms of finances, time, and emotions. This is the most widely used model for getting divorced because it has been around the longest and people are most familiar with it. It is probably the most effective model to use if one or both parents have a history of serious mental illness, domestic violence, or substance abuse issues. However, in simpler situations, more attorneys and judges are coming to the conclusion that the adversarial nature of traditional litigation probably has no place in domestic court.

If you choose this model, how your divorce will proceed is dependent on the key players—you, your spouse, and each of your attorneys. Attorneys are trained in the adversarial court system, but some attorneys are better negotiators than others and can avoid the pitfalls of the traditional, adversarial system. These attorneys can use the traditional system well. Others are trained to win at all costs, but when there is a winner, there is also a loser. Divorce should not be about one parent winning and the other losing. When it is set up that way, the true losers are the children. Divorce should be about setting up the next stage in a family's life. If both parents are relatively stable and involved, both should have the right to parent from their own homes and provide their children with all they need to reach their full capabilities.

The more conflict the divorce process brings up, the more painful it will be for all the people involved—parents and children—emotionally and financially. When you have a strong attorney who wants to get you everything he or she possibly can, even if it means increasing the tension and conflict or intimidating the other party, then the children will suffer. You want both parents to emerge from the divorce process feeling relatively good about themselves and their former spouse so they can be effective parents and co-parents.

You want an attorney who can look out for your rights and interests and who can also see the bigger picture of how the children's best interests can be addressed. This is especially important when issues such as mental health, domestic violence, or substance abuse are involved. You also want an attorney who wants to see as much of the family's assets remaining with the family (in two homes) rather than being spent on a lengthy court battle leaving them divorced but nearly broke. If you have two fair and reasonable attorneys who try to minimize the litigious nature of your divorce, this process works well. If you have an attorney who is out for the fight and the win, it can get very emotionally and financially costly. As the parents' legal battle escalates the children can't help but feel the escalating tension and hostility between the two people they love the most in this world. That can be very uncomfortable and damaging for children.

The advantage of having your own attorney is that you know you have a personal advocate, and you have a final court date when the judge will decide things if you haven't been able to before then. The disadvantage is that it can become very expensive, financially and emotionally, for you and your children.

Establishing New Patterns as a Basis for Co-Parenting

You'll want to establish new communication patterns so you can co-parent your child from two homes. Before you open your mouth to speak to the other parent think, "How will what I'm about to say to my child's other parent affect my child?" Other possible thoughts or questions are: "What tone of voice do I want to use to make this as understandable and respectful to my child's other parent as possible?" "How will what I'm about to say affect my child?" "Is this really necessary to say?"

If you can stop yourself long enough to think and ask these questions, you'll improve your communication with your child's other parent tremendously. You may need to re-ask these questions throughout your interactions, not just before you begin a conversation. You may want to write these questions down on a piece of paper and have it with you when you pick up the phone to talk to your child's other parent. That way you can look down and remind yourself to speak from a cooperative place. You may also want to jot down a list of what you want to talk about so you can stay focused.

These thoughts and questions help you remember it's not just what you say, but *how* you say it. There is an actual, verbal message in any human interaction and a *meta* message—what your tone of voice implies. During tense conversations, the meta message, the tone of voice, often comes off stronger than the verbal message, and that can result in quickly escalating emotions. You want to keep conversations as conflict-free as possible.

Thinking about what you want to say and how you want to say it before you communicate with your former spouse will help you be a considerate co-parent. You'll want to remember the following: your child is a precious human being and can be successfully loved from two different houses; you adults need to see each other as your child's other parent and learn to work together in co-parenting your child; your child has two parents and you're only one of them; both of you are needed to help raise a happy and healthy human being; your child may live in two homes, but they should be two loving homes where both parents encourage an active, involved relationship with the other parent.

If you and your child's other parent have trouble communicating or establishing a co-parenting system, a number of teaching tools are available. The Shared Parent Support Program (SPSP) can teach you effective communication skills. It was developed by Dr. Frank Leek in Sacramento, California (spsp@jps.net). The SPSP training is available throughout the country. Another skills-based program for parents is Solutions for Families developed by Dr. P. Leslie Herold of San Bernardino, California (www.solutions4families.com). He has trained therapists around the country as well. Three books that are useful for amicably establishing separate, loving homes for your children are *Mom's House, Dad's House* by Isolina Ricci,

PhD; *Learning From Divorce: How to Take Responsibility, Stop the Blame, Move On* by Christie Coates and E. Robert LaCrosse, PhD; and *Parents Are Forever* (Revised Edition) by Shirley Thomas, PhD. A book that outlines the nightmares if you fail to accomplish your goal of respectful coparenting is *In the Name of the Child* by Janet Johnston, PhD, and Vivienne Roseby, PhD.

Make the Divorce as Cooperative as Possible

During the first year or two of life, a child's main task is building attachments with other human beings and learning to trust that someone will be there for him to meet his needs. A baby needs to feel close to at least one human being. Respectful Parenting nurtures a child's sense of trust and self-confidence. Respectful Parenting helps a child form close attachments. When a child's early life is affected by a great deal of stress and tension between the parents, it negatively affects the child's cognitive, emotional and social development. If one parent essentially disappears (when the couple separates) then the child's early bonds with that parent can be temporarily or irretrievably broken. This can seriously affect a young child.

Minimizing fighting, accusations, stress, and legal battles is *essential* to your child's healthy development and long-term mental health. Parents should not talk badly about the other parent within earshot or possible earshot of their children. Each parent needs to encourage a loving relationship with the other parent even though they've chosen not to live with him or her any more. (The exceptions to this rule are when there has been ongoing domestic violence, serious mental health problems, and/or substance abuse issues. These situations will be talked about later in this chapter.)

When children of divorce feel free to love both their parents and see their parents appreciating each other, they're able to reach their cognitive, social, and emotional potential. You want to put what's in your child's best interests in front of what's in your best interests. You'll want to remember that the more stress a child experiences in his or her first few years of life, the more negatively that child's development will be affected. The impact can be short-term developmental delays or, in serious cases, it can have long term effects, negatively impacting a child's emotional, social, and cognitive development. Even if your baby is preverbal and doesn't understand the content of what's being said, she'll still be affected by what's happening around her. She instinctively senses that her environment and her life is changing. It's no longer as stable or safe as it was. The accompanying stress (from these changes) and how it's affecting her mommy and daddy affects her.

Keep Both Parents Involved

In the past twenty years, families as a whole have changed. One of those changes is that fathers are much more involved with their children than they used to be. The old "deadbeat dad" image of divorced dads doesn't seem to apply anymore. In general, the more contact children have with their fathers as young children the closer they seem to remain throughout life. The old idea of dad having every other weekend with their children does not seem to be the best arrangement for most families. If a dad is relatively emotionally balanced, wants to be involved, and is willing to be a responsible parent, the thinking these days is to maximize each parent's time with a young child.

When a parent interferes with a child's ability to visit the other parent, and the other parent is relatively healthy and involved, the child usually ends up resenting the parent's interference as they grow up. When the child is eighteen and can choose who he wants to spend time with, he often chooses to spend less time with the parent he perceives "kept him" from the other parent for "no good reason."

Exceptions to Encouraging an Ongoing, Involved Relationship with Both Parents

If your child's other parent has an untreated, serious depression, mood disorder, character disorder, problems with domestic violence, or a substance abuse problem, then your child may need to be protected from the harmful effects of being around an erratic, irresponsible, inadequate, or violent parent. A child can have supervised parenting time or therapeutic supervised parenting time in a neutral, safe setting to maintain the parent-child relationship. As the child grows up a therapist can help a child understand the situation so he doesn't feel like the other parent abandoned him, or that one parent arbitrarily kept him from maintaining a relationship with his other parent. It is rarely necessary to completely restrict parenting time between a parent and child, but this kind of complex situation will need the help of trained and experienced professionals to properly assess what's in the child's best interests.

Parenting Time Arrangements

The current recommendation for parenting time in divorce situations with two relatively healthy parents and very young children (three and under) is to have one residential parent and to maximize time with the other parent. We know it's important that both parents actively interact with their young children. An emerging idea, still being debated, is that one or two non-sequential overnights with the non-residential parent *may not* be a bad thing for young children. We don't have enough research to substantiate the claim that very young children shouldn't have any overnights with the non-residential parent, nor do we have research on whether they should have overnights. Many unanswered questions still exist for creating the best co-parenting environment for the very young child. More research with this age group will help determine what's best for very young children. Watching your child carefully is your best indication of how your child is doing.

Some children who react to changes easily will do better with an overnight or two than children who seem to have trouble with change and different environments. It's very important to design an individualized parenting plan that works for your child. If you try overnights with the non-residential parent, watch how your child reacts to these visits. If your child is in child care during the day, ask the child care providers to let you know if they see changes in your baby before or after non-residential overnights. Change the parenting plan as needed, depending on how your baby copes, not on how you cope.

A non-residential parent should spend time with a very young child frequently—ideally every two or three days for at least a few hours at a time so that parent can engage in the routines of daily life with the young baby. By feeding, changing, putting a baby to sleep, and comforting the baby, a non-residential parent creates the close ties with his or her baby that are important to the baby's healthy cognitive, emotional, and social development. A flexible parenting plan can be developed where both parents agree they will make decisions based on how the growing child is reacting (emotionally and behaviorally) to spending more time and overnights with the non-residential parent.

You can design a parenting plan that changes over time and considers your child's developing needs. Thus for the first three years one parent may be the primary residential parent and then you may gradually in-

crease time and overnights with the non-residential parent. You can increase by one or two nights a week, eventually getting to a 50/50 parenting time schedule if you both believe and see that that's in your child's
best interests. Children younger than about ten sometimes have trouble
being away from the residential parent for a week at a time so you need to
break up the time more, having the children switch in less than one-week
segments. In that case, some children do fine going back and forth frequently while others get very disorganized with frequent transitions between the two homes. Weekends of four and five day stretches, every
other week can also work well for some children. It's helpful when you
can develop some ideas for a graduated parenting plan when your child is
young, but don't set them in stone so you can be open to modifications
depending on how your child is doing.

In high-conflict, complex divorces (about 10 to 12 percent), joint legal
residence and joint decision-making may be unrealistic. In extreme situations where both parents have serious emotional or drug problems, alternative living arrangements (other relatives or foster care) may be necessary.
In these very complex families you can always appeal to the court to appoint a professional who can do a thorough investigation and recommend
what is in the child's best interests.

What to Avoid

Sometimes parents accuse each other of neglect or abuse if they want to
get back at an ex-spouse. Sometimes one parent honestly *believes* the other
parent is neglecting their child because he doesn't parent in the same manner as the other parent. Parents can make overt accusations or they can
quietly ooze, roll their eyes, and give their children nonverbal indications
of their general dislike of the other parent. When children sense any of
these things going on, it puts the children in the middle of an adult battle
zone, a place you *don't* want your child to be. It's like being a ping-pong
ball in the middle of a particularly competitive and brutal game. If a child
takes sides it produces guilt, loss, and sometimes anger from one parent. If
he stays neutral, which puts him in the middle, he gets bombarded and
bashed from both ends. The child can't win.

High-Conflict Divorce

Only about 10 to 12 percent of all divorces end up being what profession-als call "high-conflict" divorce situations. Parents in these families seem to fight almost every time a decision has to be made. They rarely agree about anything. Another pattern is they barely speak to each other so they make decisions without involving the other parent. The other parent finds out and gets angry. They start fighting over the decision. The parents believe they're fighting for what's right for their child. They don't seem to see how their fights cause more harm to their child. If there are frequent accusa-tions and counter accusations a judge may appoint someone to be a spe-cial advocate, child and family investigator, parent coordinator, legal rep-resentative, court investigator, or child custody evaluator to make recommendations to the court as to what actually is in the children's best interests.

These court appointed professionals will conduct a thorough investiga-tion and assessment of the family to figure out what's really going on, how it's affecting the children, and how it will affect the children as they grow up. They want to know if either parent is healthier (emotionally) and able to operate in their children's best interests to a greater degree than the other parent. The court appointed professional will try and teach the par-ents about family dynamics and child development so the parents can un-derstand how their continued conflicts and fighting affect their children in negative ways. The goal is for parents to reduce their conflict and be able to put their children's best interests in front of what they want for themselves. If parents can't do this, the professional will recommend living arrangements and decision-making arrangements that are in the child's best interests. These professionals can also make recommendations to the court for additional services and interventions to help these families get to a more cooperative place.

Factors That Increase a Child's Risk

In about 88 to 90 percent of divorces, parents can be civil, cordial, and even friendly with each other. Their children usually grow up well ad-justed and able to handle intimate relationships of their own. However several factors can negatively impact children such as: a) inadequate par-enting, b) continued conflict, c) children being put in the middle when parents criticize the other parent, d) children being spies at the other house, e) talking badly about a new step-parent, f) asking a child to carry a hostile message, g) asking intrusive questions about the other parent, which creates a need for the child to hide information, or h) asking a child to keep secrets from the other parent. Economic problems can cause stress for parents, which can have a trickle-down affect on the children. Major life changes including moving, changing schools, or additional marriages and divorces need to be minimized. If these changes continue to occur in your child's life, they increase your child's risk for developmental problems, behavioral problems, emotional trauma, and problems with intimacy as the child grows up.

The stress that comes along with this combination of factors can seriously affect a young child's social, cognitive, and emotional development. Your young child may begin to have nightmares. His language development can be delayed. He can talk incessantly to cover up his fears. He can begin to tantrum or escalate tantrums. He can get clingy. He can stop enjoying things he used to enjoy. He can have trouble learning or cooperating at home and at child care. If your child begins to exhibit changes in his behavior and moods, look at how you and your child's other parent are relating. See if you can communicate in a more peaceful way—perhaps by e-mail or phone instead of in person. You may need to have a neutral place for dropping your baby off and picking your baby up, so your baby isn't in the middle of a cold war or an openly hostile parental war. You may need to meet with a trained mediator, therapist, or divorce coach who can help you resolve issues in a more respectful manner.

Summary

- If you must divorce, consider all the options for the divorce process and pick the one that will work best for your family by minimizing conflict and stress.
- Your goal throughout the divorce process ought to be putting your child's best interests first.
- When both parents are relatively healthy and involved, joint legal responsibility and joint decision-making can be a creative workable solution for your young child that enables him or her to spend lots of time with both parents.
- You can design and implement a graduated parenting plan as your child grows up. If you agree to a parenting plan that changes as

your child grows up, watch your child carefully. Make sure the plan you designed years ago continues to make sense for how your child is developing. Modify the plan if it no longer meets your child's needs.

- Encourage an open and involved relationship between your children and your ex-spouse.
- Keep the conflict between you and your ex-spouse to a minimum. Any time you're ready to open your mouth in anger think and ask yourself questions like, "How will this affect my child?" "How will what I'm about to say to my child's other parent affect my child?" "What tone of voice do I want to use to make this as understandable and respectful to my child's other parent as possible?"
- Be fair to each other.
- If you've never learned how to communicate with your spouse before, learn now.
- Probably one of the worst things you can do during and after a divorce is to decide, "I didn't like talking to him (her) before and now I don't have to." It's emotionally damaging to children of any age to make the transition from one house to the other in silence or hostility.
- Up to 90 percent of divorces can be handled without a lot of acrimony.
- The first two years during and after a divorce are often the most difficult time, but life seems to level off once you've all adjusted to the changes.
- If a history of serious mental health issues, domestic violence, or substance abuse is part of your divorce, make sure you get good legal and emotional help so that you can protect yourself and your children.

Sixteen

Parental Frustrations

$\mathcal{M}$OST OF THE TIME your frustrations probably spill onto your child, or they're triggered by something your child is doing that is challenging to you. Your frustrations can also come when you're unable to change the situation in front of you or when your expectations of how things should be don't match how life is. Like when your two-year-old puts her hands on her hips and says things like, "I don't have to do that," or "I'm bigger than you!" or "You're not the boss of me!" These confrontations are exacerbated if you happen to be hungry, tired, distracted, stressed about something else, or overworked. Then instead of keeping your cool, laughing it off, negotiating, walking away, ignoring it, knowing through and through that you don't have to engage, or taking a time-out, you may find yourself yelling, crying, whining, screaming, grabbing them, or dropping to your child's level and doing such things as sticking out your tongue.

Sometimes, it's not just you and your child struggling through a situation, although you two may be the only ones present. It's you, your personal history demons, and your child. Unfortunately your child doesn't have a clue that he isn't just dealing with Mommy or Daddy. In fact, you may not realize how much of your frustration is due to your own internal battle between the present and your memories (conscious and unconscious). This includes how it was done to you, the current situation at hand, how you'd like it to be (your own expectations), how you'd like to handle it today, and what your parents might think about how you want to handle it today. The room is actually emotionally charged and crowded, and the struggle is more complicated than it appears.

At other times you may be frustrated when your expectations don't fit your child's developmental abilities. For instance, when you expect or want your home to be orderly and your young child just can't seem to put away things that have been used so the house has that cluttered, lived in look, both you and your child can become frustrated. Your expectations are not matching your child's developmental abilities. Many young children are not naturally neat and orderly because they're easily distracted by something interesting that catches their curiosity. As a result you may ask yourself, 'Whose home is orderly when at least one young child lives there?' Around the time you're returning to work from maternity leave, look around. When it's completely unclear where the hours in the day are to work, nurture, nurse, change diapers, shop for food, prepare meals, eat, wash dishes, do laundry, sleep, and clean, remember: something has to give. Choose at least one item on the list and figure out a way you don't have to do it yourself or how you can lower your standards to give yourself a break.

Even if you need to have a sense of orderliness around you, if you're juggling work and family, or even just juggling a multiple-child family and no outside-the-home job, you need to give somewhere in your life. One strategy is to spontaneously change your plans and expectations as the day unfolds. Rather than sticking to prearranged ideas that no longer apply because of things like a child who won't take a nap, an earlier nap than planned, a grumpy parent or child, bad weather, or an unplanned tummy ache, simply change your plans. Flexibility and spontaneity will enable you to avoid countless unnecessary power struggles with your child.

Here are some Respectful Parenting strategies for when you're feeling at the end of your rope and you want to be gentle and kind with your child.

- **When you're feeling stuck about what to say or do, when you're about to say something you don't want to say, quickly give yourself a time-out.** Take a time-out, even if it's only a minute to breathe deeply. You may have the luxury of going into another room for a little while if another adult is around to make sure your child is safe. If you're the only one home and you can't leave your child alone, you may simply want to say, "I need a time-out so I can do this differently. I really want to be loving right now." Sometimes just hearing yourself saying that is enough to clue you into slowing down and responding from a different place.

- **When you're stuck, remind yourself of how you want to respond.** Form a complete picture with details of how you want to look as you're responding, what you want to say, and how you want to feel. Rehearse your behavior in your mind and it'll be easier to do in real life.
- **Slow down so you can react differently.**
- **Ask yourself, "How important is this?"** After you decide the relative importance, alternatives will kick in.
- **When in doubt, ask for help.**
- **If necessary, decide to deal with it later.**

Take Care of Your Own Issues

If you were hit, spanked, yelled at, or abused as a child, then during these highly frustrating, tense times when your otherwise darling small child is testing your limits, and your limits are frayed to begin with—watch out! These are danger zones, where you're most likely to do what you unconsciously and consciously remember. Your memories may be exactly the kinds of scenes you promised yourself you would never inflict on another human being. Take a time-out and create in detail the scene of the way you want to parent your child today. Separate your present-day self from your yesterday self. Look in a mirror and see yourself today, so you can re-establish who you are and how you want to behave *today.*

If you get stuck in an old automatic loop, you can get upset by judging your actions and words, and being angry at yourself for contemplating or doing what you had promised yourself you never would. So now you're frustrated with your child's behavior in the here and now; upset, angry, or disappointed with your own behavior in the here and now; mourning or angry that your past is infringing on the present; and generally stuck.

When something in your parental bag of tricks needs fixing, use the resources at your disposal such as your partner, a friend, a child care provider who knows your child, a therapist, a parent support group, parenting classes, a parent training audio CD, a parent chat group on the web, or a parent phone hotline. You're not alone. That's why there are so many outside resources available. People use them, or they wouldn't be there. There's always room for expanding your parenting options, and for personal growth, if you're willing and open to suggestions. You don't need to be at the end of your rope, even if you just want another idea, take full advantage of the resources out there, and appreciate yourself for having the courage to learn, and grow.

If you grew up in an alcoholic home, every community in the country has Al-Anon meetings, and most even have special Al-Anon meetings for people who grew up in alcoholic homes called, "Adult Children of Alcoholics" (ACA or ACOA) meetings. Although Al-Anon was originally formed as a support group to help family members and friends of alcoholics, some meetings are open to people who grew up in dysfunctional homes even where alcoholism wasn't present, because the resulting problems are so similar. Sometimes people find, after going to meetings for a while, that there was more drinking involved in their family of origin than they had originally consciously remembered.

Al-Anon meetings can be enormously supportive and helpful if you're trying to do things differently. They cost nothing, and are usually available throughout the day and evening. Check your local phone directory or call information and ask for the Al-Anon number nearest you. When you talk with them, ask them to send you a meeting schedule. Pick a convenient meeting and go. Sometimes people find it really difficult to walk into those rooms for the first time. They're scared of what they'll find. What you'll find is some people similar to you, who want to untangle themselves from their past, and who want a better quality of life for themselves and their families. Anonymity is an important part of the Al-Anon program, so don't worry about gossip outside of meetings or people knowing that you went. "Who you see here, what you hear here, when you leave here, let it stay here," is a greatly respected saying that is adhered to among Al-Anon members.

A Bag of Tricks

Short of using outside resources, there are some things you can do to untangle yourself and diffuse the situation. A phone call to another parent as a way of gaining a different perspective, a break, or advice and support might be the best thing for you. A nice relaxing bath may help. You can even invite your child in so you can both calm down. Help from a partner may be unavailable, but if your partner is available either in person or by phone, use him or her for some relief or a more objective perspective. Some parents also suggest praying, which can be helpful, especially when it's already a part of your life.

All the parents who were quoted in this book thought this was an important chapter, because no matter how well you want to parent, no matter how good your intentions are, no matter how well you really do parent, sooner or later, you'll go through those parental testing days. Just as the sounds radio stations make when they test the emergency broadcast systems can jar your body, wait to see how jarring your "wonderful" toddler or two-year-old can be. I hope that the suggestions contained on these pages will help provide a broader perspective on your situation when you're feeling frazzled or stuck. All parents have been there.

If you can't reach a friend when your frustration is mounting to a breaking point, try opening to this chapter during times of extreme stress. You may find a solution. Some parents have made a literal grab bag. Take the suggestions offered in this chapter, write each one on a piece of paper, put them in a paper bag, twist the top, and put it in a convenient location (the kitchen or laundry room). When in doubt, pull out a suggestion and try it. If it doesn't work or doesn't appeal to you, pull out another. Just the act of using the bag may lighten your spirits and enable you to deal with your child differently.

The best advice is to have fun. Lighten up. This is only one moment in both your lives. Whatever you are going head-to-head about probably isn't that important in the greater scheme of things. Step back. Give both of you the room to reconsider your ultimatums and your rigidly held positions. When you do that, watch the tension melt. Time-outs are marvelous inventions. When parents use time-outs to figure out how else they can be handling a situation and emerge with creative, calm ideas, their children seem to need time-outs less frequently.

Grab Bag Suggestions

If you're going to make a grab bag, here's a beginning list of what to put in the bag. Put one suggestion on each piece of paper:

- Keep things simple.
- Prioritize. Think and do first things first.
- Look at the bigger picture.
- Lighten up.

- Back off and let the argument dissipate on its own.
- Back off and let your child cool off on his or her own.
- Detach a little and let your child find his or her own solution.
- Be a comforting or sympathetic parent rather than an all-knowing problem solver.
- Know your own and your child's low energy times and plan your schedule around them.
- Ask yourself, "How can I be flexible now?"
- Apologize as soon as you realize you're behaving or speaking in a way you don't like. It usually stops a downward spiral.
- Have food prepared in advance for stressful or rushed times.
- Take a parental time-out.
- Look at the situation with a sense of humor.
- Take a warm bath.
- Wash your face.
- Take a walk with your child.
- Punch pillows together.
- Bang pillows onto a mattress.
- Call a friend.
- Speak with a partner or spouse.
- Call a parent support line, a hotline, or a crisis line.
- Raise your eyes toward the sky and say, "Help!" (More formal prayer works as well.)
- Tell your child that you don't like how things are going and you'd like to change what's happening.
- Ask your child if she likes how things feel right now and if she says, "No," then say, "Me either . . . Let's figure out a way to feel more peaceful. Can you help?"
- Remember that both you and your child are human.

When I was interviewing parents for this book, I asked them to be honest and talk about what they do when their best parenting techniques don't seem to be working. Even though the ideas behind Respectful Parenting are sound and work a lot of the time, these methods will not result in perfect parent-and-child interactions. All parents and all children are human. Part of being human is being imperfect. Life is challenging sometimes. Parenting is often a challenge. Parents need to take their creativity and their common sense to their fullest potential when they are faced with frustrating situations. Here's what some of them said—feel free to jot down these and other ideas for your grab bag.

What Parents Say

Cindy: My frustration comes in when I get into this head space where I'm telling myself, "I should be able to redirect this behavior," only I can't. And the more I'm in there, trying as hard as I can to redirect the situation, the more frustrated I become and the more intransigent my daughter becomes. When I realize I'm stuck, getting more stuck by the minute, and can back off to give both of us breathing space, the better we do. It's like we're both trapped in a corner (so to speak) with no way out unless one of us, and usually it has to be me, recognizes the situation and goes, "Oh, there's a roomful of space behind me. I don't need to stay trapped in this corner with you. I'll just slowly take a few steps back. There, now I can see a bigger picture. I get it. That wasn't working."

Sometimes retreat and quiet is the most heroic and useful way through a frustrating situation. When I do that, we both calm down, reevaluate our struggle and can offer each other alternatives. Sometimes I need to realize that I can't redirect this behavior. I need to stop trying and just wait this one out. But not when we're in the corner, verbally duking it out. At that point we're both lost in the emotional intensity and neither of us can see a way out.

* * *

Bonnie: I get really frustrated when those old voices in my head start saying things like, "I'm obviously not good enough to fix this." When I can hear that old voice and consciously counter it with, "No, that's not true. What is true is her frustration. She's entitled to being frustrated sometimes. I'm her mother, and that's all." I'm not supposed to always make it better or take away her emotional discomfort, otherwise how will she learn to take care of herself when I'm not around? I have to detach sometimes. Not try to fix it. Let it be hers. And know I'm being a good mother. That takes some talking to myself and countering those old negative messages I picked up in my youth.

* * *

Sylvia: Sometimes I get frustrated because I don't know if I can laugh at something or if I need to be serious. Like the other day, my son who's almost three was playing in the cat's litter box. He was digging with the shovel. I immediately saw the humor and had to hold back from laughing because I was afraid if I did, he'd do it again and not understand my explanation of why he couldn't do that. I know he loves playing with sand, and the shovel was right there. Instead of laughing, I explained, using a serious tone of voice, that the cat box was off limits, it was actually dirty and needed to be handled carefully by an adult with gloves on, or we could get sick from it. He didn't quite get it. As he questioned me, I became more serious. I think he finally did get it, because he hasn't played in there since.

The majority of my frustration came later as I second-guessed myself, wondering if I could have handled it differently (meaning better) and realizing I'm really unsure about when I can use humor and when I have to be the "Mommy" à la my mother's style. It's frustrating. Talking to friends helps, but I don't always have the time.

* * *

Linda: One day when my two-and-a-half-year-old daughter and I were really into it, arguing away, each adamantly sure she was right, I just stuck my tongue out at her. It wasn't deliberate. I guess I had seen my kids do it to each other or friends often enough and had done it with my siblings, so it was there someplace and out it came. My daughter looked shocked for a millisecond, and then we both cracked up laughing. It completely diffused the situation. I kind of like that kind of solution every once in a while.

* * *

Sylvia: Mealtimes at our house can be an excellent opportunity for frustration. Let's say my son is finished eating, or more likely he's pausing and we're still eating. He wants us to pay attention to him, while we'd like to have a few minutes of adult conversation. It's obviously a conflict in the making. One day, my son was sitting on his dad's lap, and started waving his hands in front of his dad's face. His dad warned him to stop or he'd have to get down. Our son didn't listen and kept waving his hands, annoying his dad. Finally his dad said, "You're bugging me, please get down until after I finish eating. Then you can sit in my lap again."

After he finished eating, our son came up to him and asked, "Can I bug you now?" We laughed. It's those wonderful, humorous, spontaneous remarks that can diffuse a tense situation, and come at the most needed times. I love when things like that happen.

* * *

Bonnie: When I've had an upsetting or frustrating time with my thirteen-month-old daughter, I try to take some time and rationally create in my mind the bigger picture. After all, what is really happening here? Is this particular argument, power struggle, or independent move worth so much within the greater scheme of her life and mine? By looking at the bigger picture—her life, my life—I usually drop what it was I was feeling so adamant about. It's not that important. It also helps me when I can talk about it with my husband later and get his support about my earlier dilemma and my resolution of it.

* * *

Cathy: There are times when I've had to stop my son from doing something when he's been frustrated either by what he was trying to do, or by being stopped before he wanted to stop. Afterward, I feel like the mean mommy. I know that probably stems from wanting so much to do it differently than my mother did it with us when we were younger.

In any event, when those things happened I used to try and make up for it later, feeling like I had to do something really special so he wouldn't see me as a mean mom. It helped when this book presented the perspective on limits as a natural, necessary and positive part of parenting.

Really, most of the time what happened that made me afraid I was a "mean mom" was that I set appropriate limits, which he had been warned about or which had been negotiated with him earlier. So wanting to just have a pleasant time later, rather than pushing to do something really special is a more respectful, healthy approach.

* * *

Bonnie: Sometimes when I get into a hard place with my young daughter, I have to stand back and reevaluate my goals. I often find my goals are unrealistic. I'm getting frustrated by trying to attain unrealistic goals. One of my unrealistic goals is wanting my daughter to be happy all the time. Another unrealistic goal is trying to be the perfect mother to make up for how I was mothered. And my other unrealistic goal is trying to do too much in too short a time and then getting angry because my daughter is not going along with an unrealistic adult time schedule. I try to look at the frustrating situation and see what my goal is, decide if it's realistic, and go from there. When it's one of these unrealistic goals, I can kind of laugh at myself, let it go, and go on. My tension and frustration dissipate when I realize I'm being unrealistic and I can simply back off.

* * *

Kate: My husband travels a lot with his job; sometimes he's away for three- and four-day stretches. I've found I need to keep things simple when he's gone. Dinners aren't elaborate, but they're nutritious. I try to keep everything we do as simple as possible, asking myself along the way, "Does this really have to happen right now?" or "What happens if I don't do this right now?" If I don't overburden myself with things to do and concentrate on the essentials like enjoying my son, I'm okay. If I start doing too much by the time my husband gets home, I find myself meeting him at the door and saying, "Bye, see you," and I'm out of there. And that's not fair to him. He's been working hard those three and four days, too. So, when I remember to keep it simple, our family runs a lot more smoothly when he's gone and when he returns home.

* * *

Cathy: I've learned that the afternoons, especially late afternoons, are a low-energy time for my son and for me. It's the time we're most likely to get frustrated with each other. Preparing dinner used to be a major source of frustration. He needed my attention. I needed to be cooking. I solved that frustration by preparing our dinner meal before noon. At that time he's full of energy, often entertaining himself or join- ing me in preparing the meal. Then, in the late afternoon, when we're both tired, drained, and most likely to get into it, I just have to pop something in the stove or microwave and our meal is cooking smoothly and usually served without any frustrat- ing experiences. It's been a wonderful solution.

* * *

Bonnie: I'm the kind of person who has always liked finishing something once I've started, like a letter or cooking a meal. It was difficult for me at first because I'd be in the middle of something and my daughter would wake up from a nap, or want to nurse, or cry. I believed in responding immediately, but there were times I responded with annoyance or frustration because I was being interrupted. I quickly realized my responses were absurd. I learned it's okay not to finish things. I've been getting less rigid and more flexible over the last ten years or so, but having this wonderful little baby girl has taught me and pushed me into being much more flexi- ble than I knew I could be . . . and so much faster than I would have gotten to on my own. Now, if I know I want to eat a meal at a certain time, I'll start two hours before, even if it's a simple meal because I want to leave time for interruptions to play, nurse, or soothe her as she needs or wants. If I finish early, fine, but with the extra time, I can relax and enjoy her and what I'm trying to do without feeling frustrated.

* * *

Linda: Diaper changing is often a hard time for us. My daughter doesn't like her diaper being changed. She moves around a lot and protests while I'm changing her. In the mornings I'm fine and stay calm easily, knowing this has to get done and it's too bad she doesn't like it. But a couple of times now, in the late afternoon I've yelled at her to stay still. I realize immediately it's ridiculous for me to lose my temper with her because she's squirming and making it difficult for me to diaper her. Both times I've apologized immediately and talked it through with her, telling her, "Mommy's sorry she yelled but sometimes it's hard for me to stay patient when I have to change your diaper and you keep moving around, making it harder to change you and making the whole process longer and worse than it has to be." I feel better after I've apologized and explained. And she seems to listen. It's easier when my husband is home because then one of us plays and distracts her while the other changes her diaper, and that helps. Then she's not fussy.

* * *

Bonnie: Sometimes I feel like my needs conflict with my daughter's. Like when I'm hungry and she needs to nurse. Or she needs to nurse and I need to sleep. At times like that, especially if my blood sugar is low, I can feel the irritation well up inside me. I can stop it if I remember that she has a job to do at this time in her life, and her job is being a baby and voicing her needs. I have a job too, and my job is being her mother and taking care of her needs. We really aren't in conflict, we're complementary.

One solution we've worked out is that my husband makes me a sandwich when he makes his in the morning before leaving for work. That way, if she's hungry and needs to be nursed, and I'm hungry and need to eat, I can eat the sandwich he made while she nurses. I used to put her down and she'd cry for five minutes (which I didn't believe in and which really jarred me) while I made myself a sandwich. Now we both get to eat at once.

I don't really like it when those old feelings from my childhood well up automatically, but at least I can use the new thinking I've picked up along the way to stop the old messages and deal with her the way I want to today. When I don't catch them, I try to deal with the guilt that inevitably seems to arise when I think I haven't been the perfect mother.

* * *

Sarah: At times when I find myself going head-to-head with my two-year-old son over something, anything, what to wear, what to eat, or how to play with him, I'll simply say, "You know what? Mommy needs a time-out. I'm getting frustrated right now because we're disagreeing and neither one of us is giving in. I'm just going to go in the next room for a minute so I can reconsider the situation and calm down. I'll be right back." The reality is, he usually follows me in, so I don't really get a time-out. But it's kind of a time-out, because he's usually quietly hovering rather than pursuing the argument. It serves the purpose of stopping or at least pausing the power struggle.

I've learned I don't have much time before he starts in again, but I can usually quickly take a few deep breaths and get back to feeling my age instead of being right there in the throes of a two-year-old's power struggle. It's funny, when I first tried this method and he followed me in, I tried to get him to leave me alone so I could get a true time-out all by myself . . . but it backfired and we started arguing about him leaving me alone. It seemed easier for me to give up on the idea of a time-out alone and settle for a time-out where I could bury my head if need be, and he could hover quietly for at least twenty seconds and give me a little bit of breathing space.

If I had stuck with my picture of what a time-out would be for me, I would never have gotten any relief at all. And then I'm not sure where I would be. Would I like more time? Sure, but since he can't seem to give me more, I'll take what I can get and use it as best I can. I think that's part of respecting his limits, too. He can't seem to allow me an alone time-out, but he can give me a little quiet time. I've discovered that's workable. I can do what I need within his limits.

Seventeen

Life Wasn't Going to Change this Much . . .

CAN YOU REMEMBER BACK to a time when having a good night's sleep was the norm rather than a rare event? Can you remember when it would take a particularly stressful set of events to interrupt your sleep? Do you remember a time when you and your partner were into a particularly passionate period? Can you recall when you would sit around and daydream about what your life, as a parent, with your own family would be like before having a child?

Years ago I saw Bill Cosby do a wonderful comedy routine about his pre-child fantasies versus the reality of being a father. To paraphrase him: My wife, my child, and I were going to go skipping through a field of wildflowers in slow motion. Our faces would radiate love in slightly out-of-focus soft pastels, like those artsy films. The sun would be shining. I'd be holding my wife's hand on one side and my child's on the other. Instead, when we had our first baby, reality hit. Family life was far from a romantic, hazy, film of a small family running in slow motion through a field of wildflowers. In real life the baby cried, we were exhausted, and nobody had the energy for running anywhere, slow motion or not. But we loved each other.

What were your dreams, your musings, your ideas, and your ideals? How do they compare with life today? Do you even have free time after your child goes to bed to imagine and compare or are you too tired? Have you gotten any good laughs from what you thought versus what is? It's probably not what you thought it would be, and if you can appreciate what it is, you'll enjoy the differences more.

People seem to approach parenthood with one of eight primary patterns:

1. **Panic-stricken:** "Oh, no! What are we getting ourselves into?"
2. **Laissez-faire** (with varying amounts of confidence): "It'll be okay."
3. **Rigid:** "I know exactly how this will be. I'll still be working, we'll have a nanny so I can continue working, and I'll know my child is getting quality one-on-one care."
4. **Self-Centered:** "Life won't be changing that much . . . I'm not going to let a little child tell me how to run my life."
5. **Relaxed, confident, flexible:** "I haven't a clue. I'll figure it out as I go."
6. **Simplistic, positive, loving:** "I just want to be a loving and patient parent."
7. **Idealistic and humane:** "I'll never hit my child and rarely if ever yell. It's just not necessary."
8. **Knows-what-doesn't-want:** "I won't be one of those completely devoted parents whose child becomes the center of their universe" or "I won't be like my mother/father."

All the parents I interviewed for this book said something along the lines of, "Most of my original ideas didn't pan out. I had to wing it once my baby was born. I didn't know my ideas would be so far off. I was pretty sure I knew myself well and how I'd react, but once our baby arrived (or soon after our baby arrived) it was clear our pre-baby notions of family life just weren't going to apply."

How has it been for you? How do you feel about abandoning or modifying your original plans? Did you have trouble giving them up? Are you surprised with life as it is, rather than how you imagined life would be? What has surprised you?

Be Open

If you're reading this book as you're getting ready to start a family, my recommendation is: don't have rigid expectations of this child, yourself, or even your mate. Watch and learn about the unique family you are becoming as it evolves around you. Let your family life develop as it will. Talking about parenting philosophies with your partner and having some ideas to help you get started is useful. Understanding your partner very well and having him or her understand you is also an important starting point. From all the parents I talked to, it's clear that family life has turned out to be different from what they had imagined. They also reported that the stronger their preconceived notions, the more difficult it was for them to give them up and be creative with the situation at hand.

Most families said the mother's life had changed more significantly than the father's life. Somehow the mother was more readily able to give up or modify things like sports and working out. Her schedule, especially when nursing, was affected more than the father's. That is not to say that fathers' lives do not change, just that mothers find their lives changed more. When interviewing couples, fathers agreed, especially in cases where the father was the main breadwinner.

"Acceptance of what is," and "this too shall pass" are great bases for launching respectful parenting. Laughing at the differences of what you thought being a parent would be versus what it is in real life helps a lot also. Facing and accepting the so-called intrusions that don't fit into your preconceived notions, helps enormously. This seems to be adding up to the old expression, "go with the flow," corny as it may seem, it does help. It allows you to be flexible and creative. Throw in some consistency and you have it made.

In this chapter, parents share some of their perceptions of how their lives have changed. The examples are often humorous, sometimes touching, sometimes surprising. All the parents I interviewed found they had cut back on a lot of things they used to do, such as camping, movies, dinners out, romantic evenings, making love, golf, reading, working out, cleaning, or skiing. For the most part, they truly didn't mind. Instead, they all talked about how much their children had added to their lives. They used terms like, "meaning," "joy," "love," "satisfaction," "appreciation," and "richness." After all, what's a few less tennis games when you're watching your infant turn over for the first time?

At a parent support group, where the topic was "Adjusting to a New Baby," a few moms were talking informally afterward, and their conversation went something like this:

"I can't believe it's been almost seven years since I went camping. I mean camping—backpacks, tents, that kind of thing. We used to do that all the time."

"I used to love camping. I had even built up the courage to go camping by myself. It was so great! I never went backpacking, just car camping."

"You did? I used to borrow friends' dogs to go camping, but I never went all by myself. Now if my girls were to want to do that, I'm not sure what I'd do. Things were different when I was doing it."

"We used to camp a lot, too! I can't believe that I find myself driving down the highway now, looking enviously at those trucks with camper shells over them, or even some of those big recreational vehicles I used to put down so much when my husband and I were in our cute little two-person backpacking tent. I never thought I'd see any value to those gas guzzlers. But I'm telling you, I'd love to have one. I could see us camping again if we had one of those."

"We bought one this year."

"You did?"

"Yeah, we actually did. Not one of the big ones. Ours is a pop-up tent trailer. But it has heat, hot water, and its own bathroom. I decided between my getting up at night, and my child's needs, I wanted to camp, but tenting—it didn't sound appealing. I wanted some conveniences like hot water for washing my face. You know, I just wanted it to be a little easier since I knew camping with a child would already make it a little harder."

"Hey, how many does it sleep?"

And they all laughed as they invited themselves to share the camper. After their camping conversation, they talked about some other humorous changes they had experienced since becoming mothers. Then they went on to talk more about their children, and their joy was so apparent, it truly shined through.

What Parents Say

Sarah: When I was contemplating getting pregnant, I had a difficult time imagining how a child would fit into my busy life. It was more than busy; it was full. I was content with my lifestyle and had been for a long time. I remember saying to my husband, "I can't imagine how life will be if we have a child. But I can't imagine even more being old and not having an adult child around. So I guess if I want the benefits of an adult child, I have to go through the little child part."

My husband didn't seem bothered by not knowing how we'd fit a baby into our lives. He was confident that when a baby arrived we'd be okay. My mother reassured me that not knowing how a baby would fit into my life shouldn't stop me from having a child, because once a baby arrived I'd figure it out. She was confident in my abilities to do so. Someone else suggested that if I didn't try to imagine how a baby would fit in, I'd probably be a better parent because I wouldn't have preconceived notions and I'd be able to roll with the punches more easily. That sounded reasonable to me.

I went with the no-expectations formula. I didn't spend time imagining what it would be like. I did, however, have some definite ideas popping into my head of what it wouldn't be like: I knew I wouldn't be this doting, joyful, appreciative mother, enraptured by her infant, baby, toddler, two-year-old. Not me. I was a Career Woman——I had my own interests! A stay-at-home mom? Never. Not this woman! A wannabe-stay-at-home mom? Not me. But guess what? I became this enraptured, enthusiastic, caring, giving, loving Mom who has refused to acknowledge any "favorite time" of my child's life because it has all been terrific.

When people have said, "Your son is how old?" invariably they reply enthusiastically, "That was my favorite age!" I quietly wonder to myself, "So if that was your favorite age, has it been downhill from there for you?" I don't get it. Any stage of development in front of my face has been interesting, and usually intriguing, exciting, and challenging to boot. See what I mean about reality being different from expectations, even the nonexpectation kind?

Has my life changed? Enormously! In ways I couldn't have foreseen. I'm so grateful for the changes. I appreciate my son's presence, because without it, I would still have my old busy life, which I believed was so full and satisfying. From my perspective today, nothing in life has been as satisfying, meaningful, or joyful as watching my child grow and develop. He has inspired me incredibly!

* * *

Linda: I remember when my company held my going-away-for-maternity-leave party. I was going around telling everyone, "Don't worry, I'll be back." I really didn't imagine that I wouldn't. I liked my job a lot. It wasn't a career, but it was a nice job. Look at me, two-and-a-half years later, pregnant with my second child. I can't imagine going back to work. When did it happen? I think even before she was born. Right before. But me, not working? I just couldn't have seen it as a possibility before. Yet as soon as she was born I knew. I knew I couldn't and wouldn't go back. We were just too close. She needed me. And I couldn't imagine leaving her. Me?

We don't do things without her. I mean, we really don't. I think my husband and

I have been out to dinner maybe twice in the last two-and-a-half years. At first we didn't because it would have been too hard on her. And now she's just so much fun. We'd be missing out on her doing something. This is especially true for my husband. He already feels like he misses out on too much because he has to work. So for us, it's not a sacrifice. It's what we want to do. But a few years ago, would I have seen my life like this? Never. We saw all the new movies. I never imagined life would be like this. But it is. And it's great!

* * *

Sarah: I've been amazed at how strongly I react, even in the middle of the night, from this place that says, "I need to take care of this, no matter what!" I mean I can rouse myself from a sound sleep, cope with little sleep, and react to the slightest change in noise indicating something is different and better be checked immediately. I was never like that before I had my son. It's this instinctive, primitive drive that takes over. Before I had my son and I would try to imagine what it would be like, I expected to be more detached, that I'd let my husband take care of it. But there's almost a vigilance about my reactions that has surprised me. Yet it feels so natural.

* * *

Bonnie: Since my daughter's birth I keep getting better and better at doing what feels right instead of agonizing, intellectualizing, discussing, and deliberating my actions. There's so much less of that. I never imagined it would be this way.

* * *

Linda: Having my daughter has taught me to set priorities. Up until last year (before she was born) I always thought, if I could only figure "it" out, I could do it all. Now I know I can't. I liked life in all its boxes and places before. I felt better when I could get life in those manageable boxes. Is it a relief now? Kind of. But now I have to deal with these constant changes. Yet, prioritizing is easier knowing I can't accomplish all I want to, and there is no "it" to figure out.

* * *

Kate: Life has changed a lot. I feel a lot closer to my husband since my son's birth. Now we're not just a couple, we're a family too. That seems to have more ties. I think my husband sees this as an opportunity to be with his son in a way his father never was with him. Our son is only nine months old, and my husband is already talking about fishing and skiing trips they're going to take. I feel like I'm mending stuff from my mom. I'm not sure how I am or why I'm feeling that, but when I pick him up because he's crying, every time, it feels good, and something feels better inside me too. We'd often get spanked when we were crying. I can't see the sense in that. So, yes, life is changing, for the better from what I can see so far.

Nothing is as simple as it used to be. Not that that's bad. He's been much more of a reward than anything else, but I was always such a spontaneous person. You can't be as spontaneous. Well, you have to think about things like laundry, because now there's a little baby who needs clean diapers and changes of clothes because he's more vulnerable to changes in weather. If you're going on an outing, you have to have all kinds of layers and extra layers in case he poops through them, which involves some planning in advance. I'm learning, but it's just not completely natural for me. But like I say, it's definitely worth it.

* * *

Cathy: I think one of the biggest changes I've experienced since my son was born was in recognizing my values about parenting and how that has affected my friendships. I hadn't expected my friendships to change so much. For instance, at work, during breaks when we talked, I was so intrigued with what my child was doing, I often steered the conversation to talking about our kids. And to my surprise and sometimes horror, I found how differently I was parenting than my coworkers who I had considered friends before. When I heard their stories of how they handled their children, I just couldn't be friends with them anymore. I clammed up in horror a few times. It was so uncomfortable. As a result, I've become pretty alienated at work. That's been disappointing.

I just can't be friends with people who parent in certain ways, because I no longer respect them. In fact I'm appalled with how they sometimes treat their children. For instance, one woman I had known a long time, and considered a work friend was talking about her eighteen-month-old, and said, "Damned if he didn't crawl around, pull the plug in our water bed, and all this water came gushing out. I just went over there, put the plug back in the bed, picked him up, and gave him a spanking. He had been told about that plug. He knew better than that." Stories like that made me cringe. I just couldn't say anything. Spank an eighteen-month-old? Spank at all?

I became hungry for people who treated their children with respect and dignity and found myself constantly disappointed. I hadn't realized how important it was to be around people who parent the way I do. And I hadn't realized how widespread yelling and spanking still is today. I realized quickly how strong my values toward respecting children (including infants) were. And although it's been lonely, I've needed and wanted to stick with my newly identified values. It's meant a lot to me, and I think to my son.

* * *

Carl: Before I had my son, I had one personal thing in my office, a clay mug I drank my coffee from. That was it. Everything else had been provided by my employer. By the time my son was four months old, I had a 2' x 3' photo collage of my son, my wife, and me. And it's been growing since then.

One of the things I started noticing when my son was about three months old was that I had become much more tolerant of my coworkers' moods. I had learned about moods from my son. I have always been a rather private person, probably viewed as aloof, standoffish. Most of that was because I had little tolerance for people and their idiosyncrasies, including mood changes. I didn't know how to deal with them. But I found my son's moods so intriguing, so simple, so impersonal (he wasn't out to get me); he was just being human when he cried, smiled, laughed, or stared. It seems to have generalized to my understanding of people. It sure makes my life easier.

Before he was born, I had been afraid about how I'd be, because I knew you were supposed to be able to be there for a baby, and I always needed a lot of alone space. I think my wife and I both figured she'd have to compensate, when I had to get away. But so far, I haven't had to go away. I've been so intrigued, so involved ... and it feels so good. Maybe those years of therapy have finally come together and they're clicking in me. He sure is helping though ... in ways I never imagined. I know it's easier to be around me because I'm more tolerant and understanding of other people. And I've learned it from him. He's only nine months old now. I wonder what else I'll be learning from him.

* * *

Steve: Before I became a father I had absolutely no experience with children. We're talking no cousins, no nieces, and no nephews. Everything was brand new for me. And let me tell you, the change was all for the better for me. It was difficult for my friends, but easy for me. Let me give you an example. My son was born December 29. For the first few days I just went around saying, "Wow." On New Year's Eve some friends had rented a room in a hotel to have a small, private party, maybe up to twenty people. The hotel was catering it, and I knew it was going to be a fun, nice party. But as the night went on, there I was in the hospital, holding my new baby, or watching my wife nurse our new baby. I started thinking, "I've got a brand new family. It's a new year, and I have a new family. I think I'll stay right here." And I did until around 1:00 a.m.

Then I went home for a few hours of sleep before I went back to greet my new family on New Year's Day. I knew I could have still gone to the party, my friends would have been glad to see me ... but I just wanted to be with my family, then get some sleep so I could be with my family again. And that was only two days after my son was born. I know that was different behavior for me. My friends didn't understand. But I felt so good about it.

* * *

Cindy: My daughter is the most important person in my life. Trying to raise her to be a healthy, confident person as she grows up is what I want to be doing right now. I'm realizing it's the most important thing I can do in my life. My career is on hold indefinitely, and that's fine. We're going to make do with less so I can be home with her. I didn't know I'd feel so strongly about this before she was born, but my decision feels firm and right. As an infant she wanted to be held and nursed all the time. And I did. After a few months as she began to enter babyhood I had certain expectations that this would change, only it didn't. I read some of Dr. Sears's books and found she fit many of the characteristics of a high-need baby. I found I had to be more patient and put my expectations aside for her. My needs from the past aren't as important as they once were. I can set them aside for her. I didn't know it would be so easy to do.

When my daughter was about one year old, my husband and I went on our first date since her birth. We went to the movies. The two of us sat there, watching, and saying quietly to each other, "Wow! This is incredible." We had forgotten what movies looked and sounded like on the big screen. We had been renting videos at home from time to time, but this was something else! It was so big. It was so bright. The sound was so clear. We were actually at the movies. We were actually away from the house, away from our daughter. It had taken a whole year. Incredible!

I'm glad I was in my middle thirties when I had her. I know I couldn't have given this much ten years ago. But now, I know I'll have time later. She'll only be this young and this needy for a short time, and I can do things like ski later.

* * *

Rhonda: I used to need a lot of time to myself. Before my daughter was born, I'd get home an hour before my husband. I'd look forward to that hour alone where I could just be myself. I didn't have to answer to anyone. I wasn't a professional or a wife ... just me. Now ... time alone? I never get it. Time for myself? I'm trying to get to an exercise class three times a week where there's child care on the premises . . . but my daughter isn't doing too well with that. We're trying.

It's amazing that I don't get more frustrated. Maybe because she meets my needs in ways I never thought possible. There are so many unexpected pleasures I get out of spending every day with her, watching her learn, being there with her. I probably would have been more selfish ten years ago, but now . . . this is the best thing that ever happened to me.

* * *

Sarah: My husband came home one day, took one look at me, and started laughing. I had no idea what was so funny until I looked down at my sweater. There, across and down the length of my navy blue sweater were the white remains of at least four burpings from my month-old child. I do remember thinking, as he spit up the first time, "I should change my sweater . . ." But burp number two quickly followed, and by number three a while later I figured, "Why bother?" I mean, why dirty two sweaters? I was about to explain all this when my still laughing husband said, "You would never have looked like this a month ago." Ah yes, how quickly life can change.

* * *

How did it happen that I may as well not even go into a video rental store because I don't recognize any titles? And when you read the backs of the boxes they all sound great, but you know they're not. You don't want to be bored if you're going to fight your exhaustion and actually stay awake for two hours after your child falls asleep. I can remember before I got pregnant thinking how I certainly would never let my life get so small that I wouldn't know the current movies to see or good six-month-old movies to rent. Certainly I'd have a babysitter at least once a month. Oh, I had seen what parenthood did to some people and I wasn't going to fall for it. I was going to be different. My life wouldn't change that much.

So how did it happen? Let's see: it took me till my son was eighteen months to even have enough of an outside interest that I thought seeing a film at home might be kind of nice. By the time I got to the video store a few months later, I didn't recognize any of the titles, and I went home empty-handed. Okay, so going to the video store didn't work so well. I was going to start to follow my own advice and get out with my husband at least once a month. No big deal right? Right, except for teething discomfort (how could we leave him?), unreliable babysitters, busy babysitters, and finally success. I had combed the newspapers for reviews, picked a movie, looked forward to seeing it, checked the paper for times and locations, and then arrived at the theater only to find a different movie on the marquee. The paper was wrong! Another time, the movie theater was closed for renovations. Another time the line was long, and by the time we got to the window to buy our tickets, the movie we wanted to see was sold out. We laughed at our lousy luck, grabbed a quick bite to eat, and then high tailed it back home to our son.

I thought life was full and complete before. I really did. But now, looking back, I can't believe I ever thought that. What my son has offered me has been so much more rewarding than writing a paper, having a project funded, finishing a project, a great ski run, a fun round of golf . . . you name it. My perspective on life has changed so completely.

I don't even mind being out of shape. Someday, when he's older and in school I'll probably get to that. It's just one of those things (like a clean organized house) I've given up so I can be with him more and enjoy his childhood. It's been incredibly worth it. I wouldn't trade my life today for my life before for anything!

Thank You

I WANT TO BEGIN by thanking Harper Lee, the author of *To Kill a Mockingbird*. I read her book quite a few times when I was growing up. I've always remembered what Atticus Finch told his daughter, Scout: "To really know a person, you've got to get in their shoes and walk around in them for a couple of days." I loved how gentle yet strong Atticus was as a father. Little did I know that Atticus was sowing the seeds for Respectful Parenting.

In high school and early college I worked in the special services department of the YM/YWHA in Little Neck, New York. The director, George Singfield, taught me a lot as an early role model, mentor, and friend.

In graduate school I was privileged to work with Dr. Carl Whitaker doing co-therapy with families at the University of Wisconsin. Carl encouraged me to trust my instincts, be creative, meet the family where they were, and, "shake up their apple cart so the apples don't come back down in the same place."

Dr. Carole Campana, a developmental psychology professor and practicing psychologist, read an early version of a manuscript of anecdotes about my first couple of years as a mother. She called me, excited. "This is great stuff. You have something here. You're treating Matthew differently than anything I've read before. What's your theory?"

"Theory?" I asked, confused.

"Your theory behind what you're doing. I've read hundreds of developmental psychology books and you're onto something. If you included some ideas as to why you're doing what you're doing, this would be a fabulous book."

I realized that what I was doing with my child was based on what I had learned in my clinical office while working with adults and their families. I had never put a name on it, but Carole spurred my thinking, and I began calling my theory Respectful Parenting. I even went on to get a Service mark on Respectful Parenting. The theory of Respectful Parenting developed slowly while I was working with people who shared their lives, their struggles, and their growth with me. While working with them I realized we needed new ways of parenting so children could grow into more confident adults. I want to thank everyone who came into my office.

I want to give heartfelt thanks to the parents who allowed me to interview them so I could include more examples of Respectful Parenting.

In the months before this book was "birthed," the following people helped complete the journey: Katherine Dennis was the copy editor who spurred me on to do even more . . . it's hard to stop editing once you start; Barbara Werden (BarbaraWerdenDesign.com) did a superb job with the cover and book design; Lori and Ted Garcia (www.tlcunlimited.com) provided their creativity throughout the process for logos and other design items; Michael Bedwell patiently reviewed several drafts of the manuscript; and Hattie Cutcliffe and Alex Wiberg proofed the final draft. I also want to thank Kemi Chavez who believed in this project and signed on to market the book; it has been a great partnership so far.

A number of people contributed photos for the book. I want to thank Margie and Greg Ahern, Marti and Jamie Arnold, Kemi and Shane Chavez, Sam Jaffe and Myung Oak Kim, and Timothy McCarthy.

On the more personal side, I would never have started this project in its initial form, nor had a mother's perspective on Respectful Parenting, without my child and all he has taught me. Being Matthew Jacob McCarthy's mom has been a joyous, creative, and sometimes challenging experience. Thank you for coming into my life. You are dearly loved.

My parents, Bill and Elaine Baum, provided me with role models I was free to learn from, modify, take, and change. It was in their home that I began my lifelong quest of learning, loving, and appreciating those significant people around me. My parents have grown up beautifully, even as they helped me grow up.

This book is intended to be the first in a series of books for parents taking them from birth through the teen years. I hope you enjoy reading it as much as I enjoyed writing it.

JOANNE BAUM, PhD

Recommended Reading

Bailey, Becky A. *Easy to Love, Difficult to Discipline.* New York: William Morrow and Company, 2000.

Bailey, Becky A. *Conscious Discipline.* Ovieda, Florida: Loving Guidance, Inc., 2001.

Behrmann, Barbara L. *The Breastfeeding Café.* Ann Arbor: University of Michigan Press, 2005.

Bennett Shoshana and Indman, Pec. *Beyond the Blues—A Guide to Understanding and Treating Prenatal and Postpartum Depression.* San Jose, California: Moodswings Press, 2003; www.beyondtheblues.com.

Brazelton, T. Berry. *Infants and Mothers: Differences in Development.* New York: Delacorte Press, 1994.

Brazelton, T. Berry and Sparrow, Joshua D. *Touchpoints.* Cambridge, Massachusetts: Da Capo Press, 2002.

Civardi, Anne. *Moving House.* Tulsa, Oklahoma: EDC Publishing, 1985.

Clarke, Jean I. and Dawson, Connie. *Growing Up Again.* Center City, Minnesota: Hazelden, 1998.

Cline, Foster and Fay, Jim. *Parenting With Love and Logic.* Colorado Springs: Pinon Preess, 1990.

Coates, Christie and Robert LaCrosse, PhD. *Learning From Divorce.* San Francisco: Jossey-Bass, 2003.

Fay, Jim and Charles, Fay PhD. *Love and Logic Magic for Early Childhood.* Golden, Colorado: Love and Logic Press, 2002.

Freed, Jeffrey and Parsons, Laurie. *Right-Brained Children in a Left-Brained World.* New York: Simon and Schuster, 1997.

Gurion, Michael. *The Wonder of Boys.* New York: Penguin Putnam, 1997.

———. *The Wonder of Girls.* New York: Atria Books, 2002.

Hanson, Rick, PhD., Hanson, Jan., L.Ac., and Pollycove, Ricki, MD. *Mother Nurture: A Mother's Guide to Health in Body, Mind, and Intimate Relationships.* New York: Penguin Books, 2002.

Hendrix, Harville. *Getting the Love You Want: A Guide for Couples.* New York: An Owl Book, Henry Holt and Company, 1988.

Johnston, Janet, PhD and Roseby, Vivienne, PhD. *In the Name of the Child: A Developmental Approach to Understanding and Helping Children of Conflicted and Violent Divorce.* Free Press, 1997.

Klass, Perri, MD and Costello, Eileen, MD. *Quirky Kids.* New York: Ballantine Books, 2003.

Leach, Penelope. *Your Baby and Child.* New York: Alfred Knopf, 1997.

Lessen-Firestone, Joan. "Building Children's Brains." Michigan Ready To Succeed Partnership, 1999.

Martin, Elaine. *Baby Games: The Joyful Guide to Child's Play from Birth to Three Years.* Philadelphia: Running Press, 1988.

Mogel, Wendy. *The Blessing of a Skinned Knee.* New York: Penguin Compass, 2001.

Neifert, Marianne. *Dr. Mom.* New York: Signet, 1993.

Reichlin, Gail and Winkler, Caroline. *The Pocket Parent.* New York: Workman Publishing, 2001.

Ricci, Isolina. *Mom's House Dad's House.* New York: Simon and Schuster, 1997.

Santa Cruz Toddler Care Center, Irene van der Zande, Santa Cruz Toddler Center Staff. *1, 2, 3 . . . The Toddler Years.* Santa Cruz, California: Toddler Center Press, 1989.

Sears, William. *Creative Parenting: How To Raise Your Children Successfully From Birth Through Adolescence.* New York: Dodd, Mead and Company, 1987.

Sears, William and Froelich, Paul. *Becoming a Father.* Franklin Park, Illinois: LA Leche League International, 1991.

Sears, William and Sear, Martha. *The Baby Book: Everything you Need to Know About Your Baby From Birth to Age Two.* Little Brown Publishers, Boston, 2003.

Sharp, Linda, "Stretchmarks on my Sanity." Lincoln, Nebraska: Writer's Showcase an Imprint of iUniverse.com, Inc., 2002.

Shelov, Stephen and Hannemann, Robert, Eds. *Caring for Your Baby and Child.* American Academy of Pediatrics, Bantam Books, New York, 1998.

Thayer, Elizabeth S. and Zimmerman, Jeffrey. *The Co-Parenting Survival Guide.* Oakland, California: New Harbinger Publications, 2001.

Thomas, Shirley. *Parents Are Forever.* Rev. Ed. Longmont, Colorado: Springboard Publications, 2004.

Warshak, Richard A. *Divorce Poison.* Harper Collins Publishers, Regan Books, New York, 2001.

Zero to Three and American Academy of Pediatrics. *Nurturing Children's Development from 0 to 36 Months.* Washington, D.C., 2003.

Index

About the Author

Dr. Baum is a therapist, speaker, mediator, author, and columnist. With more than thirty years of clinical experience Dr. Baum specializes in issues faced by couples, parents, families, and individuals. Joanne also works as a divorce coach and child specialist in the collaborative law process for divorcing families. Dr. Baum travels throughout the country presenting parenting workshops, seminars, and speeches to professional groups, parenting groups, and community groups. Dr. Baum has also authored *Respectful Parenting from Birth Through the Terrific Twos*, *The Truth About Pot: Ten Recovering Marijuana Users Share Their Personal Stories*, and *One Step Over the Line: A No Nonsense Guide to Recognizing and Treating Cocaine Dependency.* She has a private practice in Evergreen, Colorado.

Weego Baby Carriers come in three versions: Weego for Newborns, Weego for Preemies, and Weego for Twins.

- *Weego gives your baby the closeness, safety and security which is so important in the early years. And the hands-free design gives you the freedom to enjoy an active life while carrying your baby.*

- *The outer pouch, in connection with the shaped inner pouch, always guarantees the "frog-like" leg position. Carrying a baby with its legs in this position is important and beneficial for the healthy development of the hips.*

- *For premature babies, we offer a special baby carrier, the Weego Preemie. As scientific research indicates, premature babies thrive with extended physical contact.*

The Weego incorporates more than 30 years of parenting experience that you can see and feel.

You can purchase a Weego soft baby carrier on our website at www.weego.com and receive a $10 discount. Simply enter 12233 on the order screen in the field for a FOW-number (Friend of Weego) or give us a call at: 970-278-1080.

We wish you the best on your exciting journey into the world of parenting.

The Folks at Weego